"A perceptive and creative interface between the thought of Carl Jung and contemporary psychedelic research, now in its rebirth, by a scholar who skillfully articulates a profound comprehension of both realms of knowledge. Those who appreciate analytical psychology and those fascinated by the promise of psychedelic studies will find this synthesis stimulating and enriching."

William A. Richards, Ph.D., Johns Hopkins School of Medicine, co-designer and principal monitor for Johns Hopkins' study on psilocybin-induced mystical experiences

"The empirical research on psychedelic drugs as adjunctive medical therapies for PTSD, end of life anxiety, substance abuse, and depression—as well as triggers for intense spiritual experiences—has exploded. This book provides a valuable framework for understanding what is happening in the mind during these transformative psychedelic experiences. Dr. Hill renders Jung's theories in lucid language to provide insights into the nature of psychedelic as well as psychotic experience and their intersection. The Jungian insights Dr. Hill provides here are invaluable for clinicians working with acute psychedelic crises and the integration of difficult psychedelic experiences. They also shed light on the robust archetypal dynamics of all psychological transformation."

David Lukoff, Ph.D., co-president, Association for Transpersonal Psychology and co-author of the *DSM-IV* category Religious or Spiritual Problem

"This is a landmark study that succeeds in building a bridge, at once robust and elegant, between two fields that have, until now, had little contact with one another. While those who recognize the therapeutic potential of psychedelic experiences are generally favorable to Jung, Jungians have tended to follow Jung himself in being suspicious of psychedelics. Scott Hill respects this suspicion, but goes on to demonstrate that both sides have much to gain, both theoretically and practically, from a sustained dialogue. Practitioners and researchers in Jungian psychology, psychedelic studies and psychotherapy, trauma therapy, and transpersonal studies will all benefit from a close reading of this timely, impeccably researched, and wisely conceived text."

Sean Kelly, Ph.D., author of *Individuation and the Absolute: Hegel, Jung, and the Path Toward Wholeness* and *Coming Home: The Birth and Transformation of the Planetary Era*

"Scott Hill's brilliant book presents a sophisticated analysis of how psychedelic experiences may be understood from the standpoint of Jung's archetypal psychology–and how Jungian psychological views could be deepened by more open-minded investigations into the world of psychedelic experiences. Psychedelics can point us, like Jung did in his way, toward consideration of the humans as integrated body-mind-spirit beings, with access to many domains of consciousness (or unconsciousness) not ordinarily encountered."

Ralph Metzner, Ph.D., author of *The Unfolding Self*
and other books, including *The Psychedelic Experience*
(with Timothy Leary and Richard Alpert)

"Scott Hill has spent a good part of his life trying to understand the paradoxical dichotomy of the LSD experience—from "rapturous psychedelic experience" to "a descent into madness"—with the goal of learning how this drug can be used appropriately for therapeutic benefit and spiritual insight. I find particularly interesting his description of Carl Jung's interpretation of the unconscious and its relationship to psychedelic experience. Jung's work resonated with Alcoholics Anonymous founder Bill Wilson, who later explored the spiritual through LSD and contemplated its use as a treatment for alcoholism. Those interested in these complex phenomena will benefit from the insights Scott Hill delivers in this book."

David Smith, M.D., fellow and past president, American
Society of Addiction Medicine, and founder of the
Haight Ashbury Free Medical Clinic, San Francisco

"Scott Hill writes insightfully about how Jungian psychology can help people understand and heal the adverse effects of difficult and even traumatic experiences that can result from the use of psychedelics. At the same time, he elucidates the therapeutic and transformative potential of these complex substances, thus helping put to rest long-standing prejudices against their responsible use. The wisdom in this book offers hope that we can heal the psychological wounds and political divisions of the past, objectively assess the benefits as well as the risks of psychedelics, and move toward a more informed and mature application of these valuable substances."

Rick Doblin, Ph.D., executive director, Multidisciplinary
Association for Psychedelic Studies (MAPS)

Confrontation with the Unconscious

Confrontation with the Unconscious

Jungian Depth Psychology and Psychedelic Experience

Scott J. Hill

AEON

First published in 2013 by Muswell Hill Press.

This new edition published in 2019 by
Aeon Books Ltd
12 New College Parade
Finchley Road
London NW3 5EP

Copyright © 2019 Scott J. Hill

The right of Scott J. Hill to be identified as the author of this work has been asserted in accordance with §§ 77 and 78 of the Copyright Design and Patents Act 1988.

All rights reserved. No part of this publication may be reproduced, stored in a retrieval system, or transmitted, in any form or by any means, electronic, mechanical, photocopying, recording, or otherwise, without the prior written permission of the publisher.

Jung, C.G., Collected Works of C.G. Jung. 1977 Princeton University Press. Reprinted by permission of Princeton University Press.
Lessing J. Rosenwald Collection, Library of Congress. Copyright © 2013 William Blake Archive. Used with permission.

British Library Cataloguing in Publication Data

A C.I.P. for this book is available from the British Library

ISBN-13: 978-1-91327-402-3

Printed in Great Britain

www.aeonbooks.co.uk

To the late Dr. Ronald Sandison, Fellow of the Royal College of Psychiatrists, and the late Dr. Margot Cutner, Analyst, British Society of Analytical Psychology, for their pioneering work with Jungian-oriented LSD psychotherapy in the early 1950s, and for their papers, which became the recovered treasure of this investigation.

It is just the most unexpected, the most terrifyingly chaotic things which reveal a deeper meaning.

C. G. Jung,
The Archetypes and the Collective Unconscious

Contents

Preface xiii
Acknowledgments xvii

Part 1: Encountering the Unconscious

Chapter 1: Jung's Confrontation with the Unconscious and Its Relation to Psychedelic Experience 3
Psychedelic Research and Theory: A Brief History 6
Jung, Jungians, and Psychedelic Experience 12

Chapter 2: Psychedelic-Enhanced Psychotherapy 17
Psycholytic and Psychedelic Models 17
    Psycholytic Therapy 17
    Psychedelic Therapy 18
    Common Features and Goals 20
Schools of Psychedelic-Enhanced Therapy 21
    Psychoanalytic 22
    Grofian 22
    Shamanic 23
    Hybrid 24
An Early Jungian Approach to Psychedelic-Enhanced Psychotherapy 24

Chapter 3: Basic Jungian Concepts and Principles 29
Consciousness and the Unconscious 30
    The Relationship between Consciousness and the Unconscious ... 32
Individuation 34
Archetypes and Their Manifestation in the Psyche 35
Dreams and Other Symbolic Products of the Unconscious 37

Chapter 4: Jung's Explanation of Psychedelic Experience 43
A Lowering of the Threshold of Consciousness 44
The Limits of Integration 46
Ronald Sandison's Response to Jung's Criticism 48

Part 2: Jungian Insights into Difficult Psychedelic Experiences

Chapter 5: Psychedelic Experience and Trauma 53
   Difficult Psychedelic Experiences as Potentially Traumatic 53
   Psychedelic-Induced Trauma 55
   Psychedelic-Enhanced Therapy as Treatment for Past Trauma 57
   The Relation of Trauma in Jungian Psychology to
   Psychedelic Experience 58
      Kalsched's Model of the Psyche's Archetypal Self-Care System 59
      Trauma and Dissociation in Jung's Psychology 61
      Trauma and Jung's Theory of the Complex 66
      Possession by Complexes in Relation to
      Archaic Psychological Defenses 68
   The Emergence of Trauma-Based Imagery
   in Psychedelic Experience 69

Chapter 6: Psychedelic Experience and the Shadow 71
   The Shadow in Jung's Psychology 71
      Personal and Archetypal Levels of the Shadow 72
      The Overwhelmingly Numinous Nature
      of the Archetypal Psyche 73
      Resistance to and Projection of the Shadow 75
   The Shadow in Psychedelic Experience 77

Chapter 7: Psychedelic Experience and Psychosis 83
   Psychosis and Psychotic States 83
   Psychedelics as Psychosis-Inducing Substances 87
   From the Psychotomimetic to the Psychedelic Paradigm 90
   The Psychotomimetic Model Reconsidered 91
   Transpersonal Explanations of Psychedelic-Induced
   Psychotic States 92

Chapter 8: Psychosis in Jung's Psychology 97
   Jung's Focus on Schizophrenic Forms of Psychosis 99
   Commonalities between Schizophrenia and Other Conditions 101
   Neurosis, Latent Psychosis, and Manifest Psychosis 102
   Reduced Consciousness and Psychedelic-Induced
   Psychotic States 104
   Accounts of Psychedelic-Induced Psychotic States 106

Chapter 9: Psychedelic Experience and Transformation 113
   The Transformative Potential of Psychedelic Experiences 114
   The Transformative Potential of Psychotic States 116
   The Transformative Potential of Psychedelic-Induced
   Psychotic States 118

Chapter 10: A Jungian Approach to the Transformative Potential of Difficult Psychedelic Experiences 121
Jung on the Healing Potential of Psychotic Experiences 121
The Painful Passage through the Shadow towards Wholeness........... 123
Treating Trauma: Integration Versus Abreaction
in Jung's Psychology 125
    Jung's Definitions of Trauma and Abreaction 126
    Grof's View of Abreaction 126
    Jung's Critique of Abreaction 128
    Drawing from Both Grof and Jung 130
The Transformative Potential of Psychedelic-Enhanced
Psychotherapy: Two Case Studies.. 130
    Dr. Rick Strassman's Report 130
    Dr. Margot Cutner's Report 132

Part 3: Jung's Psychology and Psychedelic-Enhanced Psychotherapy

Chapter 11: The Transcendent Function: Jung's Approach to Integration.................................. 137

Chapter 12: Jungian Psychotherapy 147
The Method and Purpose of Psychotherapy 147
    Gaining Access to the Unconscious... 147
    Coming to Terms with the Unconscious....................................... 148
The Relationship between Analyst and Patient 151
    The Analyst... 151
    The Dialectical Relationship 151
    The Transference 152
Dreams and Their Interpretation 154
    The Sphere of the Irrational 154
    The Purpose and Value of Dreams.. 155
    The Compensating Function of Dreams....................................... 155

Chapter 13: Implications for Psychedelic-Enhanced Psychotherapy... 157
Subject Readiness.. 157
The Therapist and the Dialectical Relationship 160
The Compensating Function 163
The Significance of the Collective Unconscious................................. 163
Integration and the Role of Ego-Consciousness................................. 166

Conclusion 173
Notes 177
Bibliography.. 207
Index.. 223

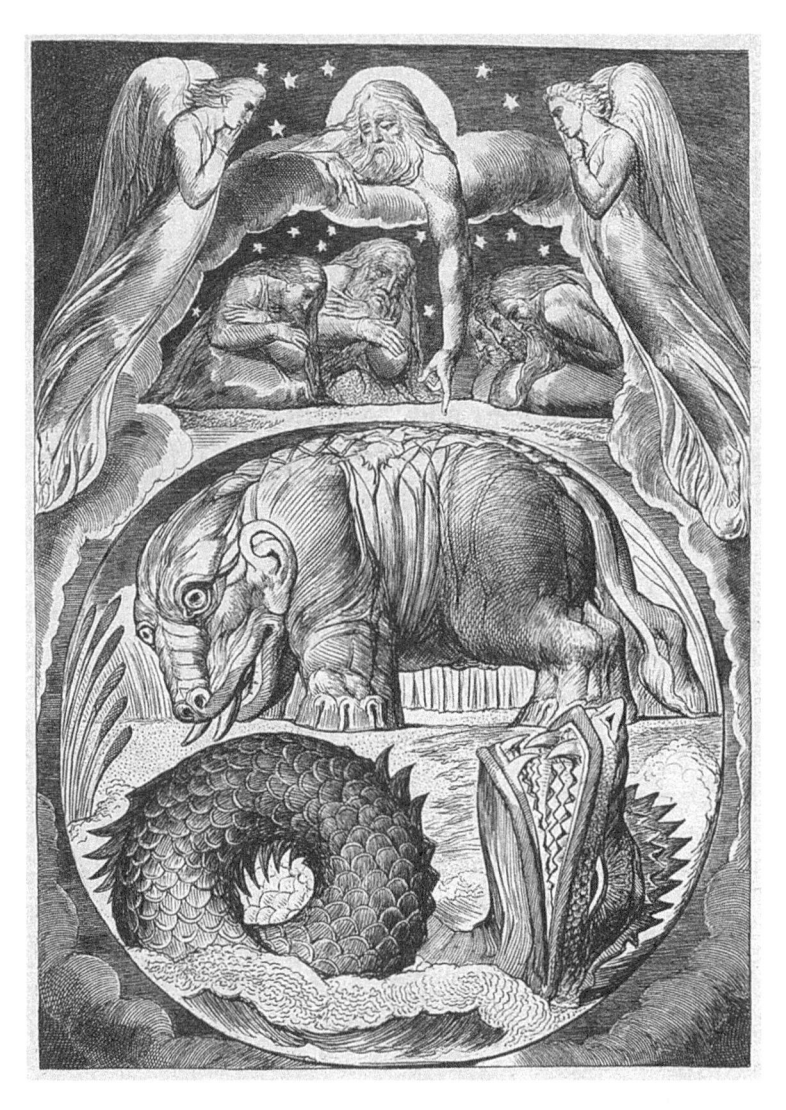

Yahweh Shows Job the Depths (Behemoth and Leviathan), William Blake
Lessing J. Rosenwald Collection, Library of Congress. Copyright © 2013
William Blake Archive. Used with permission.

Preface

> Ecstasy! . . . . In common parlance, among the many who have not
> experienced ecstasy, ecstasy is fun, and I am frequently asked why
> I do not reach for mushrooms every night. But ecstasy is not fun.
> Your very soul is seized and shaken until it tingles. After all, who
> will choose to feel undiluted awe, or to float through that door yonder
> into the Divine Presence? The unknowing . . . abuse the word, and
> we must recapture its full and terrifying sense.
>
> R. Gordon Wasson

In "The Bridge and the 'Difficult Passage,'" the historian of religion Mircea Eliade describes a mythological image that portrays a connection between this world and the beyond, a bridge that allows shamans to communicate with the gods again, as all humans did at the dawn of time. The passage over the bridge, suggests Eliade, expresses "the need to transcend opposites, to abolish the polarity typical of the human condition, in order to attain to ultimate reality."[1] The difficulty of this passage is vividly described in diverse mythological and religious traditions: Arabic texts describe the bridge as "difficult of access;" Arthurian legend describes an underwater bridge that is crossed "with great pain and agony;" and in the Christian tradition, sinners who attempt to cross this bridge are "cast into hell."[2]

I once came upon such a bridge. In 1967, at the age of nineteen, I walked over an expansive bridge on the Big Sur coast in California, swallowed a tab of LSD, and climbed into the canyon below. Having had a number of rapturous psychedelic trips earlier that year—experiences that had convinced me LSD was *the* key to a full and happy life—I looked forward to a beautiful day on a secluded beach. Instead, I descended into depths of madness and hell that I could previously never have imagined. This was the beginning of a series of terrifying psychedelic experiences, during which I struggled with the dilemma of whether I had gone insane or had discovered something disturbingly true about the spiritual nature of life. These two possibilities were bewilderingly conflated, and during each experience I struggled to resolve them in what felt like an eternal hell of confusion.

These experiences were dominated by a clear though unwelcome calling to leave what I took to be an absurd, unreal world by killing myself. This vision unfolded within a pervasive and overpowering sense of another reality, a terrifyingly immense stillness that seemed inexplicably but undeniably sacred. The profound, absolute, and seemingly transcendent nature of this stillness implicitly and mysteriously called my whole life into question, and—despite the lack of any previous religious tendency—ultimately challenged me to redeem myself by sacrificing my life on Earth to reach God in Heaven.

Let me say right off that the research clearly shows that psychedelic substances such as LSD, psilocybin, mescaline, and ayahuasca are surprisingly safe when used carefully; and I will talk about the research and well-established guidelines for safety throughout this book. The trouble was, of course, that I—and who knows how many other uninformed, immature, or foolhardy psychedelic cowboys—didn't do it right. And for some of us the price was steep.

In one way or another, I have worked to come to terms with those difficult experiences since that first day at the bridge over forty-five years ago. At a talk on psychedelics in 2002 by the comparative religion scholar Huston Smith, who had recently written the book *Cleansing the Doors of Perception: The Religious Significance of Entheogenic Plants and Chemicals,* I realized that serious people were investigating the substances and experiences that had radically changed my life. I was inspired to devote myself to learning all I could about the nature of psychedelic experiences. I decided to return to graduate school and began studying at the California Institute of Integral Studies in San Francisco, where experts in the fields of psychedelic studies and transpersonal psychology, such as Stanislav Grof and Ralph Metzner, teach. (Like many others, I had turned to the subject of psychology in the early 1970s to gain insight into my psychedelic experiences. But as much as I thrived in the University of Minnesota's psychology department, I learned nothing about such experiences there.)

It was not until I discovered Stanislav Grof's book on LSD psychotherapy that I felt I had found someone who truly understood what I had experienced. Subsequently, while writing on Jung and mythology, I realized that Jung understood, too. Of course, many people know that psychedelic substances can engender terror as well as rapture, psychosis as well as insight; but there was something about Jung's work that captured me. As I read Jung's writings—and as I saw my own psychedelic vision reflected in Jungian descriptions of the death-rebirth archetype in the myths of Gilgamesh, Inanna, Job, and Christ—I became increasingly intrigued by the possibility that my acid trips had given rise to what Jung calls "experiences of an archetypal nature."[3] I realized that I might better understand my psychedelic experiences, and those of many others, by studying Jung's psychology. His work, I eventually discovered, is especially suited to elucidating the nature of difficult psychedelic experiences. One purpose of this book is to show why that is true. For now, I will just say that C. G. Jung, like Stanislav Grof, has articulated in an especially thorough way the potentially overwhelming difficulty as well as the transformative potential inherent in deep psychological exploration. I was surprised to learn, however, that despite widespread interest in Jung's work within the psychedelic community, there exists no introduction to the nature of psychedelic experience in the light of Jung's psychology. Another purpose of mine is to address this omission, an endeavor that seems especially important at a time when research into the risks and benefits of psychedelic substances is undergoing an impressive resurgence.

Although this isn't a book about my psychedelic misadventures, it was naturally motivated by my interest to understand them. Through this work, in which scholarship became a personal process of discovery and integration and healing, I have gained both a deep appreciation for my difficult psychedelic experiences and a liberation from the craziness and fear they engendered, which had haunted me most of my life.

In addition to readers interested in the rich relationship between psychedelic research and Jungian psychology, this book should provide valuable insights to people trying to come to terms with their own "bad trips" as well as therapists treating people for an adverse reaction to a psychedelic substance. With this mixed audience in mind, my opening chapter, "Jung's Confrontation with the Unconscious and Its Relation to Psychedelic Experience," includes a brief summary of psychedelic research for readers not familiar with the field. My introduction to the practice of psychedelic-enhanced psychotherapy in chapter 2 should also be useful to these readers.[4] Chapter 3 introduces basic Jungian concepts and principles for readers new to Jung's psychology. A basic knowledge of both sides of the subject will be helpful when reading subsequent chapters.

Chapter 4 introduces Jung's explanation of psychedelic experience by introducing a hypothetical principle he called "a lowering of the threshold of consciousness." Chapter 4 also discusses Jung's views on integrating unconscious images and emotions released during a psychedelic experience. Chapters 5 through 10 examine especially challenging psychedelic experiences in light of Jung's approach to trauma, the shadow, psychosis, and transformation. My frequent reference in these chapters to the work of Stanislav Grof, John Nelson, Ann Shulgin, Ronald Sandison, and Margot Cutner, among others, demonstrates the relevance and value of Jung's insights to the fields of psychedelic and transpersonal studies. Chapter 10 includes a comparison of Jung's emphasis on integration with Grof's emphasis on abreaction in treating trauma. This leads to chapter 11's focus on Jung's core therapeutic concept, "the transcendent function," which provides a theoretical foundation for integrating unconscious material into consciousness. Chapter 12 outlines Jung's essential psychotherapeutic concepts and principles, including the dialectical relationship between analyst and patient, and the interpretation of dreams and other symbolic products of the unconscious. Chapter 13 relates these therapeutic concepts and principles to psychedelic-enhanced psychotherapy by discussing the most important implications of Jung's psychology for psychedelic-related treatment.

This book will ideally lead to further inquiry into Jungian psychology and psychedelic studies. My focus here is to explain psychedelic experience in the light of Jung's understanding of the psyche's fundamental structure and dynamics. This focus should establish a solid framework for elucidating psychedelic experience in relation to other aspects of Jung's vast body of work.[5]

Scott J. Hill, Ph.D.

ScottJ.Hill.PhD@gmail.com

Rättvik, Sweden

June, 2013

Acknowledgments

I could never have imagined that my efforts to understand the effects of my own difficult psychedelic experiences, which I had endured in solitude for years, would bring me into contact with so many goodhearted people. The pleasure of this unexpected good fortune is reflected ironically in a diary entry by J. D. Salinger's character Seymour Glass, who wrote that he was "a kind of paranoiac in reverse" because he suspected people of plotting to make him happy. Even though I can't acknowledge each one of these people individually, I hope that in one way or another I have shown my appreciation to all of them over the years for everything they have given and taught me.

Some, however, have contributed directly to this book's realization. I would like to express my gratitude to my writer brother, Doug Hill, and my dissertation committee members, Sean Kelly, Richard Tarnas, and David Lukoff. Their knowledgeable and thoughtful comments, insights, and suggestions gently but surely pushed the dissertation version of this book to a level I couldn't have reached on my own. That work unfolded in the rare atmosphere of intellectual rigor and imagination I found at the California Institute of Integral Studies in San Francisco. My work there was supported financially by the generosity of Robert Barnhart, who established the Kranzke Scholarship to advance psychedelic research.

I also want to convey my thanks to Keiron Le Grice for his excellent editorial suggestions, which significantly improved my manuscript, and for having introduced me to Tim Read and Mark Chaloner at Muswell Hill Press in London. I am grateful for their combined vision, sensibility, and expertise.

And, as surely as consciousness is nourished by the depths of the unconscious, I was sustained over many years of work on this project by my poet friend, Richard Speakes, my psychologist friend, Tom Cushing, and my wife, Ragnhild Gatu. The chances are slim that I would have undertaken this work in the first place without their wise and affectionate support.

PART 1

Encountering the Unconscious

Something empirically demonstrable comes to our aid
from the depths of our unconscious nature. It is the
task of the conscious mind to understand these hints. . . .
to understand in time the meaning of the numina that cross our path.

C. G. Jung

Answer to Job[1]

CHAPTER 1

Jung's Confrontation with the Unconscious and Its Relation to Psychedelic Experience

At a crucial point in his life, Carl Gustav Jung found himself besieged by a persistent series of especially intense dreams, fantasies, and visions. One day, fighting off fears of madness, Jung resolved to open himself to the strange impulses surging up from the depths of his unconscious mind. "Suddenly," Jung recounts, "it was as though the ground literally gave way beneath my feet, and I plunged down into dark depths. I could not fend off a feeling of panic."[1] In his ensuing vision, Jung lands in a sticky mass enveloped in darkness, and he encounters a dwarf with dry, shriveled skin at the entrance of a cave. He squeezes through the cave's narrow opening and wades through icy water until he comes to a glowing red crystal. He lifts the crystal and finds a hollow with running water. In the water, he sees the corpse of a boy with a head wound, an enormous black beetle, and a red sun rising out of the depths, before blood starts to flow out of the opening for an unbearably long time. Attempting later to engage himself fully in these images, Jung imagined trying to get to the bottom of a steep descent. On one such attempt, he found himself at the brink of an abyss, a vision that opened him to a crucial series of images that transformed his life's work. "It was like a voyage to the moon, or a descent into empty space," Jung writes. "I had the feeling that I was in the land of the dead. The atmosphere was that of the other world."[2]

While enduring what he referred to as his "confrontation with the unconscious," Jung became convinced that he was "obeying a higher will" and that he had encountered an independent psychological force that represented superior insight. He also recognized the irony that he, a psychiatrist, would encounter the same kind of terrifying imagery that so fatally confuses the insane. He appreciated nevertheless—in a way no one before him had appreciated—that such alien imagery arises from a vital universal source. This fund of unconscious images, Jung explains, "is also the matrix of a mythopoetic imagination which has vanished from our rational age."[3]

This mythopoetic imagination, Jung understood, has vanished only from our conscious mind. Dismissed, ignored, forgotten—it is always there, if we care to look. But, Jung says, "it is both tabooed and dreaded, so that it even appears to be a risky experiment or a questionable adventure to entrust oneself to the uncertain path that leads into the depths of the unconscious. It is considered the path of error, of equivocation and misunderstanding. . . . Unpopular, ambiguous, and dangerous, it is a voyage of discovery to the other pole of the world."[4]

Many who have had psychedelic experiences appreciate the extraordinary realms of inner perception and vision depicted in Jung's account. Consider, for instance, the similarity of Jung's report to Maria Estevez's description of her second psilocybin experience during a clinical study conducted at the Johns Hopkins Medical Center in Baltimore, Maryland. Feeling the initial effects of the psilocybin, Ms. Estevez said to her two medical monitors, "I'm going down." The two helped her with eye shades, headphones, and a blanket; and then, she reports, "I began to sink into another world. The descent seemed even rougher than the previous time, a rattling, lurching, high-speed roller coaster ride straight downhill through tingling geometric shapes and tunnels of textured blackness."[5]

Ms. Estevez felt assaulted and helpless during this dark and eerie descent. Despite her apprehension, she retained her intention and stayed open to what the experience presented her. As the session unfolded, she felt guided by a transcendent spiritual intelligence, and she subsequently had a vision. "It was as if all the cylinders in the lock somehow fell into alignment, the door swung open, and I found my consciousness being flooded with brilliant Light," she recounts. "I had arrived at a transcendental state, and was awestruck at the discovery. I felt a sense of joyous expansion as it opened fully to me, like entering a splendid palace."[6] Maria Estevez's psychedelic experience left her with a sense that, at the age of sixty-two, she had for the first time understood familiar religious principles. "It was as if the Light were revealing to me the innermost workings of the universe."[7] Speaking of the sacredness revealed to her, she concluded, "Previously I knew it only intellectually, but now I am certain it is real."[8]

In view of Jung's radically inquisitive approach to the psyche, his extraordinary personal confrontations with the unconscious, and his mystical sensibility, it's not surprising that people turn to his work for insights into their psychedelic experiences. Jung's understanding of the psyche, or mind, and its transformation has also earned the respect of eminent investigators of psychedelic experience and psychedelic-enhanced psychotherapy. The most prominent researcher in the field, Stanislav Grof, finds in Jung's psychology an exceptionally strong correspondence to the domains of psychedelic experience he has mapped in his own extensive investigations.

Jung knew, of course, that his explorations were outside the realm of accepted psychiatric practice. In the closing passage of *Two Essays on Analytical Psychology*, he explains that he didn't expect his readers to follow his conclusions because "the experiences which form the basis of my discussion are unknown to most people and are bound to seem strange."[9] He was less concerned with how others would understand his observations than he was with introducing what he referred to as "a wide field of experience, at present hardly explored."[10] Summarizing Jung's influence on the psychology of religion, David Wulff, author of *Psychology of Religion*, characterizes Jung as one who conveyed an attitude of openness that challenged the limits of conventional psychological inquiry, with its focus on behaviour, cognition, and the conscious mind. Jung was open especially to the irrational and the mysterious, to that which lies beyond logic and measurement, says Wulff, because he recognized "the infinity that stretches far beyond our understanding [and] the powers that lie outside our comprehension and control."[11] In this respect, Wulff adds, Jung also conveyed an attitude of humility and awe.

Jung maintained that psychology must go deeper than the intellect because "the totality of the psyche can never be grasped by intellect alone."[12] Like it or not, "the psyche seeks an expression that will embrace its total nature."[13] As a young man, Jung's goal had been to advance conventional scientific study of the psyche. Then, he reports, speaking of his confrontation with the unconscious, "I hit upon this stream of lava, and the heat of its fires reshaped my life. That was the primal stuff which compelled me to work upon it, and my works are a more or less successful endeavor to incorporate this incandescent matter into the contemporary picture of the world."[14]

Some who find their psychedelic experiences validated in Jung's writings suppose that, at one time or another, Jung must have tried psychedelics himself. He was reportedly an acquaintance of the mescaline researcher Kurt Beringer, so he could have experimented with mescaline in the 1920s, they suggest; or perhaps he tried peyote when he spent time with Native Americans in New Mexico. Many also point to Jung's *Red Book* paintings as evidence that he had used psychedelics. The imagery and themes in these paintings certainly reflect a psychedelic sensibility. Yet there's good reason to believe Jung when he says he never used psychedelic substances nor gave them to anyone else. As I demonstrate throughout this book, Jung's psychology is remarkably relevant to psychedelic experience because psychedelic substances such as LSD, psilocybin, mescaline, and ayahuasca open one to the same extraordinary realms of the psyche that Jung so courageously explored and so thoroughly elucidated—without psychedelic substances. Indeed, Jung vehemently questioned the value of psychedelics for personal growth, and he uncompromisingly opposed their therapeutic application.

Unfortunately, Jung's adamant disapproval of psychedelics has led to an enduring taboo against the study of psychedelic experiences by Jungians. Consequently, despite the exceptional relevance of Jung's psychology to psychedelic experience, Jungians have paid little attention to the subject. In this book, I address the important issues that Jung raises by considering the limitations as well as the wisdom of his critique. And I explore the penetrating insights into psychedelic experiences that are implicit in his approach to the psyche's structure and dynamics. I place special emphasis on Jung's unique understanding of a person's challenging yet potentially transformative confrontation with the archetypes of the collective unconscious. I demonstrate in particular how archetypal levels of experience associated with trauma, psychosis, and the shadow (the denied aspects of one's nature), as elucidated by Jung, can help us understand especially challenging psychedelic experiences and their transformative potential. I also show how this knowledge can lead to substantial improvements in psychedelic-enhanced psychotherapy. One of the most important ideas within the field of psychedelic studies is *integration*, the means by which potentially life-changing insights gained during psychedelic-induced states of consciousness become more than transient experiences and actually lead to concrete positive changes in one's life. Yet discussion of the integration process itself in the psychedelic literature is strikingly superficial. Jung's nuanced theory and thorough method of therapeutic integration offer, therefore, especially valuable insights into this critical aspect of psychedelic experience. Before taking up psychedelic-enhanced therapy and Jung's psychology in the next two chapters, it is worth considering the ill-fated history of early psychedelic investigation, the recent revival of government-approved psychedelic research, and the ironic affinity between psychedelic experience and Jung's psychology.

Psychedelic Research and Theory: A Brief History

By the 1940s, clinical investigators had observed that substances like mescaline and lysergic acid diethylamide (abbreviated LSD-25 or simply LSD) could temporarily induce states of consciousness that resemble the personality disturbances and the loss of contact with conventional reality characteristic of psychosis. Researchers considered the similarities between these temporary drug-induced states and psychosis to be so strong that they referred to such substances as *psychotomimetic*, or psychosis-mimicking, *drugs*.

Motivated by the research potential of a short-term, pharmacologically-generated "model psychosis," the Swiss pharmaceutical company Sandoz offered its newly discovered drug, LSD-25, to research institutions and psychiatrists in 1947. Sandoz recommended that psychiatrists could deepen their understanding of psychosis by taking LSD themselves and thereby gaining "an insight into the world of ideas and sensations of mental patients."[15] They also suggested that researchers could study how mental illness develops by giving the drug to healthy people, some of whom would most likely experience a short-term psychosis. Perhaps, they reasoned, the way healthy individuals react to this drug might provide insights into the causes and treatment of endogenous, or "natural," psychoses (that is, psychoses that originate within the mind or body). If these drugs induced psychotic reactions by interfering with the brain's neurochemistry in some way, the diseased brain of the person suffering from schizophrenia might be producing its own LSD-like substances. This line of reasoning suggested a new model for understanding the biological basis of mental illness, especially schizophrenia, at a time when the medical community was inclined to assume a physical basis for mental illnesses and to prescribe pharmacological substances to cure them. Consequently, the first phase of intense psychedelic research was initiated shortly after World War II.

Further clinical experience revealed that psychological factors played a much more significant role in responses to these substances than early researchers had appreciated. Investigators found, for instance, that patients who were carefully prepared for their drug sessions were far more likely to have life-enhancing rather than pathological experiences. Interpersonal support during the sessions was found to be quite helpful as well. Researchers were inspired by these discoveries to coin a less biased term for this complex group of mind-altering substances. In a 1954 letter to Aldous Huxley, psychedelic researcher Humphry Osmond proposed a new term in the form of a verse:

> To fathom hell or soar angelic,
> Just take a pinch of psychedelic.[16]

The term *psychedelic*, which is derived from *psyche* (mind) and *delos* (to make clear or visible) and means "mind manifesting" or "mind revealing," was popularized by Timothy Leary in the 1960s. Despite widespread association with Leary's reckless "Turn on, tune in, drop out" evangelizing and other excesses of the psychedelic 60s, the term *psychedelic* has retained currency among many experts in the field.

Lester Grinspoon and James Bakalar, of Harvard Medical School and coauthors of the authoritative *Psychedelic Drugs Reconsidered*, have defined a psychedelic drug as one that "more or less reliably produces thought, mood, and perceptual changes otherwise rarely experienced except in dreams, contemplative and religious exaltation, flashes of vivid involuntary memory, and acute psychoses."[17] They also explain that these effects are produced without causing physical addiction, craving, major physiological disturbances, delirium, disorientation, or amnesia. They are quick to add that this definition is only a rough guide because the effects of psychedelic substances (including LSD, mescaline, psilocybin, ibogaine, dimethyltryptamine [DMT], and ayahuasca) show general similarities rather than easily identifiable common characteristics.

Stanislav Grof qualifies Grinspoon and Bakalar's definition significantly by stating that a psychedelic drug acts as a "catalyst or amplifier of mental processes that mediates access to hidden recesses of the human mind."[18] That is, Grof is careful to point out that psychedelic substances don't *produce* specific psychological effects; rather, they activate psychological processes that allow one to consciously experience otherwise latent unconscious content. The person's psychedelic-induced experience therefore depends primarily on the person, not the substance.[19]

In *The Doors of Perception*, his classic book on psychedelic experience, Aldous Huxley suggests that mescaline impairs the efficiency of the brain's "reducing valve." This allows what he calls "Mind at Large" to enter a person's awareness, whereupon "all kinds of biologically useless things start to happen."[20] Huxley attributes the image of a cerebral reducing valve to a biological model conceived by Henri Bergson. In Bergson's model, the brain selects from a profusion of sensations and perceptions and by that means limits conscious experience to what is biologically useful. Mescaline, like disease, emotional shock, and mystical experience, says Huxley, has the power "to inhibit the functions of the normal self and its ordinary brain activity, thus permitting the 'other world' to rise into consciousness."[21]

Jung didn't use a generic term for the class of compounds that is now referred to as *psychedelic substances* or *psychedelic drugs* because his familiarity with the field's literature was primarily limited to early experiments with mescaline.[22] Except for mentioning LSD in a personal letter in 1954, Jung always used the term *mescaline* or phrases like *mescaline and related drugs*. His explanation of psychedelic experience, as we will see in chapter 4, is nevertheless quite compatible with both Grof's and Huxley's explanations.

An impressive body of studies on the psychotherapeutic utility of psychedelic substances has accumulated since Sandoz began distributing LSD to researchers in 1947. Grinspoon and Bakalar note in *Psychedelic Drugs Reconsidered* that more than one thousand clinical papers discussing psychedelic therapy with forty thousand patients were published between

1950 and the mid-1960s alone. Psychedelic-related investigations during this period focused on treating a wide range of disorders, including alcoholism and drug addiction, character disorders, depression, neurosis, trauma, psychosis, autism, psychosomatic disorder, and criminal pathology, as well as the emotional suffering and physical pain associated with terminal diseases.

The low incidence of significant complications within this vast body of clinical experience is impressive. In 1960, Sidney Cohen, of the University of California, Los Angeles, surveyed clinicians about negative reactions among participants in clinical and experimental studies during the 1950s. Of the five thousand individuals, some of them emotionally ill, who had collectively taken LSD more than twenty-five thousand times, only five of them (one in a thousand) experienced a psychotic reaction that lasted more than twenty hours. Cohen concluded that prolonged psychotic reactions are almost completely preventable in therapeutic settings and prolonged reactions that do occur tend to subside within a week.[23]

Cohen was not inclined to underestimate the potential dangers of psychedelics. As associate clinical professor of Medicine at UCLA, Chief of Psychosomatic Medicine at the Los Angeles Veterans Administration Hospital, and director of the Division of Narcotic Addiction and Drug Abuse at the National Institute of Mental Health in the late 1960s, Cohen repeatedly warned that the widespread unsupervised use of psychedelics was dangerous. He also expressed misgivings regarding the conditions under which psychedelics were sometimes administered by clinicians. Nonetheless, Cohen maintained again and again that psychedelic substances, when properly employed, are important research tools. "In the hands of experts these agents are relatively safe," he concluded in 1966, "but they are potent mind-shakers which should not be lightly or frivolously consumed."[24]

In contrast to the infrequency of adverse reactions during LSD's clinically-supervised stage in the 1950s, David Smith, founder of the Haight Ashbury Free Medical Clinic in San Francisco, reports that when his clinic first opened its doors in 1967, "negative acid trips or bummers, as the acid culture called them, were frequent."[25] As a result of widespread and often careless popular use of psychedelics in the 1960s, and sensational reports of their dangers by politicians and the press, even their clinically supervised use acquired negative associations having little to do with the intrinsic value of the substances themselves. The abundant body of previous research on the positive effects of psychedelic-enhanced therapy was discredited overnight, and psychedelic-enhanced therapy quickly became an unacceptable form of medical treatment. In 1970, the U.S. government passed the Controlled Substances Act, which imposed severe restrictions on research with LSD and other common psychedelic substances. Many other countries soon imposed similar restrictions. Jay Stevens, author of *Storming Heaven: LSD and the American Dream*, describes the Kafkaesque atmosphere of the time. "Those who knew the most about psychedelics were relegated to the sidelines of the debate, while those who knew the least were elevated to the status of 'expert.'"[26] The consequent legal restrictions on psychedelic research were comparable, Stevens suggests, to the Papal Court forbidding Galileo the right to continue his astronomical observations. Despite abundant historical, anthropological, and clinical evidence to the contrary, mainstream science came to view the states of consciousness induced by psychedelic substances as nothing more than pathological.

However, a number of investigators in psychiatry, psychology, anthropology, and other fields now believe the time has come for a renewed, objective inquiry into the benefits as well as the risks of these powerful substances. Pointing to their safe and beneficial use for centuries in indigenous cultures around the world, many of these investigators maintain that psychedelics have an unrealized potential for healing, growth, and transformation in modern cultures. Renewed research could lead to new forms of therapy for a wide range of illnesses. Proponents also believe that current neuroimaging technologies could yield important insights into the workings of the brain and the nature of consciousness itself.

Knowledge acquired from indigenous cultures about the respectful and skillful use of psychedelic substances, or "sacred medicines," could also foster a more mature attitude toward their use in contemporary societies, where too many people (mostly teenagers) are still misusing psychedelics. One U.S. government survey estimates that more than one million people, twelve years old or older, used a psychedelic substance for the first time in 2007 alone.[27] To former researchers in the field, it sometimes seemed that virtually the only place psychedelics were *not* being taken was under the supervision of knowledgeable and experienced professionals.

Advocates for new psychedelic research are optimistic, however. Thanks in large part to the work of the Multidisciplinary Association for Psychedelic Studies (MAPS), a nonprofit research and public policy organization, and private foundations like the Heffter Research Institute, the Beckley Foundation, and the Council on Spiritual Practices, government-approved psychedelic research appears to be on the threshold of a renaissance.[28] A growing number of basic-science and clinical studies using rigorous experimental and safety protocols are being developed with a variety of substances in Europe and the United States. Some of these studies are taking place at leading universities. They include psilocybin treatment for patients suffering from obsessive-compulsive disorder, psilocybin and LSD therapy for treating anxiety in patients with cancer and other life-threatening illness, and MDMA-assisted psychotherapy for intractable post-traumatic stress disorder in rape victims and war veterans. Other recent studies have examined psychedelic-enhanced treatments for cluster headaches, depression, alcoholism, and opiate addiction. Anthropological and ethnopharmacological research continues into indigenous peoples' use of natural psychedelic substances such as peyote, ayahuasca, and psilocybin-containing mushrooms for sacramental and healing purposes.[29]

A model clinical investigation, suggesting the potential that psychedelic substances have to improve the lives of healthy people, was conducted at the Johns Hopkins School of Medicine between 2001 and 2005.[30] This rigorous double-blind study evaluated the short- and longer-term psychological effects of psilocybin in healthy, well-educated adults who had an active interest in spiritual matters but no previous experience with psychedelics. The study concluded that high doses of psilocybin administered to carefully-screened and well-prepared volunteers under supportive conditions can occasion mystical experiences characterized by an ineffable sense of sacredness transcending time and space. Maria Estevez, whose psilocybin-induced mystical experience I described at the beginning of this chapter, was a participant in this study.

It is worth noting that participants' reactions in the Johns Hopkins study were not uniformly positive. A small number of the study's thirty-six volunteers experienced adverse reactions during their psilocybin session. These reactions included significant psychological struggle, extreme fear, and transient feelings of paranoia. Two people compared their psilocybin experience to being in a war. In all cases, these adverse effects were successfully managed with interpersonal support from the monitors, and none of the effects persisted beyond the session. Moreover, despite their struggles, most of these participants rated the experience on the whole as personally meaningful and spiritually significant, and none reported any lasting negative effects. To the contrary, a 14-month followup study showed that a large proportion of participants in the original study considered their psilocybin-induced states "to be among the most personally meaningful and spiritually significant experiences of their lives and to have produced positive changes in attitudes, mood, altruism, behavior and life satisfaction."[31] These positive changes were confirmed by friends, family members, and work colleagues who did not know about the psilocybin experience.

"Psilocybin gives us a uniquely powerful tool to study primary spiritual experience and its short and long term effects," concluded Roland Griffiths, Johns Hopkins professor of psychiatry and the study's lead scientist. The study's investigators are also promoting practices that help ensure the safety of participants in this kind of research. These practices include carefully selecting volunteers, establishing trust and rapport between monitors and participants, carefully preparing participants, and providing them ample interpersonal support during the sessions.[32]

Another of the study's investigators, Johns Hopkins psychologist William Richards, had first conducted clinical psychedelic research in the 1960s. Richards helped design the Johns Hopkins psilocybin study, and he worked closely with its volunteer participants as their principal monitor. Discussing lessons from the past and hypotheses for future psychedelic research in the *Journal of Transpersonal Psychology*, Richards includes the deeper realms of unconscious experience described by Carl Jung among the psychedelic-induced domains of consciousness having the most profound promise for psychological treatment and spiritual development in the future.[33]

Jung, Jungians, and Psychedelic Experience

The long-standing relevance of Carl Jung's psychology to psychedelic experience is emphatically reflected in the tribute that Timothy Leary, Richard Alpert, and Ralph Metzner paid to Jung in *The Psychedelic Experience*. Published in 1964, their guidebook to expanded realms of consciousness was based on *The Tibetan Book of the Dead*, to which Jung had written an appreciative commentary. Jung had also credited *The Tibetan Book of the Dead* for stimulating many of his own ideas, discoveries, and fundamental insights.[34] Leary and his coauthors considered Jung a "psychiatrist *cum* mystic" because he had committed himself wholly "to the inner vision and to the wisdom and superior reality of internal perceptions."[35]

The image of Carl Jung the psychiatrist *cum* mystic committed to the wisdom of internal perceptions certainly comes to mind when reading his commentaries on *The Tibetan Book of the Dead* and *The Tibetan Book of the Great Liberation*. "In the West," Jung wrote, "the conscious standpoint arbitrarily decides against the unconscious, since anything coming from inside suffers from the prejudice of being regarded as inferior or somehow wrong."[36] The conscious mind, he explains, naturally resists the emergence of what it experiences as "the intrusion of apparently incompatible and extraneous tendencies, thoughts, feelings."[37] In Jung's view, this alien intrusion arises from the deepest level of the unconscious, the collective unconscious, which has nothing to do with personal experience.[38] Jung finds the most startling instances of this condition in patients suffering from schizophrenia. However, he adds, in cases such as those illuminated in the Tibetan books of death and liberation, "it is tacitly agreed that the apparently incompatible contents shall not be suppressed again, and that the conflict shall be accepted and suffered. At first no solution appears possible, and this fact, too, has to be borne with patience."[39]

In his commentary on *The Tibetan Book of the Dead*, Jung discusses this resistance and ultimate surrender in terms of individuation, the process through which we relinquish our dominance over the unconscious and move toward a more balanced relationship to unconscious forces, and thereby move toward psychological wholeness: "Fear of self-sacrifice lurks deep in every ego, and this fear is often only the precariously controlled demand of the unconscious forces to burst out in full strength. No one who strives for selfhood (individuation) is spared this dangerous passage, for that which is feared also belongs to the wholeness of the self."[40]

As Leary and his coauthors recognized half a century ago, Jung's observations on the Tibetan books of death and liberation demonstrate the value of his psychological insights for understanding psychedelic experiences in general. Contemporary theorists of psychedelic-enhanced therapy have found that Jung's knowledge of the conscious mind's often terrifying confrontation with the unconscious is especially relevant to understanding difficult and potentially traumatic psychedelic experiences. Ann Shulgin, former psychedelic researcher and therapist, maintains that the degree of insight achieved in any psychedelic session depends primarily on one's willingness to face and acknowledge long-denied aspects of one's nature, the "dark side" of the personality that Jung called *the shadow*. Referring to the Buddhist analogy of encountering demon guardians at the temple's gate, Shulgin emphasizes that "the prospect of seeing what he unconsciously believes to be the core—the essence—of himself as a series of horrendous, malignant, totally unacceptable entities, can bring about a state of fear that has no parallel in ordinary life."[41]

Among contemporary theorists of psychedelic-enhanced therapy, Ralph Metzner and Stanislav Grof have most carefully documented the correspondence between their work and Jung's. Although neither attempts to establish the kind of Jungian framework that this book presents, both draw generously from Jung's theories and clinical experience to support their own theoretical frameworks. Metzner's approach to what he calls *reconciling with the inner enemy*, for instance, draws from Jung's ideas of the shadow, individuation, and the *coincidentia oppositorum*, the coming together of opposites, or the reconciliation of antagonistic aspects of one's nature.[42]

A major Jungian theme in Grof's psychology is the ego's problematic yet ultimately transformative relationship with deeper levels of the unconscious. Although Grof draws from a number of psychotherapeutic orientations, including the work of Freud, Rank, Reich, Assagioli, and Maslow, he finds in Jung's psychology the most far-reaching correspondence to the domains of psychological experience he has observed during more than five decades of investigation into what he calls *nonordinary states of consciousness*.[43]

Only two people have developed an explicitly Jungian approach to psychedelic-enhanced therapy: the British psychiatrist Ronald Sandison and Margot Cutner, his Jungian analyst colleague. Their pioneering practice of LSD therapy in the 1950s provides a valuable clinical foundation for the theoretical framework I present here, and I frequently refer to their work in this book.

Sandison, Cutner, Grof, Metzner, and Shulgin have made important contributions to a Jungian understanding of psychedelic experiences. As a general rule, however, Jungians have not explored the potential value of psychedelics. Ronald Sandison and Margot Cutner were notable exceptions to the Jungian community's emphatic remove from psychedelic investigation in the 1950s and 1960s. When not simply ignoring the subject, Jungians as a rule categorically reject the suggestion that psychedelic substances can advance psychological growth and transformation. The lack of objective discussion of psychedelic experience or reference to psychedelic-induced imagery in the Jungian literature is remarkable.[44]

There are two basic reasons for this curious lacuna, I believe. The international bans imposed on psychedelic research in the 1960s and 1970s created a significant legal barrier to psychedelic investigation for later generations of Jungians, some of whom were no doubt attracted to Jung's work because of their own psychedelic experiences. By far the most significant impediment, however, has been Jung's criticism of psychedelic therapy.[45] Several of Jung's letters reflect his conviction that psychedelics are a shortcut into realms of the unconscious for which one is inevitably unprepared.

In one of these letters, Jung replies to Alfred Hubbard, an early proponent of psychedelic therapy, who had written to Jung inviting him to contribute to psychedelic research. "When it comes to the practical and more or less general application of mescaline, I have certain doubts and hesitations," Jung replied. "The analytical method of psychotherapy (e.g., 'active imagination') yields very similar results, viz. full realization of complexes and numinous dreams and visions. These phenomena occur at their proper time and place in the course of the treatment. Mescaline, however, uncovers such psychic facts at any time and place when and where it is by no means certain that the individual is mature enough to integrate them."[46] Jung also tells Hubbard that he does not know from experience but suspects that a drug capable of opening the door to the deepest levels of the unconscious could release a latent psychosis. "It would be a highly interesting though equally disagreeable experience," Jung adds.[47]

The contentiousness toward psychedelic-enhanced therapy in Jung's letter to Hubbard is more explicit in his reply to Father Victor White. White had written about a psychiatric hospital he had visited, where LSD was being administered to patients, some of whom were experiencing religious images and visions under its influence. In Jung's response to White's letter, he wrote: "I should indeed be obliged to you if you could let me see the material they get with LSD. It is quite awful that the alienists [psychiatrists] have caught hold of a new poison to play with, without the faintest knowledge or feeling of responsibility. It is just as if a surgeon had never learned further than to cut open his patient's belly and to leave things there."[48]

The problems that Jung identifies are real and should be taken seriously. At the same time, however, Jung could not have been aware of the extensive evidence showing that psychedelic substances are relatively safe when administered responsibly. As Jungian analyst and scholar Andrew Samuels suggests regarding other issues, we need to read Jung's texts respectfully but also critically, prepared to recognize his prejudices and mistakes as well as his remarkably sound and timeless comprehension of psychological dynamics and issues.[49] I have attempted to maintain that balance here.

CHAPTER 2

Psychedelic-Enhanced Psychotherapy

Psycholytic and Psychedelic Models

After discovering the therapeutic utility of psychedelic drugs, investigation into their psychological effects focused on their therapeutic potential rather than their psychosis-inducing properties. The extensive body of clinical research, conducted in the decades after LSD was distributed to psychiatrists in the late 1940s, reflects two main models of psychedelic-enhanced psychotherapy: psycholytic therapy and psychedelic therapy. Psycholytic therapy uses low to medium doses to enhance conventional psychotherapy; psychedelic therapy uses relatively high doses to induce psychedelic peak, or mystical, experiences. Even though the distinction between the two is a common and useful one, it should not be reduced to an irreconcilable dichotomy. Indeed, the two methods share common features and goals, and some practitioners favor combining them in an integrated therapeutic program.[1]

Psycholytic Therapy

Early clinical experiments at Sandoz Pharmaceuticals, following Albert Hofmann's discovery of LSD's psychological effects in 1943, indicated that low to medium doses of LSD (between approximately 25 and 200 micrograms) could help a person recover unconscious memories in a series of psychotherapeutic sessions.[2] These initial findings led Sandoz to recommend that researchers investigate LSD's ability to intensify, deepen, and accelerate the therapeutic process. Ronald Sandison, wishing to ally LSD-enhanced therapy and Jungian analysis, coined the term *psycholytic* in the early 1960s for the low- and medium-dose model of psychedelic-enhanced psychotherapy. The term *psycholytic*, with its root *lytic* (from the Greek *lutikos*, able to loosen), indicated for Sandison the ability these substances have to loosen those psychological mechanisms that inhibit the release of unconscious memories, emotions, and images. For Stanislav Grof and others who adopted less explicitly Jungian-oriented approaches to psychedelic-enhanced psychotherapy, the term *psycholytic* refers more generally to the release of tensions by dissolving psychological conflict and resistance.[3]

As I explain in chapter 3, Jung classified the unconscious into the *personal* and the *collective* unconscious.[4] The personal unconscious contains ideas, emotions, perceptions, and other psychological elements that are derived from personal experience but which the person has forgotten, repressed, or did not consciously notice in the first place. The collective unconscious consists of the psychological content (what Jung sometimes calls *primordial images*, *thought-patterns*, or *archetypes*) that each of us has inherited from our evolutionary past and therefore shares with all other human beings. Psycholytic therapy typically, though by no means exclusively, focuses on the personal unconscious rather than the deeper, collective, or transpersonal unconscious. In comparison to conventional, non-drug-enhanced psychotherapy, the relatively low doses used in psycholytic therapy allow people to more readily and intensely become aware of unconscious memories and feelings without overwhelming their ability to communicate with their therapist and reflect on what has been uncovered. Psycholytic therapy tends to draw from the basic principles and practices of dynamic psychotherapy (prevalently Freudian psychoanalysis) with certain adjustments suitable to the drug experience: longer periods of silence, more intense therapeutic support during longer sessions, and a higher tolerance for bizarre behavior.[5]

Veteran psychedelic researcher and therapist Myron Stolaroff has found that psychedelics can be effective tools for "making the unconscious conscious."[6] Stolaroff has found in particular that low-dose sessions, as opposed to high-dose sessions, are the most effective way to become aware of and deal with those long-denied but crucial aspects of our nature that Jung called *the shadow*. But many people don't like low-dose sessions because uncomfortable feelings arise when they become aware of their shadow, Stolaroff maintains. Rather than experience these difficult feelings, they prefer to transcend them with large doses. But if we are willing to work through these painful feelings in low-dose sessions, he says, we can reach the same sublimely transcendent states that large doses open us to—with a significant benefit: having faced and acknowledged those denied parts of ourselves, we are less vulnerable to their harmful unconscious influence in our daily life.[7]

Psychedelic Therapy

Practitioners of psychedelic-enhanced therapy have nevertheless long appreciated the unique benefits of high-dose sessions. In the mid 1950s, when high doses of mescaline or LSD were shown to yield successful results in treating chronic alcoholics, who experienced mystical states of consciousness and insights into their drinking problems during their sessions, Humphrey Osmond coined the term *psychedelic* to distance this new use of psychedelics from the traditional psychotomimetic model.[8] In high-dose psychedelic therapy (300 to 800 micrograms of LSD), the psychedelic experience itself—an overwhelming, internalized experience, independent of verbal psychotherapy—is considered the significant therapeutic agent.[9] Such an extraordinary experience can bring about a temporary mystical state that can radically change a person's personality and view of life.

In psychedelic therapy, the therapist emphasizes, encourages, and supports the person's complete psychological surrender to the experience, a radical form of surrender often referred to as "ego death." The main goal of psychedelic therapy, Grof points out, "is to create optimal conditions for the subject to experience ego death and the subsequent transcendence into the so-called psychedelic peak experience. It is an ecstatic state, characterized by the loss of boundaries between the subject and the objective world, with ensuing feelings of unity with other people, nature, the entire Universe, and God."[10]

Maria Estevez's psilocybin-induced mystical experience during a Johns Hopkins clinical study, which I described in chapter 1, is an excellent example of high-dose psychedelic therapy that focuses on the psychedelic experience itself. Ms. Estevez's monitors encouraged her to internalize the process (with the help of a comfortable couch, a blanket, eye shades, and headphones) and to stay open to whatever the experience presented to her. As the session unfolded, she felt guided by a transcendent spiritual intelligence and had a vision that left her with a sense of having understood familiar religious principles for the first time in her life. Careful preparation and supportive conditions were crucial; the focus of the session, however, was the transformative psychedelic experience itself.

Psychedelic therapy is much more concerned with transcending pathological phenomena than analyzing them, says Grof. And contrary to claims that psycholytic therapy is more effective than psychedelic therapy, Grof thinks higher doses and internalizing the process deepen LSD's therapeutic effect because deeper resolution and integration takes place when the person has little choice but to completely surrender to the psychedelic experience. Total surrender is unlikely with lower doses, which, though effectively releasing unconscious memories and emotions, also allow one to avoid facing what arises during the session, Grof adds.[11]

It is not surprising that experiences of transcending time, space, and causality lacks a theoretical basis that meets current scientific standards for psychological investigation. Whereas psycholytic therapy is based on established theories of dynamic psychotherapy, psychedelic therapy lacks a conventional theoretical foundation. A theoretical basis for psychedelic therapy is understandably more difficult to develop because the ineffable, mystical nature of the insights induced by psychedelic therapy are notoriously resistant to explanation. Given these challenges, the extraordinary states elicited by psychedelic therapy are currently explained in terms of traditional religious and mystical systems as interpreted by modern transpersonal psychology.[12] As I show in later chapters, I find Jungian psychology, with its appreciation of the psyche's "religious function," especially well suited to understanding mystical experiences induced by psychedelic substances.

All in the field should agree that we have much more to learn about the relative effectiveness of psycholytic and psychedelic therapies and about how the two could be combined. Equally apparent is the need for controlled comparative studies in which each method is subjected to empirical investigation.[13] Until then, we can benefit from considering the features and goals that these two models share.

Common Features and Goals

Psychedelic therapist Abram Hoffer's description of psychedelic therapy's aim and methods illustrates well its fundamental similarity to psycholytic therapy. Despite psychedelic therapy's emphasis on mystical experience and avoiding verbal interaction during the psychedelic session, we see here the significant role that psychotherapy can play in the process as a whole:

> Psychedelic therapy [with the chronic alcoholic] aims to create a set and a setting that will allow proper psychotherapy. The psychedelic therapist works with material that the patient experiences and discusses, and helps him resynthesize a new model of life or a new personal philosophy. During the experience, the patient draws from his own past, and uses it to eliminate false ideas and false memories. With the aid of the therapist, he evaluates himself more objectively and becomes more acutely aware of his own responsibility for his situation. . . . He also becomes aware of inner strengths or qualities that help him in his long and difficult struggle toward sobriety.[14]

Conversely, even though psycholytic therapist Ronald Sandison discusses the occasional verbal role therapists may play *during* the LSD session to help patients integrate unconscious material, he had such deep respect for the psychological processes released within his patients by LSD that he tended to avoid interrupting their LSD experiences. There are no absolute rules when using these substances, he advises; maturity in therapy involves flexibility.[15]

We can say with some oversimplification, then, that the two approaches differ essentially in the emphasis placed on the role of the psychedelic experience: psycholytic therapy tends to use the psychedelic experience as an adjunct to psychotherapy, while psychedelic therapy tends to use psychotherapy as an adjunct to the psychedelic experience. The dosage, number, and frequency of sessions, and the timing of the therapist's interaction with the patient will naturally vary among practitioners within each approach. But, as Grof points out, we can reasonably assume that both approaches deal with similar psychological phenomena.[16] And, as Grinspoon and Bakalar note in their review of these two models, "the transcendent and the analytic aspects can never be entirely separated."[17] In fact, Grof proposes that psycholytic and psychedelic therapy would optimally be combined in an integrated treatment program that exploits the strengths of both.[18]

Schools of Psychedelic-Enhanced Therapy

Theorists and practitioners in the field see the psychedelic substance as only one element in psychedelic-enhanced treatment. The drug's therapeutic value is assumed to be significantly affected by factors external to the psychedelic experience itself, including the practitioner's therapeutic approach. Given the importance of non-drug factors, we can expect the therapist's school of thought, or theoretical framework, to significantly influence the practice and outcome of psychedelic-enhanced therapy. If we consider the range of theoretical frameworks and associated therapeutic goals and methods represented by, for instance, a Freudian, a Jungian, and a Grofian practitioner; each will likely relate differently to psychedelic experiences involving the personal unconscious, the collective unconscious, and transpersonal realms.

By 1970, success with psychedelic-enhanced therapy had been reported by hundreds of therapists of various persuasions, from many countries of the world, using a diverse range of psychotherapeutic methods.[19] Too often, however, the practitioner's underlying therapeutic orientation remains implicit in discussions about the nature, goals, methods, and effectiveness of psychedelic-enhanced therapy.[20] The potential for confusion caused by this situation is aggravated by the commendable tendency practitioners have to draw from a variety of theoretical orientations, borrow techniques from each other, and develop their own eclectic approach.[21] Some general trends can be identified, nevertheless.

Recent publications go a long way toward clarifying matters by surveying various theoretical frameworks.[22] With theoretical differences leading to different therapeutic practices, and with so many methodological questions to investigate, we have good reason to be as explicit as possible about the particular theoretical frameworks underlying various practices of psychedelic-enhanced therapy. Drawing mainly from Winkelman and Roberts's *Psychedelic Medicines*, I sketch here a brief overview of the most prevalent existing frameworks for psychedelic-enhanced therapy.

Psychoanalytic

Although compatible with other forms of psychotherapy, such as Jungian and Gestalt therapies, psycholytic therapy conducted in the 1950s and 1960s was dominated by a classical Freudian psychoanalytic orientation that focused on the repressed memories, emotions, drives, and conflicts of the personal unconscious. Dan Merkur proposes a contemporary psychoanalytic approach to psychedelic psychotherapy to overcome the limitations of traditional psychoanalytic assumptions. Conceiving emergent unconscious material as "co-constructions, negotiated between the analyst and the patient," and maintaining that verbal interaction between analyst and patient is essential, Merkur suggests that psychedelic psychotherapists working from a contemporary psychoanalytic perspective need to know what to say to those undergoing high-dose treatment to establish the therapeutic rapport that more typically occurs during low-dose sessions. "The task," Merkur says, "is to interpret what a patient's unconscious integrative process is trying to communicate to consciousness."[23] As I will show, I think the challenges Merkur identifies are central to effective psychedelic-enhanced therapy in general; and I think a Jungian perspective helps elucidate important questions about how and when it is appropriate, or whether it is appropriate at all, to verbally interact with a person undergoing psychedelic-enhanced therapy.

Grofian

Following his first personal experimental LSD session in 1956, Stanislav Grof started his clinical work with psychedelic drugs as an orthodox Freudian psychoanalyst using methods that subsequently became known as psycholytic therapy.[24] Discovering that his psychoanalytic framework could not accommodate the extraordinary variety of experiences and content he encountered in psychedelic sessions, Grof eventually found the Freudian orientation untenable. He subsequently "moved far beyond the narrow psychoanalytic framework to full recognition of the practical and theoretical significance of the death-rebirth process and transpersonal phenomena."[25]

Grof developed a comprehensive model of consciousness transformation that incorporates the extraordinary range of psychological and existential phenomena he has observed during decades of psychedelic research. These phenomena range from vivid sensory experiences (e.g., visual hallucinations of intricate designs) and the reliving of personal unconscious memories (e.g., a traumatic accident) to experiential encounters with birth, death, and transpersonal phenomena that suggest the human psyche is "essentially commensurate with the whole universe and all of existence."[26] Transpersonal experiences can involve an infinite variety of phenomena, including visions of and identification with various peoples, cultures, species, life forms, mythological figures, and the cosmos.

In his seminal book *LSD Psychotherapy,* Grof presents an exceptionally thorough and precisely articulated theory and method of psychedelic therapy. His framework includes preparation for a session, preventing and managing adverse effects; changes in experiences, content, emotions, and personality over a series of sessions; and the healing potential of transpersonal experiences.[27] Probably no other framework has influenced the theory and practice of psychedelic-enhanced therapy as much as Stanislav Grof's.

Shamanic

Restrictions on experimental and clinical research with psychedelics increased the importance of cross-cultural studies of indigenous peoples' therapeutic use of psychedelics, or sacred medicines. Since ancient times, psychoactive plants have been used for healing and spiritual purposes in shamanic ceremonies and rituals throughout the world. These age-old practices can provide valuable guidelines for psychedelic-enhanced therapy within cultures that lack such experience and knowledge. As anthropologist Michael Winkelman puts it, shamanic perspectives and practices provide "a broader clinical tradition within which to manage the diverse potentials of psychedelic substances."[28] This knowledge includes practices that prepare participants for the psychedelic experience, ways of optimizing the effects of the substance, and conceptual systems for understanding and managing experiences of the spirit world. Many who participate in these practices maintain that the transformation of consciousness they engender could have far-reaching consequences for the health of our beleaguered planet.

Within the rich variety of shamanic traditions, those using psychedelic medicines such as ayahuasca tend to emphasize visions and encounters with beings, or entities, of the spirit world. These visionary experiences are encouraged by ceremonies with an internal focus guided by a shaman's singing and chanting in the darkness of night. In these shamanic traditions' spirit-world orientation, the plants themselves are considered the teachers. Winkelman suggests that the states of consciousness induced by these sacred medicines activate ancient brain structures and animal powers of the unconscious. These structures and processes, which are experienced as spirits, "provide important information relevant to the dynamics of the individual and [the] unconscious," he adds.[29] Drawing from Jung's interpretation of shamanic images as symbolic manifestations of archetypes, Winkelman maintains that spirit-world images give form to the collective unconscious and thereby provide "a matrix for engaging and releasing archetypal energies, transferring [them] from the unconscious to the conscious. Shamanic visionary activities provide mechanisms for a reconnection with this archetypal ground."[30]

Hybrid

The cross-cultural study of psychedelic healing has led to new forms of group-based psychedelic therapy that combine elements of shamanic ritual healing with principles of psychedelic and transpersonal therapies.[31] Ralph Metzner calls such combined forms of psychedelic-enhanced therapy *hybrid shamanic psychotherapeutic rituals*. These rituals typically involve psychedelic plant substances, or entheogens (meaning "engendering the experience of the divine within"), such as psilocybe mushrooms, ayahuasca, or peyote. This practice also adopts certain elements from traditional shamanic ceremonies, including the gathering of participants in a circle around an alter or fire in semi-darkness, music, and an experienced guide who initially invokes the spirits of the four directions and cultivates a respectful spiritual attitude throughout the ritual.[32] Conducting sessions as neither shaman nor therapist, Marsden and Lukoff observe, the group guide attempts to create conditions that help "establish a *conscious and growth producing link* between the participant and the hallucinogenic experience."[33] In some variations, participants speak one at a time when holding a "talking staff;" in other forms, there is little or no interaction. In any case, there is no discussion or interpretation as in conventional group psychotherapy. In advance of consuming the plant substance, however, participants share their intentions for the experience; and soon after the ritual, they can reflect on their experience in relation to their intentions and what they have learned that can be applied to their lives.[34]

An Early Jungian Approach to Psychedelic-Enhanced Psychotherapy

Jungian-oriented therapist Ronald Sandison was the chief psychiatrist at Powick Hospital near Worcester, England in 1952 when he visited a number of Swiss mental hospitals. Besides visiting Burghölzli Hospital in

Zurich, where Jung's career had started, Sandison spent time at the Sandoz laboratories in Basel. He was fascinated to learn of the work being done there with LSD, and he returned a few months later to take a closer look. This time he left the Sandoz labs carrying several psychedelic-related publications and a box with 100 ampoules of LSD.

Shortly thereafter, Sandison began the first work with LSD-enhanced psychotherapy in Britain. Sandison and his Jungian analyst colleague Margot Cutner saw LSD as an instrument for advancing psychotherapy through its ability to produce "an upsurge of unconscious material into consciousness."[35] Reflecting years later on LSD's explosive popularity, Sandison came to regret the lack of appreciation among recreational users for "the esoteric nature of this remarkable substance." He recalls that those who used LSD in their clinical practice at Powick "developed a reverence for its properties, rather as the shamans of old regarded their magical plants."[36] Following extensive clinical observation, he became convinced that the drug's unique ability to release unconscious imagery made it an invaluable tool for enhancing Jungian-oriented psychotherapy, which prompted him to coin the term *psycholytic therapy*. Working with patients who took between 25 and 200 micrograms of LSD, Sandison identified three distinct types of drug-induced experiences: dream-like hallucinations, the reliving of forgotten personal memories, and encounters with unconscious imagery. Sandison describes the third type of experience as "archaic, impersonal images . . . exactly similar in nature to those experiences of the collective unconscious which patients undergoing deep analysis experience in their dreams, visual impressions, and fantasies. . . . Furthermore, these more primitive LSD experiences are accompanied by a sense of their agelessness and timeless quality which is the hallmark of the great archetypes of the collective unconscious."[37]

Sandison and Cutner published papers in the 1950s describing case studies that reflect the value of LSD-assisted psychotherapy. Reviewing these cases, Jungian analyst Michael Fordham cautioned that the "passive" process of LSD-enhanced psychotherapy, in which the substance produces unconscious imagery "by involuntary biochemical means," must be distinguished from "the patient's deliberate activity" during conventional Jungian psychotherapy.[38] For Fordham, that is, psychedelic substances diminish one's capacity to consciously engage in the therapeutic process. He is alluding here to Jung's technique of "active imagination," through which one intentionally engages with images and symbols that have emerged in dreams or fantasies by, for example, writing about them. Fordham also asserted that by far the strongest therapeutic agent in the cases he reviewed was the patient's relationship to the therapist, and that the lasting therapeutic value of the LSD experience itself is slight.[39]

Sandison agrees that the patient's relationship to the therapist is essential. Indeed, the lasting benefits of LSD therapy, he asserts, derive from the therapeutic relationship, through which the patient comes to understand and integrate unconscious material released during the LSD session. When, for example, a patient sees the doctor as her mother under LSD's influence, she can gain insight into the significance of this perception through careful work with the therapist.[40] Regarding Fordham's view that psychedelic-enhanced therapy is a passive process that must be distinguished from the active process of conventional Jungian therapy, Sandison explains that the ability "to move amongst the unconscious images is one of the most useful properties that LSD may confer on a patient;" and he compares this productive process to the technique of active imagination in conventional Jungian therapy.[41]

Fordham argues that we cannot assume that making patients aware of previously unconscious memories is therapeutic. "Therapy depends more on integrating the previously unconscious products into the ego," he says.[42] Sandison maintains, however, that integration is central to LSD therapy. Each feeling, fantasy, and image, he notes, must be explored by the therapist and integrated by the patient.[43]

One of the cases Fordham reviewed was a suicidally depressed woman who had undergone LSD therapy with Sandison. Although Sandison had reported a successful conclusion to her treatment and had found little reason to doubt her complete recovery, she attempted suicide three years later and was referred to a therapist under Fordham's supervision at the C. G. Jung Clinic in London. Only after three and a half years of painstaking work, reports Fordham, did this woman show signs of significant recovery. Fordham's criticism of LSD-enhanced psychotherapy raises the fundamental question of whether psycholytic therapy is a poor substitute for conventional, long-term Jungian analysis. When I asked Ronald Sandison in 2009 about this, he acknowledged that to some extent Fordham's criticism of LSD treatment in the early 1950s was valid. "We hadn't fully refined at that time the distinction between those patients who would do better with LSD and those who would be better off going into conventional therapy." Nevertheless, he adds, given the realities of available healthcare, where only a very small proportion of patients have the opportunity to undergo long-term psychotherapy, it would be irresponsible to not take advantage of other treatments. "If LSD is available and effective," Sandison says, "why not use it?"[44]

Sandison's Jungian colleague Margot Cutner valued LSD as an aid to deep analysis yet also believed it was essential for therapists to be aware of potential problems when working with LSD, as with any therapeutic "short cut." In her pivotal journal article, "Analytic Work with LSD 25," she asks whether LSD-assisted psychotherapy is a justifiable method for breaking through a patient's apparent resistances. Is it more appropriate to work through such resistances with conventional analytical work?[45] For many patients, she concludes, one cannot deny that auxiliary means such as LSD can be helpful. She has also found that the risks of harming patients with LSD-enhanced psychotherapy are exaggerated, "as long as the analyst is present during the crucial experiences and can represent the integrating ego-function for the patient."[46] Cutner is careful to add, however, that she always aims "to use [LSD] as sparingly as possible and to keep the *main accent on the analysis itself*."[47]

I will return in later chapters to these complex issues and the specific concepts and principles discussed in these papers by Sandison, Cutner, and Fordham. For now, I would like to emphasize the need for further research to learn about the effectiveness of psychedelic-enhanced psychotherapy compared with conventional psychotherapy. And we need to look in particular at the relative effectiveness of Jungian-oriented psycholytic therapy and conventional Jungian therapy. Regrettably, we have only one review by a Jungian analyst of psychedelic-enhanced therapy, involving only three patients. Even though I find Fordham's review to be occasionally biased and self-serving, I appreciate his engagement in the fundamental issues; and his objections raise important questions that deserve more attention by psychedelic therapists and Jungians.

CHAPTER 3

Basic Jungian Concepts and Principles

As I've said, Jung's basic theoretical and clinical work provides profound insights into psychedelic experience. Sometimes, however, we need to be patient with his way of explaining things. Jung's ideas can at times be difficult to grasp, and his writing is now and then circuitous, inconsistent, turgid, or metaphorical to the point of exasperation. Jung himself acknowledges that "the language I speak must be ambiguous, must have two meanings, in order to do justice to the dual aspect of our psychic nature. I strive consciously and deliberately for ambiguity of expression, because it is superior to unequivocalness and reflects the nature of life."[1] The occasional challenges Jung's writing can present arise to some extent, then, out of his evolving attempt to understand and describe the psyche in all its intriguing complexity. And Jung's way of writing about the psyche inevitably changed as his thinking developed through a lifetime of exploration, analysis, and reflection. He seems to have been continually searching for new ways to communicate his discoveries and express his hunches.

Many Jungians think that Jung's writing quite appropriately reflects his passionate, intuitive, and creative engagement with his subject, the dynamic psyche—especially the deepest levels of the unconscious. Sometimes, others suggest, we can best understand Jung's writing as "a flow of images," which he could only express by analogy.[2] Jungian analyst June Singer maintains that Jung bridges the intellectual abstractions of science and the direct, intuitive knowing of spiritual experience in a paradoxical way of thinking that is inconsistent with our culture's preference for precise logic.[3] I agree with these appreciative interpretations of Jung's writing style, and I encourage readers who are new to Jung's psychology to keep these explanations in mind if they encounter difficulty with Jung's writing. And if some of the definitions in this chapter seem overly abstract, I suggest that you read for a general sense of the ideas I introduce, which should become clearer as they are discussed in more concrete contexts in the following chapters.

Consciousness and the Unconscious

Jung's model of the conscious mind's relationship to the unconscious—especially the deepest levels of the unconscious—provides striking insights into the effects that psychedelics have on the psyche, including their potential to induce adverse reactions or to advance psychospiritual transformation. For Jung, a psychedelic substance causes a condition that he describes as "a lowering of the threshold of consciousness." That is, Jung understood that a psychedelic substance acts on the psyche in a way that lowers a psychological barrier between the conscious mind and the unconscious, thereby allowing unconscious images and emotions to enter and potentially overwhelm consciousness. To fully appreciate the significance of a lowering of the threshold of consciousness in a psychedelic experience, we need to understand the relationship between the conscious mind, or "consciousness," and the unconscious mind, or "the unconscious," in Jung's psychology.

Jung classifies all the contents and functions of the psyche into their conscious and unconscious aspects. The conscious aspect includes all ideas, emotions, perceptions, and other psychological elements a person recognizes or is aware of. The unconscious consists of all psychological contents and processes a person isn't aware of.[4] Generally speaking, Jung describes the psyche as "the totality of all psychic [that is, psychological] processes, conscious as well as unconscious."[5] Jung sometimes speaks of the psyche as a conscious-unconscious whole with no definite boundaries between the two.[6] But he usually emphasizes their differences and notes that the psyche is "a divisible and more or less divided whole."[7]

Jung defines consciousness as the psychological function that maintains "the relation of psychic contents to the *ego*, in so far as this relation is perceived as such by the ego."[8] Elsewhere, Jung defines consciousness as "the sum total of representations, ideas, emotions, perceptions, and other mental contents which the ego acknowledges."[9] Jung also equated consciousness with awareness, and he stressed the role of reflection and discrimination in consciousness.[10] As will become clear in chapter 4, Jung's conception of consciousness is central to his approach to integration.

The ego is the center of a person's consciousness and identity. Jung defines the ego as "a complex of ideas which constitutes the center of [one's] field of consciousness and appears to possess a high degree of continuity and identity."[11] Jung also refers to the ego as "the subject of consciousness."[12] Consciousness needs a center, explains Jung, "an ego to which something is conscious. We know of no other kind of consciousness, nor can we imagine a consciousness without an ego. There can be no consciousness when there is no one to say: 'I am conscious.'"[13] Jung often emphasizes the ego's central role in consciousness by his frequent use of the term *ego-consciousness*.

Jung's emphasis on the ego's centrality in consciousness can obscure *unconscious* aspects of the ego, such as its denied, or shadow, qualities. That is, even though the ego is highly conscious in comparison to the unconscious, the ego has unconscious properties of its own.[14] This nuanced conception of the ego recalls William James's idea of a "field of consciousness" with its indeterminate and shifting "margin" of awareness. We can't precisely outline this field, James observes; it is so vaguely drawn that we can't say exactly what we are conscious of at any particular moment.[15] Such observations remind us of the complexity and ambiguity of these hypothetical ideas.

The unconscious for Jung constitutes "all psychic contents and processes that are not conscious, i.e., not related to the ego in any perceptible way."[16] Jung points out that the unconscious is normally so unrelated to the ego that most people deny its existence altogether.[17] Even when unconscious content is recognized in the form of, say, a dream or fantasy image, we seldom appreciate it as a source of knowledge or wisdom. The essential difference between the psyche's conscious and unconscious functions, Jung notes, is that consciousness is intensely concentrated on the person's immediate field of attention within the scope of a person's lifetime. The unconscious, on the other hand, "is not concentrated and intensive, but shades off into obscurity; it is highly extensive and can juxtapose the most heterogeneous elements in the most paradoxical way."[18]

Jung classifies the unconscious into the *personal* and the *collective* unconscious. The personal unconscious contains "all the acquisitions of personal life," all ideas, sensations, perceptions, images, and emotions that are derived from personal experience, but which one has forgotten, repressed, or didn't notice in the first place.[19] The collective unconscious consists of the psychological contents and "the patterns of life and behavior" that each of us has inherited from our evolutionary past and therefore shares with all other human beings.[20] That is, underneath the personal, individual, or subjective unconscious, lies an unconscious layer that Jung usually calls the *collective unconscious*, "which has nothing to do with our personal experience."[21] He occasionally calls this deeper level the *objective psyche*, the *impersonal unconscious,* or *the transpersonal unconscious.*[22] Jungian analyst Joseph Henderson describes the collective unconscious as "that part of the psyche that retains and transmits the common psychological inheritance of mankind."[23] Jung conceives of this deeper level of the unconscious as "combining the characteristics of both sexes, transcending youth and age, birth and death, and, . . . having at its command a human experience of one or two million years, practically immortal."[24] This impersonal unconscious, he adds, seems "something like an unceasing stream or perhaps ocean of images and figures which drift into consciousness in our dreams or in abnormal states of mind."[25] But, as strange as this realm of the unconscious may seem to us, Jung maintains that we shouldn't dismiss it as worthless. In fact, Jung considers the collective unconscious an especially valuable source of knowledge and wisdom because it "contains the whole spiritual heritage of mankind's evolution, born anew in the brain structure of every individual."[26] As analyst Thomas Kirsch puts it, Jung taught us that an "openness to forms of experience beyond everyday reality is historically essential to our humanness."[27]

Although Jung repeatedly distinguishes between the personal and the collective unconscious, we must remember, as he did, that rigid distinctions between the two don't reflect the psyche's actual complexity. This more nuanced view is suggested by the title of Mary Williams' influential paper, "The Indivisibility of the Personal and Collective Unconscious."[28] Williams argues that, even though they can be distinguished intellectually, personal and collective levels of the psyche are more likely inseparable. Consider, for example, that the archetypes of the collective unconscious remain only inherited psychological patterns until they are manifested in personal experience. Williams' view has been adopted by many Jungian psychotherapists. Joseph Henderson, for example, suggests that the psyche's different levels shouldn't be separated in the therapist's mind even when patients experience their problems at only one level.[29] Such separation, Williams points out, isn't conducive to the therapeutic goal of integrating consciousness and the unconscious.[30]

The Relationship between Consciousness and the Unconscious

In Jung's psychology, the conscious and unconscious spheres complement each other in a compensating relationship. Drawing an analogy to the self-regulatory system that maintains the organism's physiological equilibrium, Jung conceives of this compensatory relationship as "an inherent self-regulation of the psychic apparatus."[31] Comparing consciousness to the focal point of vision that holds only a limited amount of content at one time, Jung characterizes consciousness as selective. "Selection demands *direction*. But direction requires the *exclusion of everything irrelevant*. This is bound to make the conscious *orientation* one-sided. The contents that are excluded and inhibited by the chosen direction sink into the unconscious, where they form a counterweight to the conscious orientation. The strengthening of this counterposition keeps pace with the increase of conscious one-sidedness until finally a noticeable tension is produced."[32] To a point, the ego can overcome this tension by increased conscious effort; but unconscious content eventually breaks through into conscious awareness in the form of dreams, fantasies, or psychosomatic disturbances. Every conscious process that goes too far, becomes too extreme, inevitably brings about a compensation. "The more one-sided the conscious attitude, the more antagonistic are the contents arising from the unconscious, so that we may speak of a real opposition between the two."[33]

The unconscious bridges the two psychological worlds by balancing, adjusting, and supplementing the one-sided tendency of consciousness through dreams, fantasies, visions, and hallucinations. But the ego experiences these unconscious manifestations as unexpected and strange. Some manifestations, like the ideas expressed by schizophrenics, are so baffling that no one can understand them. As Jung puts it, the conscious mind simply "lacks the premises which would help to explain the strangeness of the ideas."[34]

The consequences of this compensatory relationship vary. Under certain conditions, images and emotions arising from the unconscious can overpower a person's conscious mind and cause severe confusion or insanity. Yet the unconscious often brings the very wisdom that consciousness lacks. "The collaboration of the unconscious is intelligent and purposive," Jung says, "and even when it acts in opposition to consciousness its expression is still compensatory in an intelligent way, as if it were trying to restore the lost balance."[35] This observation suggests two central themes running through this book regarding adverse reactions to a psychedelic experience: the potentially antagonistic relationship between consciousness and the unconscious, on the one hand, and the transformative potential of even the most problematic reactions to unconscious images and emotions, on the other.

Jung understands and accepts that the relationship between consciousness and the unconscious is often initially challenging. He poses the basic problem this way: "Say you have been very one-sided and lived in a two-dimensional world only, behind walls, thinking that you are perfectly safe; then suddenly the sea breaks in: you are inundated by an archetypal world and you are in complete confusion."[36] What possible good could come from such confusion? Jung maintains that if we can face the confusion and darkness triggered by a confrontation with the archetypal world, we can advance psychological transformation, or individuation.[37]

Before introducing Jung's concept of individuation, I want to emphasize two fundamental Jungian principles suggested here. Psychological confusion and darkness often accompany the ego's confrontation with the archetypes of the collective unconscious. And working through this confusion and darkness is an essential step in psychological transformation. These two principles are central to my Jungian interpretation of adverse reactions to a psychedelic experience because they involve the very dynamics that elucidate the nature of such adverse reactions and their transformative potential.

Individuation

Jung defines *individuation* as "the process by which a person becomes a psychological 'in-dividual,' that is, a separate, indivisible unity or 'whole.'"[38] Understanding that Jung also sees individuation as "an extension of the sphere of consciousness, an enriching of conscious psychological life" through a constructive relationship to the unconscious, we can start to appreciate that bringing unconscious content to consciousness is central to Jung's theory of psychological development.[39] This movement toward wholeness is for Jung an extraordinarily important undertaking, a perpetual process of seeking a balanced relationship between consciousness and the unconscious. Both are essential aspects of life, and if either is suppressed, or even neglected, there can be no psychological harmony. Such a movement toward wholeness is the goal of any psychotherapy claiming to accomplish more than the mere curing of symptoms, asserts Jung.[40]

Summing up his late essay "On the Nature of the Psyche," Jung explains that his theory of the psyche leads to integrating unconscious content into consciousness. This process has remarkable effects on a person, he explains:

> It is a relatively rare occurrence, which is experienced only by those who have gone through the wearisome but, if the unconscious is to be integrated, indispensable business of coming to terms with the unconscious components of the personality. Once these unconscious components are made conscious, it results not only in their assimilation to the already existing ego-personality, but in a transformation of the latter. The main difficulty is to describe the manner of this transformation. Generally speaking the ego is a hard-and-fast complex which, because tied to consciousness and its continuity, cannot easily be altered, and should not be altered unless one wants to bring on pathological disturbances.[41]

When Jung says that the ego should not be altered unless one wants to bring on a pathological disturbance, I think he means that whenever the ego is altered by a confrontation with the deep unconscious, one risks a potentially harmful disruption of the ego's equilibrium. That potential for harm can be realized if the ego is not strong enough to weather and assimilate especially strange unconscious content that has emerged in the form of, say, terrifying images or delusional ideas. Jung is also saying, however, that psychological transformation cannot occur unless the ego *is altered* by a conscious relationship to the unconscious. Jung's description of the paradoxical necessity and danger of altering the ego in the service of psychological transformation is analogous to the risks and potential benefits inherent in psychedelic experience. We will consider this paradox throughout the rest of this book.

Archetypes and Their Manifestation in the Psyche

As we have seen, the collective unconscious contains the psychological content that each of us has inherited from our evolutionary past and therefore shares with all other human beings. Jung often discusses this content, and its effect on the conscious mind, in terms of archetypes that manifest as especially potent images, images that have been expressed through the ages in such mythological and religious motifs as birth, death, evil, and transcendence. To appreciate the demands of deep psychological exploration, and certainly serious work with psychedelics, from a Jungian perspective, we need to understand Jung's conception of the archetypes and their effects on consciousness.

Jung characterized archetypes in different ways as he refined the idea. He first used the term *primordial images* to designate universal images expressed in various forms in the world's myths and religions. Later he adopted the term *archetype* to distinguish more explicitly a hypothetical unconscious pattern from its observable manifestation as an image (in a dream, for instance). Jung's occasional references to the archetype *per se* emphasize this idea of the archetype as an underlying pattern, which we cannot observe directly, distinct from its observable manifestations in consciousness as images or emotions.[42]

Jung generally conceives of archetypes as inherited psychological patterns linked to instinct. He sometimes characterizes archetypes as "deposits of the constantly repeated experiences of humanity."[43] Although the archetypes can only become conscious in individual experience, Jung understands them to be universal "preexistent pathways which are merely 'filled out' by individual experience. Probably every 'impressive' experience is just such a break-through into an old, previously unconscious riverbed."[44] So even though archetypes developed over millennia out of such universal life experiences as birth, motherhood, and death, they are experienced differently by each person. We each experience the archetype of "the mother," for instance, in our own way.

Jung cautions that archetypes are quite difficult to understand because the intellect tends to oversimplify their multiple and paradoxical meanings. Moreover, in our experience of archetypes, their numinous, or strange and fascinating, quality always engages our emotions, making them even more difficult to comprehend intellectually. Jung concludes, nevertheless, that "insofar as the archetypes act upon me, they are real and actual to me, even though I do not know what their real nature is."[45] For these reasons, my treatment focuses on how Jung describes the subjective experience of archetypes rather than on an attempt to define their nature. As we have seen, Jung's lifework, which so richly portrays the qualities of psychedelic experience, was motivated by his own encounters with what he came to understand as the archetypes of the collective unconscious.

Given my interest in especially challenging psychedelic experiences, my treatment of archetypes tends to emphasize their problematic effects on consciousness. We shouldn't forget, however, that for Jung archetypes are universal elements of human experience, sources of psychic energy, and vital components of psychological health. For Jung, as we have seen, psychological health results from a balanced tension between consciousness and the unconscious. The archetypes become problematic, however, when consciousness becomes so one-sided that it defensively represses their manifestation, or when the ego is overwhelmed by their sudden and unexpected emergence.

Jung describes archetypes as powerful instinctive forces that consciousness experiences as "wholly unexpected, new, and even strange."[46] Archetypes can saturate consciousness "with uncanny forebodings or even with the fear of madness."[47] Archetypes surface in dreams, projections, hallucinations, and visions with a numinous effect. "They behave like highly charged autonomous centres of power—they exert a fascinating and possessive influence upon the conscious mind and can thus produce extensive alterations in the subject."[48]

These instinctual psychic patterns aren't intrinsically pathological, but their effects are especially apparent in certain forms of schizophrenia, when ego-consciousness has become overwhelmed by the unconscious. When archetypes burst into consciousness, they often trigger a psychosis, Jung explains. "They undoubtedly belong to the material that comes to light in schizophrenia."[49] The ego understandably resists the instinctive force of the archetypes. As Jung puts it, "consciousness struggles in a regular panic against being swallowed up in the primitivity and unconsciousness of sheer instinctuality. . . . The closer one comes to the instinct-world, the more violent is the urge to shy away from it."[50]

And yet, paradoxically, we are also pulled toward this instinctual archetypal world. Psychologically, says Jung, "the archetype as an image of instinct is a spiritual goal toward which the whole nature of man strives; it is the sea to which all rivers wend their way, the prize which the hero wrests from the fight with the dragon."[51] Religious and mythological imagery has traditionally provided us an essential link to the collective, archetypal, unconscious, even if we don't know it. The archetypes are what people have hitherto called gods and goddesses, and the central archetype, the Self, is what many people have experienced as God. "The idea of an all-powerful divine Being is present everywhere, unconsciously if not consciously, because it is an archetype," Jung maintains.[52] The Self, as a psychological totality, is for Jung indistinguishable from an archetypal "God-image."[53]

Jung often describes the experience of an archetype in religious terms. In "A Psychological Approach to the Dogma of the Trinity," he characterizes archetypal experience in terms of "holiness," an idea or thing that "possesses the highest value, and in the presence of [which] men are, so to speak, struck dumb. Holiness is also revelatory: it is the illuminative power emanating from an archetypal figure. Nobody ever feels himself to be the subject of such a process, but always as its object. *He* does not perceive holiness, *it* takes him captive and overwhelms him; nor does *he* behold it in a revelation, *it* reveals itself to him. . . . Everything happens apparently outside the sphere of his will, and these things are contents of the unconscious."[54]

In *Ego and Archetype: Individuation and the Religious Function of the Psyche*, Jungian analyst Edward Edinger characterizes the Self as "the central archetype or archetype of wholeness" in Jung's model of the personality.[55] Jungians find reference to the Self archetype in motifs of spiritual transformation and images of wholeness and unity such as mandalas, bridges, or the sun. The ego's relationship to the Self is often represented as a person's relationship to God, the Creator, in religious myth. For Jung, the Self is an archetype originating in the collective unconscious, and it therefore transcends an individual's personality in time and space. Our experience of the Self consequently engenders a sense of timelessness and eternity.[56] It can also engender terror because the ego experiences an encounter with the Self archetype as a subjugation. It can feel like slavery, says Edinger.[57] Jung puts it this way: "You have become a victim of a decision made over your head or in defiance of the heart. From this we can see the numinous power of the self, which can hardly be experienced in any other way. For this reason *the experience of the self is always a defeat for the ego*."[58]

Dreams and Other Symbolic Products of the Unconscious

Even though dreams are the most common and accessible form of material, or content, arising from the unconscious, many other products of the unconscious convey symbols to consciousness. When speaking of content or products of the unconscious, Jung typically speaks of dreams, fantasies, visions, and delusions. At times he refers to images, memories, and emotions. He occasionally includes hallucinations. Again, we can understand all these phenomena as material or content arising from the unconscious and manifesting in one form or another, or as Jung says of dreams, as "unconscious processes obtruding on consciousness."[59] Jung rarely made the connection explicitly, but he also viewed psychedelic-induced images, visions, hallucinations, and delusions as products of the unconscious. I will return to this parallel momentarily and again in chapter 4.

Contrary to prevailing prejudices against dreams, Jung, like Freud, regards dreams as vital sources of psychological information. In contrast to Freud, who considers dreams wish-fulfillment in disguise, Jung considers dreams "a *spontaneous self-portrayal, in symbolic form, of the actual situation in the unconscious.*"[60] (Jung's italics) Jung recognizes the possibility that a dream occasionally can be reduced to a symptom of an underlying psychological problem, but he emphasizes the symbolic nature of dreams, which may "point further and deeper, to a development still called for and a meaningfulness so far unrealized."[61] For Jung, dreams, even dreams revealing pathological conditions, are natural products of a psyche attempting to balance itself. Out of psychological confusion, Jung explains, there arises a "reconciling symbol which unites the vital need of man with the archetypal conditions" and thereby raises consciousness to a higher level.[62]

A symbol possesses complex meaning, unlike a sign, which has a fixed and relatively obvious meaning. A symbol, Jung explains, is a term, a name, or an image that, although familiar to us, implies an unknown or hidden meaning beyond what is apparent. The image of the eagle in American culture is a sign in the Jungian sense because it denotes through common usage the recognizable meanings of American might and freedom. On the other hand, in his book *Man and His Symbols*, Jung explains that the image of the eagle in Christianity is a symbol. In Christianity, the eagle symbolizes John, one of the four Evangelists. The image is derived from the Hebrew prophet Ezekiel's vision of four winged creatures, which are analogous to the four animals representing the sons of the ancient Egyptian god Horus.[63] That is, the image of the eagle in Christianity has far-reaching connotations beyond its obvious, conventional meaning.

It could be argued that the image of the eagle in American culture is symbolic to the extent that it evokes unrecognized or implicit meanings, such as the predatory dominance of other nations and peoples that empire entails. Yet even this unconventional meaning is a fixed one and therefore isn't a symbol in the Jungian sense. For Jung, symbols always have a significance that can never be exactly defined or explained. A symbol contains an unconscious aspect, and when we explore the meaning of a symbol, we eventually reach something "beyond the grasp of reason."[64] This sense of reaching something beyond the grasp of reason becomes more apparent when we consider, say, the wheel as a symbol of the divine. "At this point reason must admit its incompetence," Jung suggests. We are "unable to define a 'divine' being. When, with all our intellectual limitations, we call something 'divine,' we have merely given it a name."[65] For Jung, religious symbols arise from our need to represent phenomena that cannot be fully defined or comprehended.

Symbols in dreams and other products of the unconscious fill a comparable need. A symbol arising from the unconscious bridges the divide between the worlds of consciousness and the unconscious. The symbol is "the middle ground on which the opposites can be united," Jung explains. The symbol or dream image is "the best possible expression for a complex fact not yet clearly apprehended by consciousness."[66] The unconscious isn't rational; it speaks in illogical images, not concepts. Yet to be an effective compensating agent, and to be integrated into consciousness, the image must express a psychological reality and be understandable on some level. We do our best to translate our dream images, to conceptualize them, even though our attempts are never quite adequate because, again, the symbol always indicates something beyond our concepts.[67] Nevertheless, through symbols "the union of conscious and unconscious contents is consummated. Out of this union emerge new situations and new conscious attitudes."[68]

The LSD-induced imagery reported by one of Ronald Sandison's patients illustrates such a union. Having first become conscious of what she described as "the good and evil within me" during an earlier session, this woman became determined to overcome her fear and "go to the bottom of the sea."[69] In a later session, she had a vision of reaching the bottom of the sea, where she found four stones that formed a face. This image was indescribably ugly and beautiful at the same time, and it seemed to her to reflect the essential, sacred, nature of all existence. Through the symbol of four stones forming a face, this woman intuitively recognized that the good and evil within her formed a wholeness that was the foundation on which she had to build her personality.

As I suggested above, my Jungian interpretation of psychedelic experience is based to a great extent on the commonality between manifestations of the unconscious that Jung observed with his clients and patients—in their dreams, fantasies, visions, and delusions—and manifestations of the unconscious found in psychedelic-induced images, visions, hallucinations, and delusions. Jung indicates this commonality in several ways: He describes dreams as hallucinatory representations of unconscious material, or "the hallucinations of normal life."[70] Jung's descriptions of dreams and visions occasionally evoke the otherworldly quality of psychedelic experiences, experiences that can be described as "dreaming awake." In the sleeping state, Jung explains, the psyche "produces contents that are strange and incomprehensible, as though they came from another world."[71] He also says that "a vision is in the last resort nothing less than a dream which has broken through into the waking state."[72] And as I discuss in chapter 8, "Psychosis in Jungian Psychology," we can see the relationship between dreams and psychedelic experiences in Jung's thought by tracing the similarities he describes between dreams and schizophrenia, on the one hand, and between schizophrenia and psychedelic experience, on the other. We can see hints of these connections when Jung describes a dream as a series of apparently contradictory and meaningless images that yield a definite meaning when properly translated.[73]

As I show in the next chapter, the connections between dreams, schizophrenia, and psychedelic experiences are also based on Jung's explanation that they all are related to a lowering of the threshold of consciousness. As the intensity of consciousness is reduced in each of these conditions (to varying degrees), the conscious mind's capacity to hold back emerging unconscious material is weakened to the extent that unconscious imagery and emotions can rise and even flood into consciousness.[74] Again and again, we see Jung coming back to the fundamental insight that unusual, altered, pathological, and even religious states of consciousness—whether reflected in dream images, spiritual visions, psychedelic hallucinations, or psychotic delusions—can be understood as unconscious content arising into and sometimes overwhelming consciousness. As bizarre or even pathological as some of these manifestations may seem, Jung maintains, they all reveal processes that have meaning when understood in the context of a person's life; and they can transform that person's life when properly worked through in therapeutic analysis.

This perspective is closely related to the two principles that underlie my interpretation of difficult, even traumatic, psychedelic experiences and their integration: confusion and darkness often accompany the ego's confrontation with the archetypes of the collective unconscious, and working through this confusion and darkness is an essential step in psychological growth.

Before turning to Jung's explanation of psychedelic experience, I want to emphasize the *hypothetical* nature of these ideas. Consciousness, the unconscious, archetypes, and the Self are theoretical constructs that Jung used to describe psychological phenomena and processes that cannot be directly observed. They can only be inferred from descriptions of subjective experience, from observable effects on human behavior (such as dream images or neurotic symptoms), or from various forms of cultural expression (such as mythological or religious imagery). Problems arise when, having given names to these theoretical ideas and having seen them represented spatially in diagrams, we tend to reify them. We risk, that is, thinking of them as actual physical components. These theoretical concepts provide, nevertheless, a useful model of the psyche, and they have become an effective means by which Jungian theorists and therapists attempt to describe, understand, and treat the psyche in all its invisible complexity. Clinical psychologist Stephen Diamond points out that envisioning "the unconscious" or "the shadow" metaphorically as objective, independent, separate *entities* can help patients in therapy "establish some cognitive framework for conceptualizing their inner experience."[75] But, he cautions, both patients and therapists should never forget the strictly metaphorical nature of these terms. As we look to Jung's psychology for illumination, concepts like the unconscious, the archetypes, the shadow, and the Self can also serve us well. But we should never forget their hypothetical and metaphorical nature. As Jung puts it: "Psychology, like every empirical science, cannot get along without auxiliary concepts, hypotheses, and models."[76] As such, he cautions, they shouldn't be mistaken for the underlying reality they attempt to describe. "The atom of which the physicist speaks," he writes, "is a *model*. Similarly my concept of the archetype or of psychic energy is only an auxiliary idea which can be exchanged at any time for a better formula."[77]

CHAPTER 4

Jung's Explanation of Psychedelic Experience

Jung's psychology is remarkably relevant to understanding psychedelic experiences because psychedelic substances such as LSD, psilocybin, mescaline, and ayahuasca open one to the same realms of the unconscious that Jung so thoroughly explored in his therapeutic practice and his personal life *without* using psychedelics. Responding to Alfred Hubbard's invitation to contribute to psychedelic research, Jung wrote: "Thank you for your kind invitation to contribute to your mescaline scheme. Although I have never taken the drug myself nor given it to another individual, I have at least devoted 40 years of my life to the study of that psychic sphere which is disclosed by the said drug; that is the sphere of numinous experience."[1] Although Jung didn't mention to Hubbard that his study of that numinous sphere of experience was rooted in his own confrontation with the unconscious, he later revealed the personal basis of his knowledge in *Memories, Dreams, Reflections,* the autobiography that he and his colleague Aniela Jaffé wrote near the end of his life. Jung characterized his life as "a story of the self-realization of the unconscious," and he disclosed his intimate lifelong relationship with the deepest layers of the psyche, which began in early childhood with a traumatic fantasy and a precocious dream rich in psychospiritual symbolism.[2] Jung's psychological encounters became especially intense in his late thirties with the series of overwhelming dreams, fantasies, and visions that I introduced in chapter 1.

Reading Jung's account of these psychological confrontations, one can appreciate how closely they resemble intrapsychic encounters and insights others have experienced with psychedelics. The inherent similarity between Jung's encounters with the unconscious and psychedelic experience is graphically represented in his *Red Book,* which he created as a record of his personal psychological explorations. Many of Jung's *Red Book* paintings reflect striking stylistic and thematic parallels to the psychedelic-inspired art of ayahuasca shamans in South America.

Jung's confrontations with the unconscious unfolded during a four-year period of uncertainty and disorientation following his split with Freud in 1913. Despite the extraordinary distress these encounters caused him, they became the indispensable foundation for his lifelong study of the psyche. "The years when I was pursuing my inner images were the most important in my life—in them everything essential was decided," Jung writes.[3] "It all began then; the later details are only supplements and clarifications of the material that burst forth from the unconscious, and at first swamped me. It was the *prima materia* for a lifetime's work."[4]

Initially, Jung resisted the images bursting forth from his unconscious. Eventually, however, he submitted to them and opened himself to a process that left him feeling "menaced by a psychosis."[5] "In order to grasp the fantasies which were stirring in me 'underground,' I knew that I had to let myself plummet down into them, as it were. I felt not only violent resistance to this, but a distinct fear. For I was afraid of losing command of myself and becoming a prey to the fantasies—and as a psychiatrist I realized only too well what that meant. After prolonged hesitation, however, I saw that there was no other way out."[6] Thus, sitting at his desk and thinking over his fears one day, Jung let himself drop into that "other pole of the world."[7]

A Lowering of the Threshold of Consciousness

Jung came to understand that the psychological dynamic underlying his harrowing confrontation with the unconscious was an *abaissement du niveau mental*, a lowering of the threshold of consciousness, that allowed content from the unconscious to flood his conscious mind. Again, an *abaissement du niveau mental* (or simply an *abaissement*) is a hypothetical psychological condition that Jung characterized as a reduced intensity of consciousness, or a "depotentiation of the conscious personality" that starts with a loss of concentration or attention. This state of reduced conscious control allows a corresponding strengthening of the unconscious. In this condition, consciousness can be unexpectedly interrupted and overwhelmed by strange and disruptive images, visions, hallucinations, or delusions.[8]

Jung came to understand, then, that a lowering of the threshold of consciousness is the psychological mechanism that underlies all manifestations of unconscious content, whether in the form of dreams, fantasies, visions, psychotic delusions, or psychedelic experiences. As the intensity of consciousness is reduced in such states, Jung explains, "the check put upon unconscious contents by the concentration of the conscious mind ceases, so that the hitherto unconscious material streams, as though from opened side-sluices, into the field of consciousness."[9] Jung understood that one's threshold of consciousness can be lowered by a wide range of conditions, including fatigue, sleep, fever, intense emotion, religious and political fanaticism, intoxication, or, as he puts it, "morbid cerebral conditions in general."[10] Although such statements by Jung don't typically mention psychedelic experience, he clearly understood that psychedelics also cause a lowering of the threshold of consciousness.

Alterations of consciousness that accompany an *abaissement* become most apparent in people experiencing overwhelming emotions. In especially intense emotional states, Jung explains, "the tone of the unconscious is heightened, thereby creating a gradient for the unconscious to flow towards the conscious. Ego-consciousness then comes under the influence of unconscious instinctual impulses and contents."[11] When Jung speaks here of unconscious instinctual impulses and contents, he is alluding to the extraordinary properties of the archetypes. An archetype, Jung explains, has a particular "charge" that causes emotionally-loaded "numinous effects," which contribute to the reduction of consciousness. That is, as an archetype raises unconscious content to a "supernormal degree of luminosity," energy is withdrawn from consciousness, which is thereby weakened or "darkened."[12]

We can see that emotions play a complex role in lowering the threshold of consciousness. On the one hand, intense emotions can lower the threshold of consciousness and allow content from the unconscious to enter the conscious mind. On the other hand, when released unconscious content includes archetypal material, the emotions associated with the archetypes produce a further *abaissement*. This helps to explain how psychedelic substances can radically reduce the conscious mind's control. The substances initially lower the threshold of consciousness to such an extent that archetypal images enter consciousness. The emotions associated with this released archetypal material lower the threshold of consciousness even further. This additional *abaissement* opens the way for more archetypal material to flood the conscious mind, and so on, until one is immersed in an intense psychedelic-induced state. As long as archetypally-charged images and feelings continue to lower the conscious orientation, Jung notes, the unconscious is given "a favorable opportunity to slip into the space vacated."[13]

The conditions associated with an *abaissement* arise in relatively healthy as well as in mentally disturbed people. Yet the impact of these conditions on the psyche understandably varies depending on the circumstances in which they occur and the stability of one's personality. When the ego's control is reduced and the mind's capacity to think is weakened, the unity of the personality is more likely preserved in people with a relatively stable psyche. People lacking psychological stability are naturally more vulnerable to the disruptive effects of an *abaissement*, and hence Jung's concern that a psychedelic-induced *abaissement* could release a latent psychosis.

Of course the destabilizing potential of a psychedelic-induced *abaissement* is further aggravated when psychedelics are used carelessly.

The *abaissement du niveau mental* induced by psychedelic drugs—even in healthy people—resembles the *abaissement* that accompanies schizophrenia. Both cases involve an extreme *abaissement*, an especially intense state that tends to occur under conditions that threaten the very foundation of a person's existence. These are conditions, Jung explains, that a person can experience in "moments of mortal danger, before or after accidents, severe illnesses, operations, etc., or when psychic problems are developing which might give his life a catastrophic turn, or in the critical periods of life when a modification of his previous psychic attitude forces itself peremptorily upon him, or before, during, and after radical changes in his immediate or his general surroundings."[14]

These conditions also beautifully characterize a person's subjective perception of an especially difficult psychedelic experience. People can fear they are in mortal danger, feel their life has taken a catastrophic turn, or sense that previous attitudes are being threatened or obliterated. One can perceive even a joyously revelatory psychedelic experience as a radical change in one's immediate or general surroundings, or as a critical point in life when one's attitudes and views are abruptly modified.

Comparing an *abaissement* brought on by schizophrenia to one induced by psychedelic substances, Jung explains that mescaline and related drugs, with their "countless nuances of form, meaning, and value," cause a lowering of the threshold of consciousness that "renders perceptible the perceptual variants that are normally unconscious, thereby enriching one's apperception [conscious perception] to an astounding degree."[15] Jung's description of the psychological effects of a psychedelic-induced *abaissement* is consistent with Stanislav Grof's characterization of psychedelics as "nonspecific catalysts and amplifiers of the psyche."[16] For both Jung and Grof, that is, psychedelic substances don't cause *specific* psychological effects. Although they increase energy levels that activate psychological processes, which allows one to consciously experience otherwise unconscious content, they don't give rise to specific experiences or content. The content that arises from the unconscious during a psychedelic session, like the content that arises in a dream during sleep, is what is available in the unconscious at the time.[17] What emerges can naturally vary, then, from session to session for each person, and can certainly vary from person to person.

The Limits of Integration

In describing the psychological effects of a psychedelic-induced *abaissement du niveau mental*, Jung explains that the astounding perceptual enrichment brought about by psychedelic substances makes it impossible to integrate the experiences into consciousness. "The accumulation of variants that have become conscious," Jung says, "gives each single act of apperception [conscious perception] a dimension that fills the whole of consciousness."[18] That is, as far as Jung is concerned, one can't integrate psychedelic experiences because such experiences intensify one's awareness of formerly unconscious content to such a degree that the conscious mind becomes saturated and overwhelmed. And for Jung, both conscious and unconscious aspects of the psyche must function for integration to take place.

Jung's criticism of psychedelic-enhanced psychotherapy is based on his belief that it is impossible to integrate the unconscious content released by psychedelic substances. As I will demonstrate in later chapters, Jung's idea of integration is central to his psychology and is an essential element in individuation. Integration from Jung's perspective can be understood for now as bringing released unconscious material into a constructive relationship with consciousness. This process moves the person toward a balanced relationship between consciousness and the unconscious, toward, that is, psychological wholeness, or individuation.

To fully understand Jung's criticism of psychedelic-enhanced therapy, we need to appreciate his concern for the integrity of the psyche's conscious aspect. If at times Jung seems to value the unconscious over consciousness, it is because he is so acutely concerned with the dangerous consequences of neglecting the unconscious.[19] But he also values the conscious mind's capacity to resist the potentially overwhelming chaos of the unconscious. For Jung, integration can only occur when consciousness is stable enough to assimilate the material that arises from the unconscious.

The value Jung places on the stability of ego-consciousness is forcefully illustrated in his own confrontation with the unconscious. Jung describes his paradoxical effort to protect his conscious mind from the chaos of the unconscious even as he allows himself to drop into its depths. "An incessant stream of fantasies had been released," he writes, "and I did my best not to lose my head but to find some way to understand these strange things. I stood helpless before an alien world; everything in it seemed difficult and incomprehensible. I was living in a constant state of tension; often I felt as if gigantic blocks of stone were tumbling down upon me. One thunderstorm followed another. My enduring these storms was a question of brute strength."[20] During such experiences, Jung explains, one must differentiate oneself from the contents of the unconscious, and yet it is essential "at the same time to bring them into relationship with consciousness. That is the technique for stripping them of their power."[21]

Jung also found that maintaining the stability of his personal identity was essential to protecting his conscious personality from these tumultuous unconscious forces. As he worked through his fantasies, he needed "a point of support in 'this world.'"

> It was most essential for me to have a normal life in the real world as a counterpoise to that strange inner world. My family and my profession remained the base to which I could always return, assuring me that I was an actually existing, ordinary person. The unconscious contents could have driven me out of my wits. But my family, and the knowledge: I have a medical diploma from a Swiss university, I must help my patients, I have a wife and five children, I live at 228 Seestrasse in Küsnacht—these were actualities which made demands upon me and proved to me again and again that I really existed.[22]

In his letters discussing psychedelics, Jung repeatedly points out that psychedelic drugs make it impossible to maintain the stability of ego-consciousness necessary for a productive relationship to the unconscious. Jung maintains that the extraordinary perceptions experienced during a psychedelic session occur because "the lowering of consciousness by the drug offers no resistance to the unconscious."[23] In a letter to psychedelic therapist Betty Eisner, Jung explains that he regards the use of psychedelic drugs with suspicion even though he recognizes that they can open people to the same kinds of perceptions and experiences that occur in mystical states or in analysis. "I don't feel happy about these things," he writes, "since you merely fall into such experiences without being able to integrate them."[24]

Ronald Sandison's Response to Jung's Criticism

Jungian-oriented psychiatrist and LSD therapist Ronald Sandison agrees with Jung regarding the potential psychedelics have to bring unconscious material into conscious awareness. "The psychological basis of LSD treatment lies in its peculiar property of releasing unconscious material," he explains.[25] He also acknowledges the risks of psychosis, and even suicide, when the natural barriers between ego-consciousness and the unconscious are broken down in the absence of a carefully designed and administered therapeutic environment. He emphasizes, nonetheless, that extensive clinical experience provides ample evidence that the rate of complications in therapeutic settings is low.[26] And even though Sandison acknowledges that unconscious images and emotions released by LSD are not always integrated into consciousness, and that the failure to integrate such material can raise barriers to further psychological development, he emphasizes the capacity people have to successfully integrate unconscious material released by psychedelic drugs. The key to successful integration, Sandison explains, is that patients receive support from a skilled therapist and that they are prepared to put in the work necessary to assimilate their experiences.[27]

Sandison suggests that Jung failed to recognize that people can in fact integrate unconscious material released by psychedelic drugs and that the likelihood of successful integration is significantly increased in a therapeutic environment. Even Jungian analyst Michael Fordham, a critic of psychedelic-enhanced psychotherapy, acknowledges that case material on LSD therapy shows that Jung overstates his argument when he says it is impossible to integrate unconscious material released by psychedelic substances.[28]

As we've seen, when Jung wrote to Victor White about White's visit to a psychiatric hospital where LSD was being administered to patients, he complained that psychiatrists had found "a new poison to play with, without the faintest knowledge or feeling of responsibility." As it turns out, the psychiatric hospital White had visited was Powick Hospital, where Ronald Sandison and his colleagues had established their LSD clinic. As you may recall, Sandison had set up the Powick LSD clinic after visiting Sandoz laboratories when he was on a study tour of Swiss psychiatric hospitals in the early 1950s. On that tour, Sandison had also fulfilled his dream of "touching the hem of Jung's garment" by visiting the Jung Institute in Zurich.[29] But Jung was away somewhere in the mountains that day. Several years later, after initiating the LSD treatment program at Powick Hospital, Sandison returned to the institute in hopes of catching Jung this time. Missing Jung again, Sandison spent most of the day visiting the institute's director, Carl Meier, who warned Sandison not to talk to Jung about his work with LSD. Jung, Meier told Sandison, was greatly opposed to its use.[30]

Looking back on his clinical experience with LSD-enhanced psychotherapy, Sandison thinks he was fortunate to have learned of Jung's letter to White long after the Powick LSD unit had closed. He needed to find his own way, without being influenced by the man whom he held in such high regard. Sandison firmly believes that Jung's letter to White reflects Jung's ignorance of psychedelic-enhanced therapy. Sandison notes that Jung had read Aldous Huxley's *The Doors of Perception* the same year, 1954, that he had written to White and that Jung tended to equate LSD with mescaline.[31] In his letter to White, Jung wrote, "Is the LSD drug mescaline? It has indeed very curious effects, *vide* Aldous Huxley—of which I know far too little. I don't know either what its psychotherapeutic value with neurotic or psychotic patients is."[32]

Sandison concedes that, as Jung charged, some inexperienced therapists had no idea what to do with the unconscious material that psychedelic drugs released in their patients. Nonetheless, he maintains that Jung had fallen into the trap of voicing prejudiced opinions without knowing what responsible psychotherapists were actually doing with these drugs. Recalling the careful experimental use of LSD by other clinicians as well as his own conscientious work at the Powick clinic before legal prohibitions terminated their efforts in the 1960s, Sandison wrote: "The experience gained and memories of that short period of the true therapeutic use of LSD are valuable and precious. I believe it made a real contribution to our understanding of the human psyche, and the interaction between patient and healer." "Sadly," he concluded, "if we had more support from the analysts in the 1950s we might have been able to do a great deal more."[33]

In 1963, evaluating more than ten years of intense work with LSD therapy, Sandison observed that despite increasing certainty among therapists that psychedelic-enhanced therapy is a valuable form of treatment, many questions remain unanswered.[34] Due to restrictions imposed on psychedelic research, most of those questions remain unanswered half a century later. But the current resurgence in psychedelic research provides an invaluable opportunity to increase our understanding of the risks and benefits of psychedelic-enhanced psychotherapy. Jungians could make substantial contributions to that understanding by objectively evaluating those risks and benefits. Jungians could make particularly useful contributions to our understanding of the extent to which psychedelic substances can safely and effectively advance psychological integration. Given Jung's unique understanding of a person's challenging and potentially transformative confrontation with the collective unconscious, Jungian psychology offers especially valuable insights into the nature and transformative potential of difficult psychedelic experiences, insights that become evident in Jung's approach to trauma, dissociation, complexes, the shadow, psychosis, integration, and transformation—all of which I discuss in the following chapters.

I occasionally try to imagine the rich conversation Ronald Sandison might have had with Carl Jung that day at the Jung Institute in Zurich. I often see my inquiry into the relationship between psychedelic experience and Jung's psychology as an attempt to sort out their different views on the matter and to reach a better understanding of all the issues. As is often the case when I listen to intelligent arguments for each side of a complex question, I tend to find myself appreciating both views at one time or another. In any case, I find myself becoming more fascinated the deeper the conversation goes.

PART 2

Jungian Insights into Difficult Psychedelic Experiences

> Even the most absurd things are nothing other than
> symbols for thoughts which are not only understandable
> in human terms but dwell in every human breast.
> In insanity we do not discover anything new and unknown;
> we are looking at the foundations of our own being,
> the matrix of those vital problems on which we are all engaged.
>
> C. G. Jung
> "The Content of the Psychoses"[1]

CHAPTER 5

Psychedelic Experience and Trauma

Even though Jung's explicit discussion of psychedelic experience is quite limited, his work on trauma, the shadow, psychosis, and psychological transformation is extremely relevant to understanding difficult psychedelic experiences. The relationship between psychedelic experience and trauma is an intriguingly complex one that brings to mind the proverbial power of fire to create as well as destroy. Incalculable numbers of naive and careless trippers have been traumatized by their psychedelic experiences. When used respectfully and responsibly, however, psychedelic substances have for centuries been uniquely effective agents for healing and psychospiritual transformation. And clinical experience shows that psychedelic-enhanced therapy can be an effective treatment for healing past trauma. I look here at both sides of the subject before turning to a Jungian interpretation of psychedelic experience and trauma.

Difficult Psychedelic Experiences as Potentially Traumatic

When I speak of a difficult psychedelic experience, I refer to a psychedelic experience in which one encounters perceptions, insights, or unconscious material that cause intense confusion and suffering. Such confrontations usually occur unexpectedly and involve inconceivably strange and terrifying thoughts, feelings, and images. People undergoing an especially difficult psychedelic experience are often convinced they are insane.

A difficult psychedelic experience is commonly referred to as a "bad trip." (A "terror trip" or a descent into the "hell realms" would at times be a more apt description.) Psychedelic researcher Rick Strassman reports in his review of the literature on adverse reactions to psychedelic drugs that a difficult experience is the most common adverse reaction. He describes a difficult psychedelic experience as a temporary episode of panic lasting less than 24 hours with symptoms that include frightening illusions or hallucinations, confusion, overwhelming anxiety, aggression (which is occasionally acted-out violently), depression with suicidal thoughts or attempts, and fearfulness to the point of paranoid delusions.[1]

The extreme intensity of an especially difficult psychedelic experience is reflected in Stanislav Grof's description of psychedelic-induced ego death, which can involve "an experience of the destruction of everything that the subject is, possesses, or is attached to. Its essential characteristics are a sense of total annihilation on all imaginable levels. . . . Subjects face agonizing tension increasing to fantastic proportions and develop a conviction that they will explode and the entire world will be destroyed."[2]

Whether a difficult psychedelic experience becomes traumatic depends on a complex combination of non-drug factors that are often simply referred to as "set and setting." Set, mindset or psychological state, includes one's personality, life history, beliefs and attitudes, mood, intention, expectations, and preparation. Setting is the physical and interpersonal environment in which the experience occurs, including interpersonal support and the mindset of those providing that support.[3] Difficult psychedelic experiences are triggered by more than altered perceptions—no matter how strange those perceptions are. Difficult psychedelic experiences are a consequence of one's *reaction* to those altered perceptions.[4] Non-drug conditions will significantly influence one's reactions to a psychedelic experience and how one manages those reactions. At the risk of oversimplifying the matter, the potential for a difficult psychedelic experience to become traumatic, or in extreme cases to lead to a psychotic reaction, comes down to whether the person using the substance has any significant preexisting psychological problems (such as a latent psychosis), is carefully prepared for the experience, and is in a safe and supportive environment. These are understandably the same criteria for safe and effective psychedelic-enhanced therapy.[5]

We can determine the extent to which a psychedelic experience is traumatic by the symptoms outlined in the next section on psychedelic-induced trauma. We can determine the extent to which a psychedelic experience is a psychotic reaction by symptoms discussed in chapter 7. In addition to the following section in this chapter on psychedelic-induced trauma, I also discuss these matters in chapter 13 on the implications of Jungian psychology for psychedelic-enhanced psychotherapy. In a sense, however, this book as a whole concerns why a difficult psychedelic experience becomes traumatic and why a traumatic psychedelic experience triggers a psychotic reaction.

Despite their potential to become traumatic experiences or lead to psychotic reactions, difficult psychedelic experiences often have beneficial effects. As the saying goes, bad trips can be the best trips. Psychedelic theorists and practitioners tend to view difficult psychedelic experiences as opportunities for psychological insight and growth rather than intrinsically traumatic experiences. When safely contained within the session and worked through, adverse reactions are generally seen as a natural part of the uncovering process. Experienced psychedelic therapists often frame a difficult psychedelic session as an opportunity to face and work through painful unconscious images and feelings. Even sessions involving paranoid states and hellish visions can be deeply therapeutic if they are resolved well, says Grof.[6] Some even consider difficult experiences a natural part of psychospiritual transformation. Francesco Di Leo, a doctor at the Maryland Psychiatric Research Center, views difficult psychedelic experiences as "a formidable series of trials and ordeals consciousness has to undergo to complete one of the most remarkable processes of personality transformation man is capable of: the 'Death-Rebirth' process."[7]

Such positive views of difficult psychedelic experiences reflect primarily the many successfully resolved psychedelic emergencies witnessed by practitioners in the field.[8] I have seen, however, a certain defensiveness within the psychedelic community concerning adverse reactions to psychedelics. Still smarting no doubt from all the sensationalized stories of bad trips, some advocates emphasize the benefits of psychedelics and minimize, or ignore, their risks. *Hofmann's Potion: The Pioneers of LSD*, an excellent documentary produced by the National Film Board of Canada, emphasizes the healing and transformative potential of psychedelic substances to a fault. The film's only emphatic point addressing their risks is made by Stanislav Grof in a comment on Timothy Leary, who, Grof says, "didn't tell people about the dangers, [didn't tell them] that before you go to Heaven, you might go to Hell, or if you don't do it right, you might stay there."[9]

Given the potential for psychedelics to induce extraordinary degrees of emotional stress and even psychotic reactions of varying intensity and duration, there is no question that psychedelic experiences can be traumatic. Discussing the nature and dynamics of a psychedelic crisis, Grof beautifully encapsulates the potential a difficult psychedelic experience has to become transformative—or traumatic. A difficult psychedelic experience, Grof explains, "represents an exteriorization of a potentially pathogenic matrix in the subject's unconscious. If properly handled, a psychedelic crisis has great positive potential and can result in profound personality transformation. Conversely, an insensitive and ignorant approach can cause psychological damage and lead to chronic psychotic states and years of psychiatric hospitalization."[10]

Psychedelic-Induced Trauma

The American Psychiatric Association discusses Posttraumatic Stress Disorder (PTSD) in its *Diagnostic and Statistical Manual of Mental Disorders*

(*DSM-IV*). With its orientation toward events that threaten serious *physical* injury and *literal* death as opposed to serious *psychological* injury and *ego,* or *psychological,* death, the PTSD category seems at first to have limited relevance to psychedelic-induced trauma. By articulating characteristic psychological responses to traumatic events, however, this category provides an excellent context for discussing adverse reactions to psychedelic experiences, which are, of course, psychological events.[11]

The *DSM-IV Guidebook* emphasizes that the symptom pattern for PTSD is remarkably uniform despite great variations in the psychological history and cultural background of those who have suffered trauma. Although the guidebook's authors don't say so explicitly, the PTSD symptom pattern is also remarkably uniform despite great variations in the nature of the trauma experienced.[12] This uniformity accounts for the strong parallels between the PTSD symptom pattern identified in the *DSM-IV* and adverse reactions to a psychedelic experience. I outline here some of the PTSD symptoms that reflect these parallels.

PTSD involves a response to a traumatic event in which a person experiences "intense fear, helplessness, or horror," all of which are common emotions in a difficult psychedelic experience. Characteristic symptoms of trauma include the "persistent reexperiencing of the traumatic event," which can involve "a sense of reliving the experience" as well as "illusions, hallucinations, and dissociative flashback episodes."[13] One can naturally feel intense distress when experiencing something resembling the original trauma. The *DSM-IV Guidebook* notes that such an experience can be triggered by a wide range of stimuli or can occur spontaneously. The guidebook explains that reexperiencing a trauma can be terrifying in its own right and that the intensity of these relived experiences can lead people to fear that they are losing their minds.[14]

As I have said, PTSD symptoms aren't unusual during spontaneous recurrences of a difficult psychedelic experience, which are commonly referred to as "flashbacks." Most psychedelic flashbacks aren't as intense as these PTSD symptoms would indicate, however. Grinspoon and Bakalar define a psychedelic flashback as "the transitory recurrence of emotions and perceptions originally experienced while under the influence of the drug," and they note that flashbacks "can last seconds or hours" and can be "blissful, interesting, annoying, or frightening."[15] Most flashbacks, they report, last only a few seconds or minutes; but "occasionally they last longer, and in a small minority of cases they turn into frightening images or thoughts."[16] During my own LSD flashbacks, I momentarily relive a terrifying sense that I am literally in Hell. That is, I briefly experience the same perceptions and feelings I first experienced on LSD forty-five years ago.

(I describe one of my flashback experiences, an especially intense one, later in this chapter.)

Other characteristic symptoms of PTSD and, I suggest, of reactions to psychedelic-induced trauma, include the avoidance of stimuli associated with the trauma, the numbing of one's general responsiveness to the environment that can involve a diminished interest in significant activities, a detachment from others, and the loss of expectations for career, marriage, or children. Common trauma symptoms relevant to psychedelic-induced trauma also include increased irritability or outbursts of anger, difficulty concentrating, hypervigilance and a tendency to be startled easily, as well as significant distress or impairment in important areas of one's life.[17]

A *DSM-III* criterion describing a traumatic event as being "outside the range of usual human experience" was eliminated in the *DSM-IV* because it was too vague.[18] Still, being "outside the range of usual human experience" aptly describes psychedelic experiences in general.

Again, psychedelics have a long record of safety when used in controlled settings with appropriate safeguards. However, when used carelessly, and sometimes when used carefully, psychedelics can trigger a trauma. The potentially traumatic effects of psychedelics are implied in standard precautions for psychedelic-enhanced therapy: screening out people with pre-existing psychiatric disorders, establishing a safe and supportive setting, preparing participants carefully, and arranging supervision and follow-up by an experienced therapeutic team.[19]

Psychedelic-Enhanced Therapy as Treatment for Past Trauma

As we have seen, therapists have extensive experience using psychedelics substances to reduce a patient's resistance to repressed traumatic memories and feelings, thereby allowing the patient to come to terms with past trauma.[20] Stanislav Grof's extensive research demonstrates the potential psychedelics have to help patients recover and work through past traumatic events.[21] Grof attributes his and his colleagues' success in treating a wide range of trauma-based disorders to LSD's unique properties as an abreactive, or releasing, agent. Abreaction is the discharge of emotion and physical energy associated with an unconscious experience, especially the repressed memories and feelings associated with a trauma. During LSD therapy, patients often relive the original trauma and dramatically act out pent-up emotions. Grof encourages psychedelic therapists to allow their patients to freely work through and complete the cathartic experience. He believes this work is inherently healing, no matter how challenging the content the patient encounters. Difficult psychedelic experiences, Grof explains, "are caused by the emergence of highly-charged emotionally traumatic unconscious material. Since this material is the source of the patient's difficulties in everyday life, negative episodes in LSD sessions, if properly approached and handled, represent great opportunities for therapeutic change."[22]

The Relation of Trauma in Jungian Psychology to Psychedelic Experience

I came to more fully appreciate the way past trauma emerges in difficult psychedelic experiences when I discovered Jungian analyst Donald Kalsched's book, *The Inner World of Trauma: Archetypal Defenses of the Personal Spirit*. Kalsched discusses the unconscious images commonly revealed by adults who have suffered early childhood trauma. The dreams of Kalsched's patients consistently reveal deeply disturbing images, such as powerful demonic figures, remarkably similar to images encountered by many people during difficult psychedelic experiences. Kalsched's findings therefore clearly support the suggestion that difficult psychedelic experiences can release archetypal imagery associated with past, repressed trauma. And, despite the initial difficulty of grasping some of his ideas, Kalsched's findings suggest that terrifying images manifested during difficult psychedelic experiences can reflect the psyche's ironically destructive attempt to protect itself from being traumatized again. Kalsched's analysis of Jung's approach to trauma is especially valuable because, even though much of Jung's psychology is relevant to understanding and treating trauma, Jung rarely discussed trauma explicitly.

Kalsched defines trauma as any experience that causes "unbearable psychic pain or anxiety."[23] Even though trauma occurs under a wide variety of conditions, from physical injury and sexual abuse to the destructive psychological effects of unmet childhood needs, the distinguishing feature of trauma for Kalsched is what Heinz Kohut calls "disintegration anxiety," which stems from an event that threatens to dissolve the personality's coherence and is "the deepest anxiety [one] can experience."[24] When such trauma occurs in early childhood, before strong ego defenses have developed, the psyche relies on more primitive and dissociative unconscious defenses to protect itself. Although it is widely understood how destructive these archaic, or primitive, defenses can become in later life, Kalsched argues that we need to recognize their initial life-saving potential for the child. Kalsched suggests, that is, that the child's dissociative defenses paradoxically protect her by ensuring that she will always remain on guard. We have to realize, Kalsched explains, that the defenses preventing the early-trauma patient from trusting others and forming meaningful relationships as an adult "have literally saved the patient's life as a psychological being."[25] When trying to understand this paradoxical, and initially bewildering, dynamic it helps me to imagine parents who attempt to protect their child from life's dangers by keeping her locked up in the cellar: they protect destructively.

Kalsched's thinking about trauma-induced disorders developed out of Freud and Jung's early dialogue about the mythopoetic, daimonic, and uncanny imagery revealed by traumatized patients. Kalsched's approach to trauma-induced disorders has clear parallels to Jung's approach to dissociation, which Jung described as a weakening of consciousness resulting from a splitting of psychological content that becomes increasingly independent of consciousness.[26] Yet, as essential as a classical Jungian interpretation of trauma disorders is for treating trauma, it requires in Kalsched's view certain revisions in light of more recent findings, especially the work of contemporary object-relations and self psychologists such as Donald Winnicott and Heinz Kohut.[27]

Kalsched's work highlights the way dramatic and bizarre dream images symbolize the psyche's fragmentation and defenses. When consciously faced in therapy, these dreams images can promote healing. This insight brings to mind the work of Jungian analyst John Weir Perry, who in the 1970s advocated the transformative potential of acute psychotic episodes. Perry asserted that, with proper attention, even the apparently scattered images expressed by a person suffering acute psychic upheaval may take on coherent form and reveal meaning.[28] (I discuss Perry's work in "Jung on the Healing Potential of Psychotic Experiences" in chapter 10.) The therapeutic principles underlying Kalsched's and Perry's work strongly support the value of carefully analyzing the bizarre and often terrifying imagery associated with traumatic psychedelic experiences and psychedelic-induced psychotic states. Such analysis can reveal meaningful patterns that reflect the psyche's attempt to protect and heal itself.

Kalsched's Model of the Psyche's Archetypal Self-Care System

Kalsched is concerned with what happens within the psyche of those who experience unbearable events in their lives, whether those traumatic events be physical or psychological (for example, extreme forms of parental neglect). He has found that, in response to overwhelming pain, the vulnerable psyche creates persecutory figures that emerge in dreams and fantasies as archetypal daimonic images such as a witch, a ghostly axe man, a mad doctor, or the Devil. In a way that is initially difficult to understand, these daimonic images ironically attempt to protect the integrity of the personality by carrying out inhibiting attacks that split the psyche. Kalsched explains how these inner persecutory images function in the traumatized person's psyche to prevent him or her from becoming traumatized again in the external world.

In Kalsched's judgment, these daimonic persecutory figures reflect the dynamics of the psyche's dissociative defenses, which, again, ironically divide the psyche in an attempt to protect the personality from further trauma.[29] (The Greek root of *daimonic,* a variant of *demonic*, can mean to divide.) More specifically, unconscious imagery that Kalsched's therapy patients have reported, in combination with recent clinical research, reveals that trauma often results in psychic fragmentation that manifests as personified dyads. This dyadic structure typically takes the form of a "progressed" part of the personality that adopts a "caretaking" relationship to a "regressed" part. The progressed, caretaker part is often represented paradoxically by a threatening daimonic figure such as a witch, a murderer, or a demon. The regressed part of the personality is usually expressed through images of vulnerability and innocence such as a child or a fragile animal. These images of vulnerability and innocence represent, Kalsched suggests, the essence or core of the individual's personality, which he calls the "personal spirit."[30]

The progressed, or caretaking, part of the personality, can be represented by "a powerful *benevolent or malevolent great being* who protects or persecutes its vulnerable partner," explains Kalsched.[31] Sometimes the protector figure presents both benevolent and malevolent aspects, thereby representing a protector and persecutor in one. An excellent example of this complex protector-persecutor figure is the image of a threatening God.

Usually, however, the caretaking part is represented unambiguously, though ironically, as a terrifying figure. As such it exhibits compelling parallels to the Self's dark side, the archetype of evil.[32] One of Jung's psychological characterizations of the Devil, in the form of Mephistopheles, is as "the diabolical aspect of every psychic function that has broken loose from the hierarchy of the total psyche and now enjoys independence and absolute power."[33] Kalsched points out that the root meaning of the word *diabolical* is to throw (*ballein*) across or apart (*dia*), which is also the origin of the common meaning of "diabolos" as the Devil, "he who crosses, thwarts, or dis-integrates (dissociation)."[34]

The key principle underlying Kalsched's trauma theory is expressed in his hypothesis that violating the personality's inner core is unthinkable. If, therefore, other defense mechanisms fail, archetypal defenses will go to any length to protect this inner core. As Kalsched conceives it, the dynamic of progressed versus regressed parts of the personality makes up what he calls *the psyche's archetypal self-care system*.[35] As its name implies, this psychological system appears to emerge from the deepest layers of the unconscious because the imagery and emotions associated with it have the numinous qualities of the collective unconscious. "When the ego falls through the abyss of trauma into the darkness of the unconscious psyche," Kalsched points out, "it falls into an archetypal world which is experienced by the ego as numinous—dark or light. Unfortunately for the trauma victim, the numinous usually constellates negatively."[36]

The ultimate effect of the psyche's protector-prosecutor figures is to defend the trauma victim by becoming an anti-life force in which new situations and opportunities are experienced as threatening. The trauma victim thereby becomes isolated from reality through dissociation, addiction, depression, or schizoid withdrawal.[37] As much as one wants to change, "something more powerful than the ego continually undermines progress and destroys hope," Kalsched says, "as if the individual were *possessed* by some diabolical power."[38]

Trauma and Dissociation in Jung's Psychology

The symbolic daimon figures Kalsched has seen so often in the dream images of his traumatized patients seem to personify the psyche's dissociative defenses against overwhelming events that it is unable to integrate. Yet, Kalsched asks, "How did the internal guardian figures of this [archetypal self-care] 'system' and their vulnerable child 'clients' get organized in the unconscious, and from whence did they derive their awesome power over the patient's well-intentioned ego?"[39] To start to answer these fundamental questions, Kalsched turns to Jung's approach to psychological dissociation.

Jung demonstrated in word association tests that dissociation is the psyche's defense against the damaging impact of trauma. When physical withdrawal from injury is impossible, the psyche withdraws part of the personality by splitting itself into fragments. Memories and emotions associated with the unbearable experience are distributed to different parts of the person's body and mind, especially to the unconscious. This accounts for "flashbacks of sensation," notes Kalsched, which are often disconnected from the context in which they occur.[40] This resonates, of course, with the phenomenon of a psychedelic flashback, which often seems to come out of the blue.

Although the distribution of traumatic memories and emotions to the unconscious can initially help trauma victims go about their lives in the world, the psychological consequences can be severe. The effects of trauma can continue to haunt one in the form of what Jung called unconscious *feeling-toned complexes*, which manifest as images of frightening figures.[41] Jung observed that a trauma-induced complex can take on an independent quality that acts in tyrannical opposition to the conscious mind.

"The explosion of affect is a complete invasion of the individual," says Jung. "It pounces upon him like an enemy or a wild animal."[42] In a separate passage on hysteria, Jung adds that "the complex has an abnormal autonomy ... and a tendency to an active separate existence, which reduces and replaces the constellating power of the ego-complex. In this way a new morbid personality is gradually created, the inclinations, judgments, and resolutions of which move only in the direction of the will to be ill. This second personality devours what is left of the normal ego and forces it into the role of [an oppressed] complex."[43]

Kalsched presents extensive evidence of these attacking dissociative defenses from his therapy practice. He has observed repeatedly that, as his patients begin to consciously approach repressed trauma, "an intra-psychic [dream] figure or 'force'. . . violently intervenes and dissociates the psyche. This figure's diabolical 'purpose' seems to be to prevent the dream-ego from experiencing the 'unthinkable' affect associated with the trauma" by terrifying one into a new state of despair.[44] Ironically, these attacking figures traumatize the patient's inner world to protect him or her from becoming traumatized again in the outer world (that is, with the therapist).

The intrapsychic figures from many of Kalsched's case-study descriptions resonate strongly with the persecutory tone and images that can permeate difficult psychedelic experiences. It isn't unusual, explains Grof, for threatening or demonic images to arise, or for the therapist to assume demonic form, when a person undergoes psychedelic psychotherapy for severe trauma.[45] Ronald Sandison reports the case of a 26-year-old woman suffering suicidal depression related to her psychopathic father and the death of her mother when the woman was twelve years old. During her first LSD therapy session, she "met the spider, a huge, ugly, terrifying and menacing animal, quite out of her control."[46] In subsequent sessions, the woman had many encounters with the spider, as she reports here: "Flashes of a woman's face, I think my mother's. Continuous pictures of the four eyes of the spider and complete spiders advancing upon me (coloured green and black) . . . . The spider never touches me but seems to want to enfold me and take me bodily."[47]

Margot Cutner discusses the case of a woman in her early 30s suffering from severe depression and paranoid tendencies. As a child, this woman was severely neglected by her mother. Reporting on one of her LSD sessions, the woman says, "I saw my mother driving the sheep down the lane, and I saw a full-sized bear walking among the trees and peeping at me. I saw a wood where the trees were growing almost trunk to trunk and the ground was covered by undergrowth."[48] In this experience, Cutner notes, the archetypal images, "mainly of the Mother-archetype, emerge behind, or just after, her memory of her real mother in the nursing chair. The wood—the trees—the bear—the witch. The witch was actually seen, sitting on the chair in the clinic room. On another occasion, the image of the bear was projected directly onto the analyst after the patient had experienced 'deep longing' for her mother."[49]

Hanscarl Leuner relays the following LSD-induced vision by a 23-year-old university assistant during psychedelic-enhanced therapy. The young woman had a history of traumatizing experiences during early childhood, and she suffered from recurrent depression, aggressive outbursts against her parents, and suicidal tendencies. "I saw Hitler several times. Then something very strange happened: Hitler became my father, drove our car and came into our house. . . ."[50]

The intrapsychic figures from many of Kalsched's case-study descriptions resonate strongly with the persecutory visions that characterized my own psychedelic experiences when I was 19 years old. But the disturbing projections I encountered more recently during an MDMA-enhanced psychotherapy session showed profound parallels to the daimonic archetypal defenses that Kalsched has seen dissociate a client's psyche and interrupt therapy at a crucial point.

My MDMA therapy session took place at an improbable location: in a tent at the Burning Man festival, a week-long event held each year in the Black Rock Desert in Nevada. The festival can be described as a community experiment in radical self-expression or as a mass Dionysian revel. (In 2011, attendance was capped at 50,000 participants.) I had gone to the festival as a member of the MAPS (Multidisciplinary Association for Psychedelic Studies) psychedelic emergency response team, a group of people trained to support those suffering from adverse reactions to psychedelic substances. During the first days of the festival, I had provided support for a young woman and a young man (individually), both of whom were overwhelmed by the intensity of their reaction to the festival. The young man was struggling through an LSD trip with suicidal visions.

On the forth day of the festival, I became overwhelmed by perhaps the strongest flashback I have ever experienced. The initial terrifying sense of again finding myself utterly alone in an absurd, alien world, and facing another challenge to end my life, was so powerful that I later wondered whether I had been accidentally dosed with LSD. It's more likely, however, that I had become overwhelmed by heat, dust, the festival's otherworldly atmosphere, and unconscious memories from past psychedelic experiences stirred up by my work with the young woman and young man.

In any event, I was so disturbed by my reaction that I asked to be helped to the MAPS center, where I could be supported by others. (Although other people have no doubt experienced flashbacks of such intensity, I don't mean to suggest that such experiences are typical.) I talked with a volunteer about my past LSD trips and my history of flashbacks, and I stayed there for several hours until I felt I had fully recovered. A few days later, I talked with a man who had helped many people through adverse reactions to psychedelic trips. He suggested that this would be a good time to try an MDMA-enhanced therapy session to start to come to terms with my traumatic LSD trips. MDMA is a mild psychedelic that, without changing physical perceptions or the ability to think and speak, typically expands one's emotional awareness and generates a state of peace, empathy, and trust that allows one to less fearfully revisit past trauma. MDMA-enhanced therapy sessions can, nevertheless, be quite difficult and painful, especially for those with chronic PTSD, because the work so effectively brings up past trauma.

After careful reflection with a few experienced and knowledgeable people whom I trusted, I decided that the potential benefits outweighed the risks of a session in such bizarre surroundings. I understood, of course, that the setting might stir up my old fears, but I trusted those I would be working with and knew that more help was within reach if we needed it.

The session began after midnight. All started well. I felt peaceful within a secure atmosphere of mutual warmth and respect with my therapist and his assistant. But sometime later, as I was struggling to recount an especially traumatic LSD trip during which I had made a violent attempt to sacrifice my life in this world, I suddenly and shockingly perceived a man observing the session to literally be Satan himself. Then I perceived my therapist and the woman assisting him as Satan's demonic helpers. Ironically, I was able to tell them what I was experiencing—that the other man was Satan and that I realized they were helping him, not me; and in the painful process of working through this delusion, I gained some perspective on my projections. This process had benefits of its own, and the session led to months of fruitful inquiry into past trauma in my life. But the focus of the session had dramatically shifted from gaining insight into my self-destructive vision, and coming to terms with past trauma, to slowly working through my terror and reestablishing trust for the man and woman who were trying to help me.

Kalsched has repeatedly observed that the terrifying actions of an inner daimonic figure seem to fragment his patients' emotional experience in a way that precludes conscious awareness of pain that *has emerged or is about to emerge* in psychotherapy. In my case, it seems that my own daimonic self-care system was projected onto those around me and quite effectively blocked our attempt to understand my past traumatic experiences. Kalsched's theory that diabolical figures traumatize the patient's inner world to protect him from becoming traumatized again in the outer world suggests that the terror I felt during the session was an unconscious defense against confronting past trauma. I seemed to have come too close to the core of that original trauma. And in doing so, I experienced the unconscious fear of confronting that trauma as a threat of suffering a new trauma in the outer world, in the tent at Burning Man that night.

The key to understanding Kalsched's idea of daimonic persecutory-protective figures, I think, is to see that the daimonic figures that emerge in the psyche as a result of the original trauma paradoxically work to protect the person from re-experiencing the pain of the original trauma by continually terrifying him anew. This dynamic played out dramatically in the life of an incest victim treated by Jung, which I will turn to shortly. In her case, dissociative daimonic figures prevented her from venturing beyond her isolation to form new, potentially dangerous, relationships. Again, these psychic figures act like parents who attempt to protect their child from danger by keeping her locked up in the cellar: they protect destructively. If therapy brings the person too close to re-experiencing the original pain, daimonic figures arising from the unconscious distract the person by terrifying him or her, as they distracted me that night.

Given Jung's view that a diabolical split-off psychic function can be perceived by a person only when that function becomes an objective entity such as a dream image, it's possible that my "seeing Satan" in my MDMA session represents a significant breakthrough in my attempt to come to terms with psychedelic experiences that have haunted me for so many years.[51] Perhaps this partially accounts for the profound exhilaration and gratitude I felt several days after the session. This healing potential was also reported in each of the three psychedelic psychotherapy cases I cited above, and I will discuss in detail the transformative potential of difficult psychedelic experiences in chapters 9 and 10.

The paradoxical nature of these psychic figures explains Kalsched's use of the word *daimonic* instead of *demonic*. Both words convey positive as well as negative qualities. Both can mean fiendish, diabolical, evil, on the one hand, or "motivated by a spiritual force or genius," on the other. The Greek root of both is *daimon*, meaning divine power.[52] Thus, Socrates spoke of his daimon as his divine guide and protector. Yet *daimonic* more explicitly than *demonic* suggests benevolent as well as destructive qualities, and thus more effectively suggests the paradoxical quality of Kalsched's hypothetical psychic figures.[53]

Anticipating the next chapter on Jung's idea of the shadow, and the relationship between the shadow and trauma, I close this section with Kalsched's observation that these diabolical figures can appear as "a true *agent of death*, . . . a truly perverse factor in psychological life," which becomes a formidable resistance to life itself.[54] The primitive disintegrative energies of such figures should not be attributed to the personal shadow but rather to what Jung understood as the archetypal shadow, the dark side of the Self. We must keep in mind, however, that mysteriously ambivalent Self figures such as Satan or Mercurius, as symbols of the ostensibly evil characteristics of the psyche, represent the power to heal as well as to destroy. As such, they are diabolical forces of *transformation*.[55]

Trauma and Jung's Theory of the Complex

Before Freud and Jung, psychologists such as Charcot and Janet had discovered multiple centers of organization within the psyche, and they understood that a secondary personality could take over a person's primary personality during altered states of consciousness. Even during this earlier period, such secondary personalities were understood to be daimonic in that they had destructive powers of possession that originated in trauma yet somehow also blocked memories of the trauma.[56]

By the time of Freud's early work, it was understood that healing could be effected by hypnotically inducing this daimonic state of consciousness. But the mechanism of the disorder was thought to be either mental weakness or brain lesions, and therefore it was difficult to explain how a cure could come about by evoking, and "exorcizing," the daimon. Using hypnosis with his hysterical patients, Freud's clinical practice led him to the idea of *psychic* reality and thus a psychological theory of trauma, in which trauma resulted from a lesion, or injury, to the *psyche*. Freud then hypothesized that memories of the trauma became cut off from consciousness in what he called a "second psychical group" or a "sub-conscious complex of ideas," which resisted healing. Given the difficulty in tracing the patient's memory of the original trauma, Freud characteristically concluded that its origin lay in the patient's sex life.[57]

A significant shift occurred in Freud's theory when he came to understand that his patients were often struggling with *fantasies* of sexual trauma rather than actual traumatic events, an insight that developed into his notorious theory of the Oedipus complex. This leads us, by way of a rather truncated summation, to Jung's statement that "fantasies can be just as traumatic in their effects as real traumata."[58] Although Jung disagreed with Freud's narrow sexual interpretation of trauma's origin, he agreed with Freud's fundamental hypothesis that trauma involves a psychological element that splits the psyche and resists healing. Through his own word association studies, Jung came to understand that his subjects' associations were often blocked by emotions, which led to his theory of psychic dissociation and the idea of *feeling-toned complexes,* each with an archetypal core of images and emotions grounded in the collective unconscious. The numinous domain of the collective unconscious is potentially both awe-inspiring and terrifying—and therefore potentially traumatic. For Jung, then, this realm of archetypal images and complexes became the source of trauma-induced unconscious anxiety and fantasy.[59] "A situation threatening danger pushes aside the tranquil play of ideas and puts in their place a complex of other ideas with a very strong feeling-tone," explains Jung. "The new complex then crowds everything else into the background."[60] For Jung, then, complexes originate in the shock of trauma.[61]

Jung's model of dissociative complexes is beautifully illustrated in his patient who was a victim of incest. Except for psychedelics, this case brings together all the key elements of my inquiry: trauma, shadow, psychosis, and psychospiritual transformation. Jung's patient, a nineteen-year-old woman, had become catatonically psychotic after she was sexually abused by her older brother when she was fifteen. She had withdrawn from the world into dissociative fantasies of an alienated life on the moon, which was ruled by an evil vampire who killed women and children. Having patiently coaxed the young woman into revealing the content of her psychosis, Jung recognized meaning (as opposed to mere sexual wishes) in her psychotic fantasies. Jung's intense personal commitment to the young woman's struggle allowed her to overcome the daimonic power of her fantasy figure and relate meaningfully to another human being for the first time since her psychosis had broken out, whereupon she slowly came to recognize the necessity and value of living on Earth.[62]

In Kalsched's terms, the young woman's trauma had fragmented her psyche and given rise to the archaic, daimonic image of the moon vampire that paradoxically persecuted and protected her by drawing her vulnerable ego into a delusional isolation from the outer world. That is, the psychotic imagery of her primitive self-care system protected her from injury by ensuring that she would never trust anyone again. Jung's patience, empathy, and authentic engagement with the archetypal nature of her psychic reality helped her overcome her psyche's primitive, daimonic defenses and return to an authentic life among people in this world.

The insufferable nature of the young woman's trauma gave rise to a metaphorical form of representation in her psyche that Jung characterizes as ultimately redemptive. This brings to mind the relationship between trauma and religious imagery. In his book *God is Trauma*, Jungian analyst Greg Mogenson writes, "It is not just that God is unknowable and unimaginable; it is that we reach for 'God' most earnestly when imagination fails us. . . to stand before an event for which we have no metaphors is to stand in the tabernacle of the Lord."[63] And, Mogenson suggests, the path to healing lies in slowly, painfully working and reworking the symbols that arise from the unconscious in response to trauma. This alludes to the creative work with symbolic unconscious imagery that Jung calls *the transcendent function*, to which I return in chapter 11. Kalsched notes that Jung's dissociative model *"includes a religious or numinous background to the imaginal psyche which seems ... crucial in understanding severe forms of character pathology and [their] primitive defenses."*[64] I would add that the psyche's religious or numinous background also seems crucial in understanding the *transformative potential* of these trauma-induced defenses, which I discuss in chapter 10.

Possession by Complexes in Relation to Archaic Psychological Defenses

Despite emphasis on the psyche's mental and spiritual functions in later Jungian theory, Kalsched views affect as the basic functional unit and key organizing principle of Jung's psychology. Jung himself had said that "the essential basis of our personality is affectivity. Thought and action are, as it were, only symptoms of affectivity."[65] Life experiences associated with a strong emotion become organized around a feeling-toned complex, which Jung characterized as "a collection of various ideas, held together by an emotional tone common to all," and which he called "a higher psychic unity."[66] Jung's affect orientation has not been fully appreciated, Kalsched suggests, because *feeling* later came to mean "valuing" as one function of consciousness in Jung's typology, along with sensation, intuition, and thinking. When Jung speaks of feeling-toned complexes, however, he uses *feeling* to mean "emotion" or "affect."[67]

As part of the psyche's symbol-generating nature, says Kalsched, a feeling-toned complex tends to take form in dreams, fantasies, and other manifestations of the unconscious as a personified image, or being, which interacts with the conscious ego.[68] Jung speaks of such a complex-based image as an "image of a personified affect."[69] Complexes constitute, then, according to this psychological interpretation, the people who populate our dreams, the hallucinatory voices that haunt schizophrenics, and the figures, ghosts, demons, or spirits of our visions.

More or less autonomous complexes exist in everyone, "even in so-called normals," Jung maintains. Yet, he explains, "in those states where the complex temporarily replaces the ego, we see that a strong complex possesses all the characteristics of a separate personality.... somewhat like a small secondary mind, which deliberately (though unknown to consciousness) drives at certain intentions which are contrary to the conscious intentions of the individual."[70] The extent to which these complexes disturb the ego depends on their autonomy, which is influenced by their emotional intensity. The superstition that insane people are possessed by demons has a certain validity, notes Jung, because these people are affected by autonomous complexes, which can behave independently of the ego and completely overpower the patient's self-control. Jung even refers to some forms of psychosis as a *"complex disease."*[71]

In his essay "The Psychological Foundation of Belief in Spirits," Jung distinguishes between unconscious autonomous complexes of a personal nature and those of an archetypal nature. Those of a personal nature, which are related to an identifiable painful event in one's life, tend to be comprehensible even if disturbing. A person confronted by a complex embedded in the archetypal psyche, however, experiences it as utterly foreign and irrational; and she can understandably perceive its influence as literally coming from outside her. Hence, the notion of being possessed by a spirit. Experiencing a complex arising out of the archetypal psyche "is felt as strange, uncanny, and . . . fascinating," says Jung, and "the conscious mind falls under its spell, either feeling it as something pathological, or else being alienated by it from normal life."[72] The eruption of such alien content from the unconscious, Jung also notes, is a symptom of mental illness, and in his judgment this occurs "when something so devastating happens to the individual that his whole previous attitude to life breaks down."[73] If, on the other hand, this alien content can be translated into the language of consciousness in some form, it can have "a redeeming effect," Jung says, suggesting the healing and even transformative potential of complexes.[74]

Jung's possessing spirits correspond to the persecutory-protective daimonic figures Kalsched has so often encountered in the unconscious images of his traumatized patients. Jung's spirits and Kalsched's daimonic figures both arise uncannily out of the collective unconscious with a terrifying impact. "As the affect-images of the collective layer of the psyche, archetypes structure the most archaic and primordial (primitive) emotional experience in images," writes Kalsched.[75] "If we can imagine the volcanic storms of affect that rampage through the [child's traumatized] psyche, we get some inkling as to why the forms given such affect are themselves archaic, i.e., images of daimons or angels—of titanic, god-like 'great beings' which threaten to annihilate the immature ego. Potentiated by severe trauma, these inner figures continue to traumatize the inner world."[76]

The Emergence of Trauma-Based Imagery in Psychedelic Experience

The cases that I presented above of the three women who suffered childhood trauma and underwent LSD-enhanced psychotherapy illustrate the psychedelic-induced emergence of unconscious imagery that is consistent with Kalsched's model of the psyche's archetypal self-care system and its persecutory-protective daimonic figures. I have also been stuck by the resonance between the characteristic images and dynamics of these archetypal defenses and the psychedelic-induced visions and images I have personally encountered. Following my first difficult psychedelic experience in 1967, my subsequent psychedelic trips, and the countless spontaneous recurrences I have experienced since then, have consistently been pervaded by a sense that the world is a dark, threatening, hellish place, or is Hell itself. Because demonic imagery became so strikingly explicit during the MDMA-enhanced psychotherapy session I described above, Kalsched's insights have motivated me to consider the role of childhood trauma in my own difficult psychedelic experiences.

Kalsched's work with adults who have suffered early childhood trauma suggests that the disturbing daimonic content of my Burning Man session could have been due to more than the traumatic nature of my psychedelic experiences at the age of 19. I now consider it likely that those first terrifying psychedelic experiences in 1967 released unconscious feeling-toned complexes associated with third-degree burns I suffered at the age of two. As Kalsched explains, the unbearable images and emotions from a childhood trauma are distributed to different parts of the body and mind, especially to the unconscious; and this accounts for flashbacks of sensation that are often disconnected from the context in which they occur.[77] Considering Kalsched's discoveries and the potential psychedelics have to release unconscious images associated with past trauma, it seems likely that the LSD-induced images and visions I experienced in 1967 were, to some extent at least, a nineteen-year-old's psychedelic version—a kind of flashback experience—of what I first suffered at the age of two. And considering the possibility that the daimonic imagery I encountered during my therapy session at Burning Man reflected childhood trauma, it seems worth asking how a two-year-old boy would have experienced the doctors and nurses who were trying to treat his third-degree burns.

CHAPTER 6

Psychedelic Experience and the Shadow

The Shadow in Jung's Psychology

When I introduced the case of the young woman who had suffered sexual trauma, I mentioned that the case brings together most of the key elements of my inquiry. The shadow element played out especially dramatically for this young woman. At one point in her treatment, she improved enough to take a job as a nurse in a sanatorium. When a doctor made a pass at her, she shot him with a concealed pistol she had been carrying. (He survived; and after more treatment, she went on to live a normal life.) In her last interview with Jung, she told him that she would have shot him, too, if he had failed her. We can understand how this young woman, who had become catatonic after having been the victim of incest with her older brother when she was 15, would carry a great deal of repressed anger in her shadow.

Jung is said to have first referred to the "shadow side of the psyche" in characterizing Freud's idea of the repressed parts of the personality and its unrecognized desires.[1] But Jung later conceived of the shadow as an autonomous unconscious personality, *the other* in us that embarrasses us because the ego tends, consciously or unconsciously, to deny all negative aspects of itself. What we deny therefore coalesces in the unconscious as "the shadow," which serves a compensating function by making up for our one-sided, or imbalanced, conscious identification with what we find acceptable.[2] Jungian analyst Edward Whitmont defines the shadow as "that part of the personality which has been repressed for the sake of the ego ideal."[3] Jung defined the shadow as "the 'negative' side of the personality, the sum of all those unpleasant qualities we like to hide, together with the insufficiently developed functions [of the personality] and the contents of the personal unconscious."[4] That is, the shadow also contains undeveloped personality traits that we consider positive. We can think, for instance, of the difficulty many of us have manifesting the concern that we feel for a stranger in need of help. "All archetypes," says Jung, "spontaneously develop favorable and unfavorable, light and dark, good and bad effects."[5] We shouldn't forget that the psyche in its complex wholeness contains polarities just as surely as the physical world contains light and darkness. And even the shadow's negative aspects, such as unconscious anger, have transformative potential. (I discuss the transformative potential of the shadow in "The Painful Passage through the Shadow towards Wholeness" in chapter 10.)

In his essay "The Shadow," Jung outlines the shadow phenomenon: its personal and archetypal nature; the resistance it engenders within us and the ferocity of our consequent unconscious projections; its emotional and independent nature, which accounts for its power to overwhelm and isolate the ego; and the moral effort required for its assimilation into consciousness.[6] I draw from that essay to describe the shadow and its relationship to difficult psychedelic experiences and transformation.

Personal and Archetypal Levels of the Shadow

As we have seen, Jung frequently distinguishes between the personal and the collective unconscious. He makes a similar distinction between the shadow's personal and collective aspects.[7] Trying to draw a definite distinction between these two levels of the shadow can create some confusion, however. When Jung refers to the shadow as an archetype, for instance, it is difficult to think of the shadow as only part of the *personal* unconscious. Again, it helps to realize that sharp distinctions between the personal and the collective, both as dimensions of experience and as aspects of the unconscious, don't accurately reflect the psyche's complexity. (It also helps to remember that we're dealing with hypothetical constructs rather than actual parts of a physical structure.) Joseph Henderson identifies three interrelated and inseparable levels of the shadow: the personal, the cultural, and the archetypal, or collective.[8] Henderson's classification scheme suggests various nuanced interrelationships worth considering. I focus here on the personal and archetypal, or collective, levels.

Jung claims that the shadow "represents first and foremost the personal unconscious;" but the shadow sometimes represents the collective unconscious.[9] Jung describes the collective shadow as "that hidden, repressed, for the most part inferior and guilt-laden personality whose ultimate ramifications reach back into the realm of our animal ancestors and so comprise the whole historical aspect of the unconscious."[10]

Jung often describes the personal and collective aspects of the shadow in terms of evil. Stephen Diamond explains that Jung's idea of the shadow developed from his attempt to metaphorically articulate the psychological problem of evil in a way that was free of associations with the Christian

"Devil."[11] For Jung, evil is a consequence of excessive unconsciousness. Coming to terms with personal evil is one thing. But dealing with evil at its deepest level is quite another. Jung expresses the challenge this way: "It is quite within the bounds of possibility for a man to recognize the relative evil of his nature, but it is a rare and shattering experience for him to gaze into the face of absolute evil."[12]

When Jung speaks here of *absolute evil*, I understand him to mean the dark side of the Self, or the dark side of the God archetype.[13] Henderson maintains that Jung's truest insight into psychological reality, and his real interest, wasn't the ego and its personal shadow but the Self and its archetypal shadow.[14] This assertion is born out in Jung's *Answer to Job*, in which he analyzes Job's shattering encounter with Yahweh as a symbolic representation of a person's confrontation with the dark side of the Self.

More accurately, Yahweh represents a paradoxical combination of opposites, a *complexio oppositorum*, recalling the persecutory-protective figures in Kalsched's trauma-induced self-care system.[15] The Hebraic God, Kalsched suggests, "rages against his people, persecutes them, . . . sadistically tortures them without provocation, all the while demanding constant bloody sacrifices to propitiate his wrath."[16] Yet, Kalsched adds, this wrathful God also provides guidance and protection to his people. In *Answer to Job,* Jung describes Yahweh as "both persecutor and helper in one, and the one aspect is as real as the other. Yahweh is not split but is an *antinomy*—a totality of inner opposites—and this is the indispensable condition for his tremendous dynamism."[17]

The Overwhelmingly Numinous Nature of the Archetypal Psyche

The tremendous dynamism of the Self archetype as both persecutor and protector gives our experience of the Self, in both its sublime and destructive aspects, an overwhelmingly numinous quality. As we have seen, Jung often describes the numinous, or strange and fascinating, quality of archetypal experience in religious terms such as "holiness." For Jung, the idea of holiness represents a psychological insight of the highest value, a revelation from beyond the sphere of consciousness, that evokes overwhelming awe.[18] Jung adopted the idea of the numinous from Rudolf Otto, who in his book *The Idea of the Holy* describes the qualities of numinosity and mystery expressed in Job's encounter with Yahweh. After Otto reviews God's demonstration of overwhelming power through creations like the Leviathan and the Behemoth, he writes: "Assuredly these beasts would be the most unfortunate examples that one could hit upon if searching for evidence of the purposefulness of the divine 'wisdom.' But they . . . do express in masterly fashion the downright stupendousness, the wellnigh daemonic and wholly incomprehensible character of the eternal creative power; how, incalculable and 'wholly other,' it mocks at all conceiving but can yet stir the mind to its depths, fascinate and overbrim the heart."[19]

The psychological consequence of an encounter with the God archetype is the ego's paralyzing fear and subordination. "Either one's moral courage fails, or one's insight, or both," Jung maintains.[20] Edward Edinger observes that this alienating experience is "a necessary prelude to awareness of the Self," an insight I will return to in chapter 10.[21] Jung describes an encounter with the archetypal psyche as "the meeting with oneself."[22] This meeting, he explains, begins with an encounter with one's shadow: "The shadow is a tight passage, a narrow door, whose painful constriction no one is spared who goes down to the deep well [which leads to] a boundless expanse full of unprecedented uncertainty."[23] Jung's depiction here of a confrontation with the shadow recalls other metaphorical characterizations of an encounter with the darker nature of existence, such as a descent into the underworld, the dark night of the soul, facing one's demons, and wrestling with the Devil.[24] Such a fall into the collective unconscious can leave one feeling "delivered up," says Jung, and it has brought on cases of psychosis or "a catastrophe that destroyed life."[25]

One of my own difficult psychedelic experiences in 1967 illustrates a confrontation with the personal and archetypal levels of the shadow. After having taken LSD on the evening before moving out of a rented house, I came across a number of things I needed to pack or dispose of. Feeling hopelessly overwhelmed with the tasks before me, and recalling the kind old couple from whom we were renting the house, I was suddenly overcome with guilt at the thought that I would be leaving the house in a mess. As I stood looking down at a pile of old newspapers, I had, despite the lack of any previous religious inclination, a vision of standing below a panel of heavenly judges. It *was* the Last Judgment. Hanging my head in shame, I felt crushed by irredeemable guilt. Not only did I feel guilty for my personal transgressions, I felt profoundly ashamed for being a human in an absolutely sinful world. Life in this world was, I knew then, nothing but folly.

Standing on a beach later that night, I had the terrifying feeling that I was being pulled into the ocean to my death—and to God—and I desperately fought my way back into this world, which I knew was Hell. The dilemma I experienced that night is beautifully expressed in William Blake's image of Yahweh giving Job a glimpse of Hell (p. 75). In this image, Job seems as terrified of God as he does of Hell.

My friend and I later drove to a secluded cliff, and in windswept darkness, we threw our unwanted things into the surf below. As my long overcoat flapped violently in the wind, and as I raised a box over my head and flung it into the darkness—*I was evil incarnate*. A few months later, during my next LSD trip, I attempted to honor God's command that I kill myself to free my soul from Hell.

Yahweh Frightens Job with a Glimpse of Hell, William Blake
Lessing J. Rosenwald Collection, Library of Congress. Copyright © 2013 William Blake Archive. Used with permission.

Resistance to and Projection of the Shadow

Returning now to Jung's characterization of falling into the archetypal psyche, which can leave one feeling "delivered up," and which has brought on cases of psychosis or "a catastrophe that destroyed life;" we should recall that Kalsched's diabolical self-care figures can appear as "a true *agent of death*, . . . a truly perverse factor in psychological life," which becomes a formidable resistance to life itself. Kalsched didn't attribute such archaic disintegrative energies to the personal shadow but rather to the "archetypal shadow," the dark side of the Self.[26] The emotional nature of one's inferior personality traits makes insight into one's personal shadow difficult, notes Marie-Louise von Franz; but when shadow projections arise from the archetypal psyche, insights come with "almost insuperable difficulties."[27] Jungian analyst Lionel Corbett emphasizes that experiencing the numinous qualities of the Self, especially the Self's darkness, can engender intolerably intense fears and psychotic reactions. Terrified by experiences of the *numinosum*, Corbett explains, the conscious mind tends to ward them off rather than assimilate them.[28]

Corbett observes that the ego-controls of psychologically healthy people can allow them to experience archetypal levels of the unconscious and yet contain them within safe limits. "The more cohesive . . . the [ego], the more it can safely experience the Self by reordering itself rather than by fragmenting."[29] But, he adds, people who have consistently devalued and repressed their feelings may strongly resist the archetypal unconscious because it has become so populated with painful complexes.[30]

Job's shattering encounter with Yahweh can be understood as representing the resistance we all have to the archetypal shadow, or the dark side of the Self. The biblical book of Job reflects our fear of becoming conscious of the darkness at the core of our being, just as Job feared facing God's shortcomings. A confrontation with the dark side of our personal unconscious contradicts our image of ourselves and is deeply disturbing. A confrontation with the dark side of the Self contradicts our image of the absolute and is terrifying.

Our fear of our shadow nature at both the personal and archetypal levels is ultimately a fear of psychological death. That is, to develop psychologically, our ideal image of ourselves must die as we recognize and integrate the shadow side of our nature and become whole. In our fear, and as a reflection of our resistance, we unconsciously project our shadow qualities onto others. Or, as Corbett puts it, when we resist the emergence of unconscious content, material that is pushing to break through to consciousness becomes projected onto our environment.[31] Such unconscious projections can only be recognized, Jung maintains, with "a moral achievement beyond the ordinary. . . . Both insight and good will are unavailing because the cause of the emotion appears to lie, beyond all possibility of doubt, in the other person."[32] When I get angry at my neighbor's selfishness, for example, it could be that I'm projecting my own selfishness onto him. So our perception of the other person is obscured by that part of ourselves that we see in the other person. And we experience our own shadow in our perception of the other as strange, suspect, or perhaps even evil. This experience stems from the illusion that we know ourselves. The other becomes, then, "the carrier" of the darkness we fail to acknowledge in ourselves.[33] Jung describes the mechanism and effects of projection in this way: "It is not the conscious subject but the unconscious which does the projecting. Hence one meets with projections, one does not make them. The effect of projection is to isolate the subject from his environment, since instead of a real relation to it there is now only an illusory one. Projections change the world into the replica of one's own unknown face."[34] When the psyche's defenses block unconscious material from entering consciousness, they also isolate us from ourselves by preventing us from knowing ourselves more deeply. As a result, Corbett suggests, these defenses preclude the potentially healing and transformative effects that the unconscious can have through its compensating relationship to consciousness.[35]

The Shadow in Psychedelic Experience

After having taken psilocybin more than one hundred times, Timothy Leary tried LSD (an overwhelming dose) for the first time, and encountered his shadow:

> This experience is of course endless and indescribable. After several billion years I found myself on my feet moving through a puppet show. Where does Timothy Leary belong in this dance of illusion? I thought of my kids and walked somehow upstairs to the second-floor landing and opened the door to my daughter's room. Susan was sitting in bed, the classic thirteen-year-old with her hair up in curlers, frowning in concentration at the school book in her lap, while rock-and-roll music blasted through the room. It was Saturday Evening Post Cover Americana. The puppet doll teenager glanced up. Hi, Dad. She was biting a pencil and looking at the book. I slumped against the wall, looking with amazement at this marionette stranger, from assembly-line America. She glanced up again, quickly. Hi, Dad, what would you like for Christmas? She went on biting the pencil, frowning at the book, waving slightly at the beat of the music. In a minute she looked up again. Hi, Dad, I love you.
>
> A shock of terror convulsed me. This was my daughter and this was the father-daughter game. A shallow, superficial, stereotyped, meaningless exchange of Hi, Dad, Hi Sue, How are you Dad? How's school? What do you want for Christmas? Have you done your homework? The plastic doll father and the plastic doll daughter both mounted on little wheels, rolling by each other around and around on fixed tracks. A complete vulgarization of the real situation—two incredibly complex, trillion-cell clusters, rooted in an eternity of evolution, sharing for a flicker this space-time coordinate. And offered this rare chance to merge souls and bring out the divinity in the other, but desiccated and deadened into Hi Dad Hi Susan squeaks.
>
> I looked at her beseechingly, straining for real contact. I was stunned with guilt.
>
> With microscopic clarity, I saw the egocentricity, the sham of my devoted-father routine. Is it too late, can I come back, glorify this rare trembling opportunity? I turned and slowly walked downstairs.

Leary found his eleven-year-old son sitting on the floor downstairs watching television. He sat down next to his son, and followed his son's gaze to the television set. At one point, Leary recounts, one of the television characters "suddenly wheeled around and said, looking straight through the television tube, into my eyes, You've been dead for two seconds."[36] Understanding this as a message to him from "the cosmic playwright," written out for the obtuse in a dumbed down television drama, Leary writes, "I'd been dead for two seconds. And this is what hell is like. I could look back over the past forty years with chagrin, with pain at my blindness."[37]

Reflecting further on the impact of his first LSD trip, Leary touches on the potential a psychedelic-induced confrontation with one's shadow has to trigger a temporary psychotic reaction:

> There is a second aspect of this session from which I have never recovered. *The mind manipulation paranoia* [my italics].... Ever since that day I have had a recurring science-fiction paranoia which comes up in almost every LSD session. It starts like this: suddenly, with a click, I am [in] this new level of reality. I am suddenly on camera in an ancient television show directed and designed by some unknown intelligence. I'm the pathetic clown, the shallow, corny, twentieth-century American, the classic buffoon completely caught in a world of his own making, and not realizing that the goals and ambitions he strives for, the serious games he struggles with, are simply the comic relief, a brief clown act.[38]

Ann Shulgin, former psychedelic therapist and venerated matriarch of the psychedelic community, asserts that the degree of insight achieved in any psychedelic session depends primarily on one's willingness to face and acknowledge one's shadow. This process is grounded in Jung's psychology, but Shulgin's approach to psychedelic-enhanced psychotherapy differs in one significant respect. Jungian analysts encourage their clients to clearly see the shadow within themselves and work with it until it's consciously integrated as an ally, Shulgin points out. "A therapist working with MDMA, psilocybin, or a similar drug," she explains,

> will gently help his client to take one additional step, when he has full view of his Shadow, which, by the way, usually, but not always, takes the form of a large, powerful animal. He will urge the client to first face, then enter into, the dark figure he is meeting; he must work to get inside the beast's skin and look out through its eyes.
>
> It is here, at this point, that a battle may have to be fought, because not only does the conscious mind have to fight his own revulsion, shame, and fear of this forbidden aspect of his psyche, the mind may project on the Shadow an equal resistance to being seen or touched.[39]

Shulgin emphasizes that "the prospect of seeing what he unconsciously believes to be the core—the essence—of himself as a series of horrendous, malignant, totally unacceptable entities, can bring about a state of fear that has no parallel in ordinary life."[40]

Only recently did I appreciate the significance of the shadow in my own difficult psychedelic experiences. Attempting to understand and integrate the challenging MDMA-enhanced therapy session I described in chapter 5, in which I became overwhelmed with the conviction that I was literally trapped in the Devil's den, I became fascinated by Jung's concept of the shadow. Reflecting on the session as I read, I felt I understood the idea of the shadow, and its projection onto others, for the first time.

As I described, the session started well. But as I probed an especially traumatic memory, I suddenly and shockingly perceived a man observing the session to be Satan himself, and I realized that the man and woman I was working with in the session were his demonic assistants. Their skin now seemed bluish and cold to the touch; I thought I saw fang tips peeking out from their upper lips. With the thump of trance music and the vague cries of thousands of pagan revelers pulsating across the desert in the middle of the night, I understood that this *was* "the night of the living dead." I noticed the devilish curl of another man's eyebrow as he entered the tent dressed like some nomadic sorcerer. They were all gathering for my demise, I realized. I was going to die a horrible death at their hands—*I* was to be the burning man.

After reading in more depth about the shadow, it seemed clear that my projection of the shadow at its personal, cultural, and archetypal levels could account for a good deal of my perception of this world as Hell that night. (I say "a good deal" because I think to some extent I was also confronting the objective reality of absolute evil.) Exactly what I was projecting, I won't delve into here. But, as I've suggested, it's possible that my projections were to some extent related to unconscious images and fears from my emergency-room experience at the age of two.

As I was learning more about Jung's concept of the shadow, I was becoming fascinated by Kalsched's approach to trauma. When it became clear to me that both trauma and shadow were key elements in my own psychedelic-induced psychotic states, I started to wonder how they were related to each other in my experiences. After some reflection, I realized that the link between trauma and shadow and my psychedelic-induced psychotic states was *anger*. And anger seems to be a key link between trauma, shadow, and psychosis for others.[41] As we have seen, this was certainly true for the young incest victim. Shadow and anger also emerged during LSD therapy with two traumatized patients treated by Ronald Sandison and Margot Cutner.

Sandison's patient, who suffered suicidal depression related to her psychopathic father and the death of her mother, exhibited a "ferocious antagonism" toward her father.[42] Sandison reports that her father's chance visit to her at the hospital "put her in a most hostile and irrational mood."[43] During one LSD session, the woman reports, "I found myself under water. I thought how remarkably pretty this land of the unconscious was. Then the colours changed, and the water became green and angry looking."[44] The woman goes on to describe feeling surrounded by her father's presence in the form of a spider.

Margo Cutner's traumatized patient, who suffered from severe depression and paranoid tendencies, "became wildly hostile and aggressive" during negative phases of transference, or projection. Cutner reports that at one point she found her patient in her room, out of which she had thrown every piece of bedding and furniture except a bed and a chair: "She was sitting on her bare bed, trembling, with a face distorted with fear, hatred and horror, begging me to leave the room as otherwise she was sure she would strangle me. She also kept repeating, as she often did under LSD, that she must take her own life."[45] The patient herself reports:

> The chair began to change and I saw that it was the one that my father had cut down for my mother to nurse my brothers in. I also remembered it used to stand in the corner in the boys' room where I kept my toys, and I used to be frightened of it because I thought a witch used to sit in it. I afterwards [during the LSD session] felt I wanted to smash everything, and again later I wanted to tear things up and I prayed the nurse would come and bring some papers so that I could just tear and tear.[46]

The woman was surprised that she could keep such strong feelings hidden inside herself for so long. "I realized that I had indeed felt this dreadful anger as a little girl but had never really known about it and certainly not let it out."[47]

Considering again my own case, there is good reason to think that a two-year-old boy who suffered third-degree burns would feel a great deal of anger as a result of such an accident. If he also felt unconsciously that he couldn't express that anger, he would understandably repress it. Growing up "a good boy" by appearances, that anger would become a big part of his shadow, which would manifest in various destructive ways, including the physical abuse of his little brother, chronic stealing, and, later, alcohol and drug abuse. Using psychedelics recklessly, he becomes overwhelmed by the eruption of his own unconscious content, which is so heavy with darkness that his conscious mind breaks under the burden of it. In a state of psychotic reaction to the unbearable strangeness of this shadow material, he projects his own darkness onto the world at large and has a vision that he must kill himself to escape its evil and prove his worth to God. In the act of attempted suicide, he acts out his repressed anger and avoids coming to terms with his own shadow.

CHAPTER 7

Psychedelic Experience and Psychosis

Psychosis and Psychotic States

Modern psychiatric research has revealed the extreme complexity of psychosis, a disorder affected by a wide range of factors, including genetic elements, developmental history, biochemical changes, situational circumstances, and sociocultural influences. The term *psychosis* has been historically defined in different ways, none of which has been universally accepted by psychiatrists.[1] Earlier definitions used by the American Psychiatric Association (APA) were so broad that the term *psychosis* covered any disorder that "resulted in 'impairment that grossly interferes with the capacity to meet ordinary demands of life.'"[2] Later APA classifications for psychosis use much more restrictive criteria. In classifications such as Schizophrenia, Schizophreniform Disorder, and Brief Psychotic Disorder, the term *psychotic* refers to "delusions, any prominent hallucinations, disorganized speech, or disorganized or catatonic behavior."[3] Some earlier definitions included characteristics that were clearly biased against transpersonal and psychedelic-induced states of consciousness, such as "a loss of ego boundaries" and "prominent hallucinations that the individual realizes are hallucinatory experiences."[4] The *DSM-IV* classification Substance-Induced Psychotic Disorder makes a refreshing distinction by referring to "delusions or *only those hallucinations that are not accompanied by insight*" (my italics).[5]

In his book *Healing the Split: Integrating Spirit Into Our Understanding of the Mentally Ill*, transpersonally-oriented psychiatrist John Nelson defines psychosis as "any one of several altered states of consciousness, transient or persistent, that prevent integration of sensory or extrasensory data into reality models accepted by the broad consensus of society, and that lead to maladaptive behavior and social sanctions."[6] Even though this definition undervalues the integration of experience into *unconventional* reality models and doesn't recognize that some of history's sanest people suffered social sanction for "maladaptive" behavior, Nelson's treatment is on the whole quite evenhanded and useful. To begin with, he points out that his definition of psychosis also describes potentially adaptive altered states of consciousness. Among these, Nelson includes mystical rapture and the effects of certain consciousness-altering drugs.[7]

Nelson's approach to psychosis recalls Stanislav Grof's insight that the same transpersonal experiences that lead to a psychotic breakdown can, under the right circumstances, bring about spiritual insight.[8] Given the complexity of psychosis and its ambiguous symptoms, which can indicate transformative as well as destructive altered states of consciousness, we clearly must be able to distinguish potentially transformative from destructive psychotic states. Grof's model highlights two criteria that are especially useful in making this distinction. We have to take into account the triggering mechanism that brings forth extraordinary unconscious content. (Was it drug-induced?) And we must consider the person's attitude toward and ability to integrate such content.[9] It isn't the *content* itself that is problematic, as unconventional and bizarre as that content might be. As Nelson puts it, the difference between what he calls a "benign," or beneficial, spiritual emergency and a schizophrenic break has everything to do with the way one integrates the content of the experience.[10]

Nelson's and Grof's transpersonal approaches to extraordinary, or "nonordinary," states of consciousness provide a Jungian-compatible context for my investigation of psychedelic-induced psychotic states. The field of transpersonal psychology and psychiatry emerged out of the meeting between Western mental-health practices, Eastern spiritual traditions, and the psychedelic culture in California during the 1960s. The field was inaugurated in 1969 with *The Journal of Transpersonal Psychology*; and it focuses on experiences that go beyond our ordinary sense of personal identity "to encompass wider dimensions of the psyche and the cosmos," including spiritual and religious experiences.[11] In their survey of the field, *Paths Beyond Ego: The Transpersonal Vision*, Roger Walsh and Frances Vaughan point out that "the study of consciousness and altered states of consciousness is central to transpersonal psychology."[12]

C. G. Jung is one of transpersonal psychology's most respected forefathers because he viewed transpersonal experience as a valid subject for psychological investigation. His inquiry in this respect is compatible with many of the field's central concerns. Unlike Jung, however, many transpersonal psychologists have been profoundly affected by their own psychedelic experiences, and for this reason the field has elucidated the nature of psychedelic experience in ways only implied in Jung's psychology.[13] Transpersonal theory and research therefore provide an especially suitable context for appreciating the relevance, value, and implications of Jung's insights into psychedelic experience, on which I focus in the next chapter.

John Nelson integrates mainstream neuropsychiatry and transpersonal psychiatry with Eastern philosophy; and he applies them to the task of understanding what he aptly calls the "sudden unnamed terrors" of psychosis.[14] Many of Nelson's insights are clearly consistent with and even derive from Jung's psychology. Nelson relates many of his own ideas to such Jungian concepts and principles as the collective unconscious, archetypes, the shadow, the psychological significance of myth, and the need for those with fragile ego boundaries to avoid powerful techniques for expanding consciousness. Nelson credits Jung with having uncommon insight into "the Source of consciousness . . . accessible to all sentient beings."[15] He refers to this source of consciousness as "the Spiritual Ground" (suggesting his debt to Michael Washburn's Dynamic Ground).[16] Nelson discusses psychotic states within a transpersonal conception of consciousness as a universal nonphysical reality that infuses all matter and assumes a variety of forms. For Nelson, human consciousness and altered states of consciousness (whether sane or psychotic) arise within this universal consciousness, or Spiritual Ground.

Nelson's transpersonal ontology brings to mind Jung's concepts of the collective unconscious and the archetype of the Self. But even though Jung's later writings can be interpreted as pointing in this direction, Jung didn't acknowledge a transpersonal ontology that included the immaterial, extrapsychic reality that Nelson suggests. That is, Jung's avowed view regarding the ontological nature of the collective unconscious was that it was *psychologically* transcendent to ego-consciousness. My focus in this book is on Jung's phenomenological descriptions of how people experience these transpersonal realms. Whether these realms are psychologically or ontologically transcendent, and whether, despite his consistent agnostic stance on this question, Jung's actual view changed over time, is not for my present purposes relevant.[17]

Nelson's conception of psychosis is especially valuable for my inquiry because he distinguishes "benign psychotic states that herald spiritual emergence" from "malignant [psychotic] states that portend retreat to primitive mental levels."[18] He distinguishes, that is, "profound breakthroughs of higher consciousness from malignant psychotic regressions that permanently submerge the self in primitive areas of the psyche."[19]

Nelson presents a developmental model of consciousness and selfhood that stems to some extent from Michael Washburn's theory of the ego and the Dynamic Ground. For Washburn, as the ego develops in childhood, a psychic membrane, or self-boundary, is formed that establishes our sense of identity and at the same time isolates us on a conscious level from the Dynamic Ground of reality, which eventually becomes alien to us. Because this psychic membrane always remains semi-permeable to the vital Ground, Nelson explains, the ego is always vulnerable to "catastrophic fragmentation" by sudden upsurges of energy from it.[20] This model of selfhood and consciousness suggests that altered states of consciousness, whether benign spiritual emergencies or malignant regressions, can be understood as changes in the permeability of the self's psychic boundary. Within this context, we can conceive of psychedelic-induced psychotic states as dramatic infusions from the vital Ground that overwhelm the self. This perspective is clearly consistent with Jung's idea of a lowering of the threshold of consciousness and with the Jungian interpretation of psychedelic-induced psychotic states that I discuss in the next chapter.

Nelson points out that people who suddenly become infused by life's most fundamental reality can naturally find it a terrifying force that carries them into madness. But even people whose spiritual practice has enabled them to gradually reopen themselves to this reality may encounter unexpected and frightening openings, or spiritual emergencies, that can become problematic if handled badly. Such openings can be even more terrifying to unprepared trippers, of course. In any event, we need to distinguish between relatively benign psychotic states and pathological psychotic states that can deteriorate into chronic psychosis.[21]

Making these distinctions can be challenging because benign and malignant psychotic states share many characteristics (characteristics that are also common to psychedelic experiences). According to Nelson, these include:

- Shifts in the relationship between self and Ground, or between consciousness and the unconscious, which one can experience as anything from blissful to terrifying
- Shifts in attention away from ordinary concerns
- Changes in one's experience of time and space
- Changes in one's perception of the material world and reality
- Different forms of logic leading to bizarre ideas and extraordinary insights ("Ideas that are obviously true in one state of consciousness may be absurd in another, and vice versa."[22])
- Unusual emotional coloration of ordinary events leading to insights into arbitrary social conventions or to terrifying paranoia
- Changes in self identity (including identification with other life forms or the whole universe) leading to insights and spiritual growth or confusion and fear
- Changes in behavior, from extreme introversion to intrusive acting out[23]

Psychedelics as Psychosis-Inducing Substances

The understanding of the relationship between psychedelic-induced psychotic states and natural psychosis changed as researchers became more knowledgeable about the psychological effects of psychedelics. In the 1890s, when the idea of schizophrenia was taking shape, researchers viewed "mescaline intoxication" as a potential chemical model for psychosis. In 1927, Kurt Beringer issued a comprehensive survey of mescaline's effects that described their similarity to psychosis.[24] His view was supported by later research, including a clinical study of mescaline-induced psychosis in 1940 by G. T. Stockings. Stockings gave mescaline to himself and people suffering from schizophrenia and observed that he could induce a wide range of abnormal states, including hallucinations, paranoia, delusions of grandeur and persecution, catatonia, mania, religious ecstasy, and suicidal impulses.[25] Stockings concluded that "mescaline intoxication is indeed a true 'schizophrenia' if we use that word in its literal sense of 'split mind,' for the characteristic effect of mescaline is a molecular fragmentation of the entire personality, exactly similar to that found in schizophrenic patients."[26]

In the 1940s and early 1950s the relationship between psychedelic experience and natural psychosis was assumed to be so strong that psychedelic substances were referred to as *psychotomimetic drugs*. This view led to a new approach to investigating the biological basis of mental illness, especially schizophrenia.[27] If psychotic reactions to these drugs were caused by some fundamental interference with the brain's neurochemistry, this seemed to indicate that the diseased brain of the person suffering from schizophrenia might be producing its own LSD-like substances.[28]

Albert Hofmann's historic first self-experiment with LSD certainly lent credence to the notion that psychedelics can induce psychotic states. In *LSD: My Problem Child*, Hofmann gives a detailed account of that experiment, an experience he describes as a "most severe crisis."[29] Feeling dizzy, anxious, and at the same time wanting to laugh, Hofmann rode his bicycle home from his laboratory with his assistant. While resting at home, his furniture assumed grotesque forms, and the lady next door, who had brought him milk to drink, became "a malevolent, insidious witch with a colored mask."[30]

> Even worse than these demonic transformations of the outer world, were the alterations that I perceived in myself, in my inner being. Every exertion of my will, every attempt to put an end to the disintegration of the outer world and the dissolution of my ego, seemed to be wasted effort. A demon had invaded me, had taken possession of my body, mind, and soul. I jumped up and screamed, trying to free myself

from him, but then sank down again and lay helpless on the sofa. The substance, with which I had wanted to experiment, had vanquished me. It was the demon that scornfully triumphed over my will. I was seized by the dreadful fear of going insane. I was taken to another world, another place, another time.[31]

Hofmann's own psychedelic-induced psychotic state and early research on mescaline intoxication led Sandoz Pharmaceuticals to offer LSD samples to psychiatrists and researchers in 1947 in hopes of shedding light on the nature and causes of natural psychosis.

Harvard University psychiatrist Max Rinkel summarized the psychotomimetic paradigm in 1958 when he concluded that "the psychotic phenomena produced [by psychedelic substances] were predominantly schizophrenic-like symptoms. . . . Rorschach tests and concrete-abstract thinking tests showed responses quite similar to those obtained with schizophrenics."[32] In *Psychedelic Drugs Reconsidered*, Grinspoon and Bakalar outline the grounds on which psychedelic-induced psychotic states can be compared to natural psychosis, especially schizophrenia. Despite great variations, people suffering from schizophrenia share certain characteristics, which provide a basis for comparison to psychedelic-induced psychotic states. Grinspoon and Bakalar note that common characteristics of schizophrenia include:

- The reality of persons suffering from schizophrenia tends to be incoherent and incompatible with consensus reality.
- Persons suffering from schizophrenia do not distinguish between external and internal events, and they "confound perceptions with memories, wishes, and fears."
- "Reading inappropriate meanings into innocuous situations, they often begin to believe that everything happening around them is somehow directed at them, and they develop what are known as ideas of reference, feelings of influence, and delusions of grandeur or persecution."
- Persons suffering from schizophrenia also become suspicious and terror-stricken, and they often experience hallucinations of threatening, mocking, and accusing voices.[33]

When classifying different types of schizophrenia, Grinspoon and Bakalar distinguish between acute, or short-term, and chronic, or long-term, schizophrenia.[34] Research indicates that psychedelic-induced psychosis is typically a very temporary condition that shows the strongest correlation to acute schizophrenia, which Grinspoon and Bakalar characterize as having "a relatively sudden onset . . . , often in a previously normal person, [which] often ends in full recovery after a period of several days to several months, although it may recur."[35]

The distinction between short-term and long-term psychoses is an important one for my investigation of psychedelic-induced psychosis. Although I sometimes use the term *psychosis* interchangeably with the term *psychotic states*, the focus of my inquiry is on short-term psychedelic-induced psychotic *states*, not on long-term psychosis brought on by a psychedelic experience. Even though psychedelic experiences can elicit a long-term psychosis, such tragic developments are relatively rare and, based on emergency admissions at hospitals in the 1960s (the vast majority of which were short-term cases), long-term psychedelic-induced psychoses tend to be attributable to significant preexisting psychiatric disorders.[36]

Grinspoon and Bakalar's review of the research suggests a "startling resemblance between schizophrenic and psychedelic experience."[37] A number of papers "find the effects of psychedelic drugs and the symptoms of schizophrenia to be almost the same."[38] The studies that Grinspoon and Bakalar reviewed showed that both conditions involve:

- "heightened sensory responses"
- "symbolic projection"
- "changes in time sense and feelings of regression in time"
- "preoccupation with usually disregarded details"
- "impairment of judgment and reasoning"
- "unusually strong ambivalent emotions: on one hand, anxiety, dread, suspicion, guilt, fear of disintegration, and on the other hand, awe, bliss, a sense of certainty, feelings of extraordinary creative awareness or spiritual breakthrough, dissolution of the self in a greater unity"[39]

The extreme variability of schizophrenic symptoms also corresponds to the extraordinary variety of psychedelic experiences, a finding consistent with Grof's description of psychedelics as "nonspecific catalysts and amplifiers of the psyche."[40] "It is not surprising," Grinspoon and Bakalar conclude, "that psychedelic drugs were long regarded as a potential tool of special value in the study of endogenous psychosis."[41]

But, they add, psychedelic-induced psychosis also differs in significant respects from schizophrenia. In the late 1950s and early 1960s, when many studies had compared psychedelic experience and psychosis, most researchers concluded that although there are symptomatic resemblances, the clinical syndrome of psychosis as a whole is significantly different than psychedelic-induced psychosis.[42] Some of the notable differences between psychedelic effects and psychosis that Grinspoon and Bakalar highlight include:

- Psychedelics predominantly induce visual hallucinations rather than the auditory hallucinations (imaginary voices) of schizophrenia.

- Those using psychedelics experience more perceptual changes and their mood is rarely apathetic.
- Psychedelics can induce the symptoms of other psychological disorders besides schizophrenia.
- People suffering from schizophrenia cannot associate their altered states with a drug they have taken, and they therefore fall easily into an involuntary psychotic state. (Understandably, people who are not aware that they have taken a psychedelic drug are more likely to suffer a psychotic reaction.)
- Psychedelic experiences typically last six to twelve hours in contrast to the more open-ended duration of a psychosis, which can leave its victim feeling it will never end.[43]

Charles Grob notes that the central argument against the psychotomimetic model was forcefully articulated in 1959 by Manfred Bleuler. (Manfred Bleuler is the son of Eugen Bleuler, who coined the term *schizophrenia* and was Jung's chief physician at Burghölzli Mental Hospital in Zurich.) Schizophrenia, Bleuler maintained, is characterized by "the gradual and inexorable progression of a symptom complex that included disturbed thought processes, depersonalization and auditory hallucinations, evolving into a generalized functional incapacitation."[44] And although psychedelics may have improved our understanding of natural psychoses, Bleuler asserted that they had taught us nothing about the origin of schizophrenia.[45] Stanislav Grof notes that generations of scientists have endeavored unsuccessfully to understand the nature and origin of schizophrenia, and he describes it as "one of the greatest enigmas of modern psychiatry and medicine."[46]

From the Psychotomimetic to the Psychedelic Paradigm

As we have seen, there were early indications that the psychological effects of these mind-altering substances were more complex than the psychotomimetic paradigm indicated. The first experiments conducted in the mid 1940s with LSD by Sandoz Pharmaceuticals had shown that low-dose LSD therapy sessions could help people recover unconscious memories and feelings, which would presumably advance treatment. Still, researchers remained intensely interested in LSD's psychotomimetic properties through the 1950s.[47]

But when high doses started to be used, unexpected effects were discovered. Humphry Osmond and Abram Hoffer had intended to treat chronic alcoholics by exploiting the psychotomimetic effects of mescaline and LSD to reproduce the terrifying hallucinatory experiences that typically occur during alcohol withdrawal or very heavy drinking.[48] Contrary to their expectations, Osmond and Hoffer found that successful treatments resulted from the ecstatic mystical states induced by psychedelic substances. Instead of terrifying alcoholics into sobriety, high-dose psychedelic sessions had healed them through spiritual insight. Osmond and Hoffer thereby discovered that psychedelics could do much more than induce temporary psychoses, and a new theoretical framework emerged. Osmond coined the term *psychedelic* to indicate that these substances could induce life-enhancing visions as well as pathological states.[49] (Given Stockings' observation in 1940 that mescaline could induce religious ecstasy as well as pathological states, it is more accurate say that Osmond and Hoffer *rediscovered* the life-enhancing properties of psychedelics. And we shouldn't forget that Stockings had discovered something known for ages by indigenous people throughout the world.)

"It became increasingly obvious," Grof reports, "that the LSD-induced state had many specific characteristics clearly distinguishing it from schizophrenia."[50] The chemical-psychosis model became discredited, then, because it promoted a simplistic view of psychedelic experience and a reductive explanation of the biochemical origin of schizophrenia. Neither view was convincingly supported by empirical data.

The Psychotomimetic Model Reconsidered

Many important questions about the relationship between psychedelic experience and psychosis remained unanswered, however, and some investigators returned to studying that relationship in the 1980s.[51] Even critics of the psychotomimetic paradigm acknowledge that the profound psychological changes induced by LSD provide valuable insights into abnormal mental states.[52]

Despite good reasons for abandoning the psychotomimetic model, I think it is useful to reexamine the parallels between psychedelic-induced psychotic states and natural psychosis for reasons other than those traditionally advocated. To begin with, as Grinspoon and Bakalar say, "the similarities between some kinds of psychedelic experiences and some forms of schizophrenia remain impressive despite the divergences."[53] Nelson notes that although theorists have abandoned psychedelic experience as a model for psychosis because the psychedelic experience differs greatly from *chronic* schizophrenia, the first stages of an acute psychosis (when, for instance, visual hallucinations are more prominent) show an unmistakable resemblance to a psychedelic experience. The altered states of consciousness associated with both conditions "stretch self-boundaries into unfamiliar areas of Ground consciousness, for better or worse."[54]

And, in fact, even suggested differences between psychedelic-induced psychotic states and schizophrenia aren't always valid. Experienced psychedelic users would recognize many of the following states that Grinspoon and Bakalar describe as characteristic of schizophrenia alone:

- "The schizophrenic is taken by surprise and driven involuntarily into the altered state."
- The schizophrenic crisis lasts much longer than six to twelve hours [the typical duration of a psychedelic experience].
- The person suffering from schizophrenia does not know whether his or her condition will ever end.
- "The schizophrenic is drawn by forces out of his control into an [unknown world], with no assurance of return."[55]

Even though the chemical-psychosis model has fallen out of favor for good reason, it still has value. Whereas the psychotomimetic paradigm tried to use psychedelics to provide clues to the nature, causes, and treatment of natural psychosis, I am proposing that we in effect turn the chemical-psychosis paradigm on its head. That is, existing knowledge about the nature, causes, and treatment of natural psychosis can elucidate the nature, causes, and treatment of psychotic reactions to a psychedelic experience.

Objections to the psychotomimetic model deserve to be addressed. But its flaws shouldn't prevent us from investigating the relationship between psychedelic experience and psychosis to better understand psychedelic crises. As Grinspoon and Bakalar conclude in their discussion of psychedelics and psychosis: "Psychedelic experiences should not be identified with an acute endogenous psychosis, especially if the purpose is either to glorify psychotics or to denounce drug users. But it would also be a mistake to ignore the similarities. As we have seen, the overlap in symptoms is often striking, the causes might yet turn out to be related, and there might even be implications for treatment."[56]

Acknowledging a seed of truth in the anti-psychiatry movement associated with R. D. Laing, Grinspoon and Bakalar add that if we accept the potential implications for treating psychosis that may be revealed by psychedelic research, "we may also have to admit that psychosis can sometimes produce insights."[57] This conclusion touches on the *transformative* potential of a psychedelic experience and even psychedelic-induced psychotic states, to which I will turn in chapters 9 and 10.

Transpersonal Explanations of Psychedelic-Induced Psychotic States

Clearly, as with any inquiry into the nature of psychedelic experience, we need to keep in mind that reactions to psychedelic experiences vary greatly from person to person and even from session to session for the same person. We also need to remember that set and setting significantly influence a psychedelic experience. I want to establish, nevertheless, some general explanations of psychedelic-induced psychotic states from the field of transpersonal psychology.

Even though the most common psychedelics in the Western world—LSD, psilocybin, mescaline, and ayahuasca—each have a unique chemical makeup, they all affect the mind in the same general way.[58] Nelson, as we have seen, accounts for psychedelic-induced psychotic states in his transpersonal model of self and consciousness. From his perspective, the semi-permeable nature of the self's psychic membrane leaves it vulnerable to "catastrophic fragmentation" during altered states of consciousness. Psychedelics can thereby dangerously overwhelm the ego. If one's sense of self is annihilated during a psychedelic experience, Nelson says, a person who is unprepared and not supported by an experienced guide, can be carried terrifyingly into madness.[59]

For Grof, psychedelic-induced psychotic states result from a person's attitude toward and response to an extraordinary experience. It isn't the content of the experience that causes a psychotic state, as bizarre as that content might be. Rather, Grof says, "the individual's capacity to keep the process internalized, 'own' it as an intrapsychic happening, and complete it internally without acting on it prematurely is clearly associated with the mystical attitude and indicates basic sanity. Exteriorization of the process, excessive use of the mechanism of projection, and indiscriminate acting out are characteristic of the psychotic style in confronting one's psyche."[60] Grof explains that a psychotic state represents "an interface confusion between the inner world and consensus reality."[61] That is, in a psychotic state, one projects unconscious images of, say, demons and death onto the external world and reacts to them as though they are materially real. This condition distinguishes someone in a psychotic state from someone in a mystical state: a person in a mystical state can discriminate between the two realities.[62]

Christina Grof and Stanislav Grof give a dramatic example of the failure to contain the process internally. Their innovative work with psychospiritual crises led to the idea of "spiritual emergency," a critically difficult stage of psychospiritual transformation. Such crises, they say, often occur in nonordinary states of consciousness and are typically described in spiritual literature as "rough passages along the mystical path."[63] According to the Grofs, a symbolic confrontation with death is often a vital part of spiritual growth. To move into a new state of consciousness, an old way of living has to "die." The ego must be destroyed. "Although [ego death] is one of the most beneficial, most healing events in spiritual evolution, it can seem disastrous," they point out.[64] When one is struggling with ego death, they explain, there is the potential for "a very tragic misunderstanding" in which the need for ego death is confused with the necessity to kill oneself. People in the throes of ego death can be "driven by a forceful inner insistence that something in them has to die. If the internal pressure is strong enough and if there is no understanding of the dynamics of ego death, they may misread these feelings and act them out."[65]

Apparently the challenge to contain the death-rebirth process internally isn't unusual during deep psychedelic exploration. In "The New Psychotherapy: MDMA and the Shadow," Ann Shulgin suggests that the pull toward literal death in serious psychedelic work can be so strong that she adamantly prescribes a mandatory pre-session contract between therapist and client. This contract includes the rule that, should the client "see the friendly death door and know, that by stepping through it, you can be done with this life, you will NOT do so during this session."[66] As Shulgin explains: "The death door is an actual experience that most explorers in the world of the human psyche will eventually encounter. It takes many forms, all of them gently welcoming, and its message is 'Here is the way back home, when you decide to return.'"[67]

Whether experiencing "the death door" is a psychotic or a mystical state, would depend, in terms of Grof's criteria, on the person's attitude toward and ability to integrate the content of the experience without exteriorizing the process, or acting it out, as I did in my attempt to honor what I perceived as God's command to kill myself. Clearly, as Shulgin's example suggests, a skillful psychedelic guide could mean the difference between life and death for someone unable to make this distinction.

Cultural factors also help account for psychedelic-induced psychotic states. Ralph Metzner, speaking from personal experience dating back to his doctoral studies under Timothy Leary and Richard Alpert at Harvard University, describes the vehement resistance psychedelics have encountered from mainstream groups in America and Europe. Metzner describes himself as "one of the psychedelic researchers who saw the enormous transformative potential of 'consciousness expanding' drugs . . . [and who was] eager to continue the research into their psychological significance."[68] Why, Metzner wonders, did the dominant culture demonize and criminalize the same kind of substances accepted as sacraments in the Native American subculture only a century earlier? After observing and participating in a variety of Native American sacred healing ceremonies that did *not* use peyote or other entheogens, Metzner concludes that such ceremonies must have provided a pre-existing structure that naturally incorporated psychedelics once they were introduced into Native American culture. These pre-existing ceremonial structures were simultaneously spiritual, medicinal, and psychotherapeutic, so that body, mind, and spirit were treated as a unity. This, Metzner argues, stands in stark contrast to the dominant Western culture's compartmentalization of medicine, psychology, and religion into seemingly incongruent fields of knowledge, each of which "separately considered the phenomenon of psychedelic drugs and were much too frightened by the unpredictable transformations of perception and worldview that they seemed to trigger. The dominant society's reaction was fear, followed by total prohibition. . . . The fragmented condition of our whole society is mirrored back to us through these reactions."[69] Clearly, although understandable within their cultural context, these reactions were excessive and harmful. And this fragmentation in our culture is reflected in our psychological fragmentation as individuals. We fear the deep unconscious, try to hold it at a safe distance, and flee from it—by way of a psychotic reaction, if necessary. Opportunities for exploration, discovery, integration, and transformation are thereby truncated.

The fear of psychedelics goes quite deep in our culture's psyche. Between the fourteenth and seventeenth centuries in Europe, indigenous healers—usually women who practiced nature-based witchcraft medicine with psychedelic plants such as datura, henbane, mandrake, and belladonna—were condemned by the Church, which saw psychedelic plants as Satan's tools.[70] Similar forms of persecution were inflicted on native peoples by Spanish conquistadors. Again, because psychoactive plants and fungi such as morning glory seeds, peyote, and psilocybe mushrooms were used by native peoples for religious purposes that were alien to their conquerors, these sacred medicines were seen as the Devil's weapons against Christianity.[71]

Given that psychedelic experiences often involve visions and perceptions of a demonic nature, it is worth considering whether, or to what degree, such visions and perceptions stem from these historical prejudices, or whether these historical prejudices grew out of early psychedelic-elicited unconscious images of a demonic nature. In any case, it is certainly safe to say that the eradication of traditional pagan and shamanic knowledge left a legacy of ignorance that could predispose modern users of psychedelics to react fearfully and even psychotically to alien aspects of the psychedelic experience. Our modern secular culture's dismissal of religious symbolism in general, including Judeo-Christian symbolism, would seem to further alienate contemporary users of psychedelics from the irrational imagery that they can encounter. Andrew Weil (whose book *The Natural Mind: An Investigation of Drugs and the Higher Consciousness* offers a thoughtful reflection on the hypothesis that we humans have an innate drive to alter our consciousness) notes that scopolamine, the psychoactive alkaloid in the plants commonly used by medieval witches, can take people into other worlds "populated by monsters and devils and filled with violent, frenzied energy."[72] Moreover, he adds, witches in medieval

Europe used these psychedelic plants "to have the experience of flying and to meet the Devil in their visions."[73] It is understandable that contemporary users of psychedelics who are ignorant of these traditions, and ignorant of the potential psychedelics have to induce such dark visions, could react psychotically to encounters with, say, Satan in their psychedelic experiences.

CHAPTER 8

Psychosis in Jung's Psychology

Jung's early research on psychosis, and especially his observation of schizophrenia's manifestation in his patients' archaic, mythological imagery, influenced his pioneering theory of archetypes and the collective unconscious. For Jung, these conceptions became indispensable in explaining the imagery, psychic splitting, and distorted reality of his patients.[1] We know from Jung's *Memories, Dreams, Reflections* that these ideas also developed out of his own confrontation with the unconscious. We get a sense of the connections Jung sees between psychosis and the archetypal psyche from his characterization of the archetypes, which, he says, "live in a world quite different from the world outside—in a world where the pulse of time beats infinitely slowly, where the birth and death of individuals count for little. No wonder their nature is strange, so strange that their irruption into consciousness often amounts to a psychosis. They undoubtedly belong to the material that comes to light in schizophrenia."[2]

When Jung talks about the risks associated with active imagination (his method for integrating consciousness and the unconscious through creative engagement with dream or fantasy images), he mentions a condition that he describes as temporarily indistinguishable from schizophrenia. Jung characterizes this condition as a "psychotic interval," which can occur when unconscious material with a high energy charge temporarily overwhelms the conscious mind.[3] That is, Jung understood that his method of active imagination could bring about a short-term psychotic reaction similar to a psychedelic-induced psychotic state. Although differences between the two conditions (such as the way a psychedelic intensifies the reaction) should not be dismissed, their similarity indicates again the relevance of Jung's psychology to psychedelic experience.

Jung's approach to psychosis in general sheds light on the relationship of psychotic states to trauma, to overwhelming confrontations with the shadow, and ultimately to transformation. Jung's approach to psychosis also helps us understand the strange and deeply disturbing psychological experiences of healthy people. He reminds us that so-called normal people often seek help for peculiar, unaccountable experiences, and that these people occasionally suffer pathological symptoms.[4] Due to our overrational character and our alienation from the primeval psychic energy of "the original mind," Jung warns, we are at the mercy of "the psychic 'underworld.'"[5] Our alienated condition is manifested in symbolic messages from the unconscious that express themselves in a strange and incomprehensible language, which cries out for interpretation.[6] The terrors of the psychotic, in other words, are an extreme form of our common condition. As Jung puts it, "in insanity we do not discover anything new and unknown; we are looking at the foundations of our own being, the matrix of those vital problems on which we are all engaged."[7]

We have seen that a person can react psychotically to a trauma, to a confrontation with the shadow, to an invasion of ego-consciousness by autonomous unconscious complexes, or to the numinous power of the Self archetype. To better understand these psychotic reactions, we will now look more closely at Jung's explanation of psychosis.

In the broadest terms, Jung viewed psychosis as both a psychopathology and a revealing manifestation of the psyche's attempt to heal itself. As he developed his idea of the collective unconscious, Jung understood that psychosis involved an invasion of ego-consciousness by contents from the collective unconscious. Although he never refrained from viewing psychosis as a mental disorder, he had the revolutionary insight that meaning could be deciphered from apparently senseless psychotic utterances. Jung was also the first to appreciate that the same content invading consciousness during a psychosis can potentially regenerate the personality.[8] If patients can be helped to understand the metaphorical nature of this strange and disturbing content, they can recover.[9]

Later chapters will demonstrate the regenerative effects of symbolic content emerging from the unconscious during psychedelic-enhanced therapy. These cases involve images that initially caused patients terrifying confusion. Images of being eaten alive by alligators or needing to gather five heavy stones from the bottom of the sea could easily have been interpreted as only senseless psychotic utterances had the attending therapist not appreciated the metaphorical nature of these unconscious manifestations and their healing potential. When, for instance, Margot Cutner recognized the archetypal symbolism in a patient's perception of being buried alive in a pit, and could encourage her to stop fighting against that image, the woman started to gradually overcome her psychotic tendencies.[10]

I started to overcome my own delusional vision (that I had to kill myself to get to Heaven) only after I could appreciate the vision metaphorically, as a symbol for the necessity of psychospiritual death and rebirth. The image of the bridge in this vision also became a pivotal symbol. Over the many years that I have experienced spontaneous recurrences of my LSD-induced trauma, my initial, momentary reaction has almost always been a terrifying sense that I must return to the bridge, where it all started, to die. Taken metaphorically, the bridge has become for me a symbol of finding a connection between this world and the beyond, of uniting opposites, of becoming psychologically whole. Edward Edinger suggests this possibility when he speaks of communication between the conscious personality and the unconscious. Archetypal forces, he says, "bring images of themselves as gifts to the ego, symbols that remind the individual of his suprapersonal connections."[11] In this light, the pull I have felt so many times over the years to return to the bridge reflects an enduring need to reconnect to the depths of my unconscious, to my spiritual depths.

Jung's Focus on Schizophrenic Forms of Psychosis

Jung focused on the schizophrenic forms of psychosis, which he describes as "all those hallucinatory, catatonic, hebephrenic, and paranoid conditions, not showing the characteristic organic process of cellular destruction," and which he distinguished from manic-depressive forms of psychosis.[12] In his earliest writings, Jung refers to schizophrenia as *dementia praecox* (premature dementia). He later adopted the term *schizophrenia*, which means "split mind." The condition was given that name by Eugen Bleuler, who was Jung's chief physician at Burghölzli Mental Hospital in Zurich as well as his teacher and dissertation advisor.[13]

The schizophrenic forms of psychosis are, Jung explains, "the real mental diseases; that is, they supply the main population of our mental hospitals."[14] In 1907, with the publication of *The Psychology of Dementia Praecox*, Jung adopted the revolutionary position that schizophrenia was primarily a *psychological* disease and not, as was widely believed at the time, a disease having physiological origins.[15] The clinical term for the psychological origin of a condition is *psychogenesis*. Thus Jung's oft-repeated phrase "the psychogenesis of schizophrenia" and the title of volume 3 in his collected works, *The Psychogenesis of Mental Disease*. Following Bleuler, Jung initially suspected that a metabolic toxin caused schizophrenia. He eventually rejected this theory, however, in favor of the view that psychological causes were primary, even though they had psychosomatic effects. In a later essay, "Schizophrenia," Jung wrote:

> Whereas at that time [50 years earlier], for lack of psychological experience, I had to leave it an open question whether the [origin of schizophrenia] is primarily or secondarily toxic, I have now, after long

practical experience, come to hold the view that the *psychogenic causation of the disease is more probable than the toxic causation*. There are a number of mild and ephemeral [short-term] but manifestly schizophrenic illnesses—which begin purely psychogenically, run an equally psychological course (aside from presumably toxic nuances) and can be completely cured by a purely psychotherapeutic procedure. I have seen this even in severe cases.[16]

As I have suggested, Jung steadfastly maintained that psychotic delusions and hallucinations are meaningful psychic productions, not random nonsense. For Jung, then, schizophrenia has as much of a "psychology" as normal mental life, with one notable difference: whereas the ego is *the* subject of the healthy person's experience, the ego is only *one* of a number of experiencing subjects for the schizophrenic. In schizophrenia, Jung explains, "the normal subject has split into a plurality of subjects, or into a plurality of *autonomous complexes*."[17] The ego, that is, can become overwhelmed by the emotional tone of a complex, which accounts for the disease's destructive nature. Such a profound and dangerous split in the psyche is brought on by what Jung describes as an extraordinary "psychological moment."[18]

In his essay "Schizophrenia," Jung describes a mescaline-induced *abaissement* to illustrate the pathological potential of ordinary complexes. As we have seen, for Jung, a complex is a collection of unconscious images with a common emotional tone and an archetypal core. This archetypal core, with its archaic, chaotic affect and mythical imagery, is rooted in the numinous, collective unconscious, which is potentially awe-inspiring and terrifying. And there lies the complex's potential to produce the devastating psychic reactions that precipitate schizophrenia. In the relatively healthy person, such archetypal affect and imagery has a much better chance of being integrated. "In contrast to this," Jung says, "the schizophrenic compensation almost always remains stuck fast in collective and archaic forms, thereby cutting itself off from understanding and integration to a far higher degree."[19] Although such archaic material appears much more often in the mind of the schizophrenic, Jung notes that in so-called normal people these numinous "dream-products" can appear in situations that threaten the very foundations of a person's existence, a parallel between so-called normal people and schizophrenics that I will return to shortly.[20]

Given the impressive similarities between psychedelic-induced psychotic states and schizophrenia, Jung's focus on schizophrenic forms of psychosis suggests that his approach to psychosis provides a useful foundation for understanding psychedelic-induced psychotic states. Jung's emphasis on the psychological origin and treatment of schizophrenia also provides a useful foundation for applying his methods to treating adverse reactions to psychedelic experience.

Commonalities between Schizophrenia and Other Conditions

The interest researchers have shown in the similarities between schizophrenia and psychedelic experience is reminiscent of Jung's radical insight into the similarities between schizophrenia and a wide range of other psychological conditions, from dream states and neuroses to occult phenomena and "those vital problems on which we are all engaged."[21] In his late essay on schizophrenia, for instance, Jung compares schizophrenia and the psychological fragmentation he observed in a young spiritualist, in whom

> contents from the unconscious appeared that were unknown to her conscious mind, and formed the manifest cause of the splitting of personality. In schizophrenia, too, we very often find strange contents that inundate consciousness with comparative suddenness and burst asunder the inner cohesion of the personality, though they do this in a way characteristic of schizophrenia. Whereas the neurotic dissociation never loses its systematic character, schizophrenia shows a picture of unsystematic randomness, so to speak, in which the continuity of meaning so distinctive of the neurosis is often mutilated to the point of unintelligibility.[22]

In dreams, too, Jung observes a schizophrenic-like breakdown of content into "random, absurd, fragmentary" material that requires the same methods of analysis to be understood as does schizophrenia.[23] Although there exists the significant difference that dreams occur in the sleeping state, when elementary operations of consciousness are mostly obscured, Jung became increasingly convinced that "there was a far-reaching analogy between schizophrenia and dreams."[24]

In his description of schizophrenia, Jung mentions the similarities and differences between schizophrenia and the effects of mescaline and related drugs. The empirical evidence available at the time indicated that schizophrenia and the disturbance of consciousness brought on by these drugs were not identical.[25] But Jung recognized that these drugs, like schizophrenia, act by lowering the threshold of consciousness, which potentially leads to consciousness becoming overwhelmed by unconscious material.[26]

Another basis for comparing schizophrenia and other psychological conditions, such as dreams and psychedelic states, lies in the phenomenology of the complex. Jung describes complexes as fragmentary personalities or splinter psyches that can manifest as the actors in dreams or the voices in hallucinations. In all cases, Jung says, complexes appear in personified form when consciousness doesn't suppress them, "exactly like the hobgoblins of folklore who go crashing round the house at night."[27] Jung notes that the origin of complexes is often a trauma that causes a dissociative split in the psyche. In their more pathological manifestations, Jung adds, complexes are objects of inner experience that "are not to be met in the street and in public places. It is on them that the weal and woe of personal life depends; they are the *lares* and *penates* who await us at the fireside and whose peaceableness it is dangerous to extol.... Only when you have seen whole families destroyed by them, morally and physically, and the unexampled tragedy and hopeless misery that follow in their train, do you feel the full impact of the reality of complexes."[28]

We see Jung coming back again to the fundamental insight that unusual, altered, and even pathological states of consciousness—whether manifested as dream images, spiritual visions, psychedelic-induced images, or psychotic delusions—can be understood as consciousness becoming overwhelmed by unconscious content. As bizarre as such manifestations may seem, Jung maintains that they all reflect unconscious patterns, structures, and dynamics that have meaning when understood in the context of a person's life. Even today, with new and valuable perspectives on psychosis, Jung's approach to the apparently random and absurd manifestations associated with nonordinary states of consciousness seems refreshingly insightful.

Neurosis, Latent Psychosis, and Manifest Psychosis

When Jung finished his work at Burghölzli Mental Hospital and started his private psychotherapy practice in 1909, he was surprised to discover that a relatively high number of his patients were latent, or potential, schizophrenics. Latent schizophrenics have schizoid dispositions but their psychosis hasn't yet overwhelmed their conscious capacity. He suspected that these patients were unconsciously avoiding the asylum by seeking psychological consultation. Jung estimated that he had seen as many as ten latent schizophrenics for every manifest case. It wasn't unusual, he says, for a neurotic to turn out to be a latent psychotic in treatment. And sometimes during treatment, such patients were known to fall into a psychosis.[29]

With respect to treatment, Jung explains, latent schizophrenics and manifest schizophrenics have essentially the same complexes and therapeutic needs as neurotics.[30] In all cases, conscious operations are disrupted by the spontaneous intervention of an unconscious complex (with different degrees of severity, of course); and the resulting dissociation can create one or more secondary personalities. The fundamental difference between these cases lies in the maintenance of the primary personality's unity.

Neurotics have a more unified and coherent personality foundation whereas potential schizophrenics have a much higher risk of this foundation giving way to a disintegration in which their thought processes become incoherent and their relationship to their surroundings breaks down.[31] The latent schizophrenic feels threatened by chaotic psychological events and terrifying dreams of catastrophic destruction, says Jung. "He stands on treacherous ground, and very often he knows it."[32] The treacherous ground the latent schizophrenic stands on is a potentially overwhelming complex or set of complexes characterized by archaic and chaotic affect and mythical imagery that can bring about a severe dissociation within the psyche.[33] Jung's description of the latent schizophrenic's vulnerability to overwhelming unconscious content clearly supports the suggestion that people with significant mental health problems should not use psychedelic substances without the full support of experienced and knowledgeable mental health professionals.

The neurosis, explains Jung, is "a relative dissociation, a conflict between ego and a resistant force based upon unconscious contents."[34] In other words, despite some degree of dissociation found in a neurotic person, the conflict between his ego and the intruding unconscious images reflects a relatively successful attempt by the psyche to unify the personality's split condition. The split-off figures that emerge from the schizophrenic's dissociation, on the other hand, take on highly exaggerated or grotesque identities that violently oppose consciousness. As Jung explains it,

> they torment the ego in a hundred ways; all are objectionable and shocking, either in their noisy and impertinent behaviour or in their grotesque cruelty and obscenity. There is an apparent chaos of incoherent visions, voices, and characters, all of an overwhelmingly strange and incomprehensible nature. If there is a drama at all, it is certainly far beyond the patient's understanding. In most cases it transcends even the physician's comprehension, so much so that he is inclined to suspect the mental sanity of anybody who sees more than plain madness in the ravings of a lunatic.[35]

As this quote illustrates, Jung frequently qualifies descriptions of chaotic and incomprehensible unconscious content as *apparently* chaotic and incomprehensible. This qualification reflects his view that although this content is chaotic and incomprehensible for the subject in real and painful ways, it is potentially meaningful to the therapist, and perhaps also eventually to the patient. It is to Jung's enduring credit that he recognized that there was nothing abnormal about the *content* of the psychosis, the images of which justifiably can be compared to the content of dreams. (Jung observed no difference between the dreams reported by people suffering from schizophrenia and the dreams of other people.) Only when unconscious content overwhelms consciousness, and becomes a person's reality, can we speak of actual psychosis. But again, even in an actual psychosis, the content is ultimately meaningful when analyzed with care.[36]

The overwhelmingly strange and incomprehensible visions, voices, and characters associated with an invasive unconscious complex can pull the ego into its orbit, says Jung. If the ego identifies with this strange content, it has relinquished its power to resist the onslaught of unconscious forces and its depotentiation has reached a fatal level. The case of Jung's psychotic incest victim, who found herself living on the moon with a tyrannical vampire, is a good example: her conscious personality fatally identified with the visions and characters that arose from her unconscious after her traumatic abuse. "Neurosis lies on this side of the critical point, schizophrenia on the other," Jung says.[37] We should take Jung's description of a clear-cut point between neurosis and schizophrenia as a simplified representation of a psychological continuum. It is the *relative intensity* of the complex and its affect that distinguishes the neurotic from the latent schizophrenic, the latent schizophrenic from the full-blown schizophrenic, and the so-called normal person from the others. "In normal people and in neurotics," Jung observes, "the affect that binds the complex together produces symptoms which could easily be interpreted as milder, preliminary forms of schizophrenic symptoms."[38]

Just as we came to see the wisdom of not separating the personal and the collective unconscious, we need to understand that sharp distinctions between neurosis, latent psychosis, and manifest psychosis don't reflect the psyche's actual complexity. The similarities Jung sees in these conditions suggest an important principle for understanding psychedelic-induced psychotic states. These similarities suggest, that is, that we can better understand the nature of psychedelic-induced psychotic states when we see what they share with a wide range of other conditions, not simply schizophrenia.

Reduced Consciousness and Psychedelic-Induced Psychotic States

The previous discussion about the relative intensity of a complex, and by implication its potential impact on consciousness, brings us back to the *abaissement du niveau mental* in Jung's explanation of psychosis and psychedelic experience. Although an *abaissement* causes a decrease in the ego's capacity to function, the ultimate impact of an *abaissement,* and whether it will precipitate a psychotic reaction, depends on the stability of the individual's personality and her awareness of what is happening. Jung indicates that the personality's unity is more likely preserved in relatively healthy people, whereas those with a less stable ego are more likely to succumb to overwhelming unconscious eruptions. Such eruptions can seriously damage the personality's unity in people suffering schizophrenia, or even latent schizophrenia. In such cases, Jung says, "the cleavage between dissociated psychic elements amounts to a real destruction of their former connections."[39]

Jung's distinction between the capacity that different people have to withstand and integrate potentially dissociative invasions of unconscious content helps explain why some people react psychotically to a psychedelic experience and other people do not. Yet we have to keep in mind that set and setting always contribute to the effects of a psychedelic experience and can determine whether a difficult psychedelic experience will trigger a psychotic reaction. For a latent schizophrenic, the setting of the session and the interpersonal support the person receives would be especially important. These other factors will influence the intensity of the *abaissement* in the first place. For example, a person's threshold of consciousness will be lowered to a greater extent if he is forced to struggle with the extra confusion of an insecure environment.

To appreciate the relevance of Jung's idea of an *abaissement du niveau mental* to psychedelic-induced psychotic states, consider again the general conditions that can bring about an extreme *abaissement* in psychologically healthy people. These are conditions, explains Jung, "that somehow threaten the very foundations of the individual's existence, for instance in moments of mortal danger . . . or when psychic problems are developing which might give his life a catastrophic turn, or in the critical periods of life when a modification of his previous psychic attitude forces itself peremptorily upon him, or before, during, and after radical changes in his immediate or his general surroundings."[40] Jung's description of the conditions that can lead to an extreme *abaissement* in psychologically healthy people is an excellent characterization of a person's subjective perception of an especially challenging psychedelic experience. That is, people undergoing an especially challenging psychedelic experience fear that they are in mortal danger that threatens the very foundation of their existence, feel that their life has taken a catastrophic turn, or sense that previous attitudes are being threatened or obliterated. Recalling Grinspoon and Bakalar's definition of a psychedelic substance as one that "produces thought, mood, and perceptual changes otherwise rarely experienced except in dreams, contemplative and religious exaltation . . . , and acute psychoses," we can say that by definition psychedelics bring radical changes in the subjective experience of one's immediate and general surroundings.[41] This is, of course, especially true of an overwhelming psychedelic experience.

Recalling that the archaic and numinous "dream-products" associated with schizophrenia can appear in relatively healthy people when they are subjected to conditions that threaten the very foundations of their existence, and recalling that profound splits in the psyche are brought on by what Jung characterizes as an extraordinary "psychological moment," consider the following accounts of psychedelic-induced psychotic states.[42] These are all reports by or about relatively healthy people.

Accounts of Psychedelic-Induced Psychotic States

Author and journalist Arthur Koestler was prepared for his first experimental psychedelic session by a quiet and gentle psychiatrist associated with the University of Michigan. Koestler understood that one's mindset plays a significant role in the experience. But despite his entering the session in an anxious and depressed state following an unpleasant encounter the day before, he volunteered for the experiment because he liked the doctor and the pleasant atmosphere of Ann Arbor, Michigan. Koestler was also encouraged by the doctor's cautious explanation that, based on his limited experience, the effects of psilocybin, in comparison with LSD and mescaline, were "relatively harmless and entirely on the pleasant, euphoric side."[43]

As Koestler lay on a couch with his eyes closed, his experience began with "luminous, moving patterns of great beauty, which was highly enjoyable." Directing the strong beam of light from a table lamp straight at his closed eyes, he experienced an effect that "was quite spectacular—rather like the explosive paintings of schizophrenics, or Walt Disney's *Fantasia*." When he found he could "walk out of the show" at any time by merely opening his eyes, Koestler congratulated himself on his "sober self-control, a rational mind not to be fooled by little pills."[44]

But as he sensed the tape recorder in the room becoming obtrusively loud, and as a previously imperceptible reflection from its reel became the revolving beam of a miniature lighthouse that seemed to be sending secret signals, Koestler experienced "the first symptom of a chemically-induced state of insanity."

> The full effect came on with insidious smoothness and suddenness. Dr. P. came into the room, and a minute or two later I saw the light and realized what a fool I had been to let myself be trapped by his cunning machinations. For during that minute or two he had undergone an unbelievable transformation.
>
> It started with the colour of his face, which had become a sickly yellow. He stood in a corner of the room with his back to the green

wall, and as I stared at him his face split into two, like a cell dividing, then reunited again, but by this time the transformation was complete. A small scar on the doctor's neck, which I had not noticed before, was gaping wide, trying to ingest the flesh of the chin; . . . the face became a smirking, evil phantasm. Then it changed again, into a different kind of Hogarthian vision.

Koestler noticed similar bizarre changes when others entered the room: "One of them, the jovial Dr. F., was transformed into a vision so terrifying—a Mongol with a broken neck hanging from an invisible gallows—that I thought I was going to be sick; yet I could not stop myself staring at him. In the end I said: For God's sake let's snap out of it, and we moved into another part of the room, where the effect became weaker."[45] Even though he retained the ability to move about at will for the duration of the session, Koestler reports that he had lost complete control over his perceptions: "I was powerless against the delusions. I kept repeating to myself: But these are nice, friendly people, they are your friends, and so on. It had no effect whatsoever on the spontaneous and inexorable visual transformations."[46]

Koestler's reflections on his "chemically-induced, temporary psychosis" touch on the relation of psychedelic-induced psychotic states to past trauma:

> I had met the mushroom in the wrong state of mind, owing to that incident on the previous day, which had awakened memories of past experiences as a political prisoner, and of past preoccupations with brainwashing, torture, and the extraction of confessions. The phantom faces were obvious projections of a deep-seated resentment against being 'trapped' in a situation which carried symbolic echoes of the relation between prisoner and inquisitor, of Gestapo and GPU.
>
> Poor Dr. P. and his nice colleagues had to endure what they would call a "negative transference," and serve as projection screens for the lantern slides of a past, stored in the mental underground. Thus I was a rather unfortunate choice for a guinea pig—except perhaps to demonstrate what mushroomland can do to the wrong kind of guinea pig; and I suspect that a sizable minority of people who try for a chemical lift to Heaven, will find themselves landed in the other place.[47]

* * * *

Walter Houston Clark, dean and professor of psychology at the Hartford School of Religious Education, co-founder of the Society for the Scientific Study of Religion, and author of *The Psychology of Religion*, participated in a group psychedelic session under the supervision of Salvador Roquet. Dr. Roquet had developed an especially extreme form of psychedelic therapy, "psychosynthesis" (not to be confused with Roberto Assagioli's non-drug psychosynthesis), which drew from Roquet's psychoanalytic training and his knowledge of indigenous healing practices in Mexico. Using a variety of psychedelic substances (including dissociative drugs) and media (including horrific images of human brutality) in marathon group sessions, Roquet intentionally forced participants into traumatic psychedelic experiences and temporary psychotic states to have them confront their fear of death and achieve psychospiritual rebirth.[48]

Clark's group session began after a brief period of exercise to pleasant music. The room was darkened and images from multiple projectors appeared on the walls. "They included every aspect of life from pictures of nature and handsome men and women, sometimes nude, to every imaginable ugliness, with an emphasis on violence and death," writes Clark.[49] Following administration of the drugs, a film with death as its subject was shown as the tempo of the projected pictures was stepped up. Clark, who was in his early sixties and was given "a low to moderate dose of LSD," writes:

> The music, at first soft and harmonious classical works, was raised in volume until it became a cacophony accompanied by blinking strobe lights to magnify the confusion and sensory overload. At that time a paranoia that I had never before experienced grew upon me. The expressions on the faces of Dr. Roquet and his assistants became demonic. I conceived the idea that they had been specially appointed by the Inquisition to drive me out of my mind—incidentally their precise purpose for the aim of the therapy was to fragment the defenses of the patients through a temporary psychosis. I strode to confront the therapeutic team and denounced them in no uncertain language—hardly my usual style. Another patient pounded his fists on the table with force so violent that he was in danger of destroying the expensive electronic equipment set on it. The other patients expressed their agitation by similar demonstrations, some weeping, others gesticulating, some embracing others, one or two vomiting; a few were quiet throughout. A visitor spirited in from the outside world would have concluded that it was the disturbed ward of a mental hospital.[50]

After describing another period of soothing music and rest, following which the participants were encouraged to exercise or dance as they liked, Clark reports:

> I began vaguely to feel that I had learned something, yet the whole affair seemed a kind of descent into Hell. The therapeutic team had not yet completely lost its demonic quality when a patient next to me

vomited over himself and the floor. As I was considering what I should do to help, the doctor's wife and a clinical psychologist armed themselves with vomit bags and towels and proceeded to the scene. To my amazement, tears were running down their faces. Instantly I concluded that those I had mistaken for demons were really angels. All the time I had been in Heaven rather than Hell.[51]

* * * *

Between 1990 and 1995, Dr. Rick Strassman conducted clinical research at the University of New Mexico on the effects of DMT, an especially powerful psychedelic that induces very sudden effects. Strassman limited his study to psychologically stable volunteers with previous psychedelic experience. Nevertheless, 25 out of 60 volunteers had adverse reactions ranging from minor to terrifying and dangerous. The majority of these reactions were extremely brief. Strassman also notes that although great care was taken to provide a psychologically warm and supportive environment, the research setting (questionnaire administration, blood drawing, and experimental manipulations) couldn't help but predispose his volunteers to negative responses. This conclusion assumes that DMT itself does not predispose subjects to such responses.[52]

Strassman describes the powerfully upsetting experience of Ken, a 23-year-old student at an alternative health college. Strassman reports that 14 minutes into the DMT session Ken looked shaken. Ken later reported: "There were two crocodiles. On my chest. Crushing me, raping me anally. I didn't know if I would survive. At first I thought I was dreaming, having a nightmare. Then I realized it was really happening. . . . It was awful. It's the most scared I've ever been in my life. I wanted to ask to hold your hands, but I was pinned so firmly I couldn't move, and I couldn't speak. Jesus!"[53]

* * * *

In an essay titled "On Being Mad," Humphry Osmond describes a session undertaken in more beneficial circumstances by a 34-year-old psychiatrist in good health. I quote the psychiatrist's own report at some length because it is an especially good example of a psychedelic-induced psychotic state experienced by an apparently stable person. The psychiatrist reports that about forty minutes after taking 400 milligrams of mescaline

> a sense of special significance began to invest everything in the room; objects which I would normally accept as just being there began to

assume some strange importance. . . . In the many thousand stitches of a well-worn carpet, I saw the footprints of mankind plodding wearily down the ages. Barbed wire on a fence outside was sharp and bitter, a crown of thorns, man's eternal cruelty to man. It hurt me.

. . . . I ran my fingers over my old corduroy slacks and, as I did so, the most vivid memories began to well up in my mind of dangerous times in the past when I had worn them. Memories of the London blitz, of seagoing during the war. . . . Gradually I began to feel that I was not merely recalling, but re-experiencing the past. The room had peeling white wallpaper, and behind this was a patch of green, a milky jade green. I was much interested in this patch of green until I realized that I was looking at the winter sea, and that if I stayed there any longer, I would see a ship sinking in a storm, and that once again our ship would plow through those unhappy survivors in pursuit of a submarine. . . .

John, sitting in the chair opposite, became the focus of my attention, and as I gazed at him he began to change. I might have been looking at an impressionist portrait of him and, as I thought of this, he leered at me in an unpleasant way. The lighting changed, the whole room was darker and more threatening and seemed to become larger, the perspectives changing. . . .

Edward came with the recording machine, and by the time they had set it up I was in the full flood of the psychosis. I hadn't met Edward before, and when he brought the machine to me, the unfamiliarity made me afraid. He urged me not to be afraid of it, but as he brought it closer it began to glow, a dull purple which turned to a deep cherry red, and the heat of it overwhelmed me as when a furnace door is opened in your face. . . .

I also noticed that my hands tingled and had a curious dirty feeling which seemed to be inside my skin. I scrutinized one hand and it appeared shrunken and claw like. I realized that beneath the dried leathery skin was bone and dust alone—no flesh. . . .

I asked for some water. I drank the glass which John brought, and found that it tasted strange. I wondered if there might be something wrong with it: poison crossed my mind. . . . I looked into the glass of water. In its swirling depths was a vortex which went down into the center of the world and the heart of time. My companions dragged me away from the water for a walk. . . .

One house took my attention. It had a sinister quality, since from behind its drawn shades, people seemed to be looking out, and their gaze was unfriendly. . . . Then we came to a window in which a child was standing, and as we drew nearer, its face became pig like. I noticed two passers-by who, as they drew nearer, seemed humpbacked and twisted, and their faces were covered with wens [cysts]. The wide spaces of the streets were dangerous, the houses threatening, and the sun burned me.[54]

These are only several of the many accounts of psychedelic-induced psychotic states I could include here. I will close this section with Osmond's conclusion to his essay "On Being Mad." "We should listen seriously to mad people," he writes, "They tell us of a purgatory from which none returns unscathed. They tell us of another world than this; but mostly we don't hear, because we are talking at them to assure them that they are mistaken. Sometimes, when they might make their escape, we do not heed, or even unwittingly drive them back into hell. The least we can do for these far voyagers is to hear them courteously and try to do them no harm."[55]

CHAPTER 9

Psychedelic Experience and Transformation

In the fields of transpersonal psychology and psychedelic studies, transformation is generally considered to be change, development, or healing of a psychological or spiritual nature. Parsing *transform* into *trans* as "beyond" or "change" and *form* as "structure" or "essence," I generally think of transformation as a fundamental change in one's personality. Many in these fields suggest that psychological and spiritual development are integrally related aspects of psychedelic and therapeutic experience.[1] Although my discussion of transformation will at times emphasize *psychological* development and will at other times emphasize *spiritual* development, I don't make hard and fast distinctions between the two. I therefore often use the term *psychospiritual* transformation because I view the changes I discuss as psychological or spiritual, or as some indefinable blend of both. In this regard, I find Jung's psychology, with its phenomenological description of subjective religious experience, an insightful and useful guide to the psychospiritual characteristics of psychedelic experience.

In *Shadow, Self, Spirit: Essays in Transpersonal Psychology*, Michael Daniels notes Jung's repeated refusal to draw metaphysical conclusions from psychological experience. Daniels concludes, correctly I think, that transpersonal psychologists should "bracket as far as possible ALL metaphysical assumptions in what should essentially become a phenomenological examination of experiences of transformation."[2] Nevertheless, as Jungian scholar Sean Kelly points out, it should not be forgotten that Jung came to the conclusion that there is much more to the psyche than can be conveyed through psychological explanation.[3] Jung demonstrates this attitude in his conclusion to "A Psychological Approach to the Dogma of the Trinity." "These considerations have made me extremely cautious in my approach to the further metaphysical significance that may possibly underlie archetypal statements. There is nothing to stop their ultimate ramifications from penetrating to the very ground of the universe. We alone are the dumb ones if we fail to notice it. Such being the case, I cannot pretend to myself that the object of archetypal statements has been explained and disposed of merely by our investigation of its psychological aspects."[4]

The idea of transformation runs all through Jung's work. Quite generally, for Jung, transformation is psychological development involving temporary ego regression as one becomes increasingly conscious of unconscious material and thereby moves toward psychological wholeness.[5] Although Jung took pains to discuss spirituality in psychological terms, and although he takes a consistent agnostic stance towards extrapsychic realities, his idea of transformation is inherently related to what he conceived as the psyche's "religious function."[6]

In the original version of *Psychology and Religion*, Jung characterizes religion as "the attitude peculiar to a consciousness which has been altered by the experience of the numinosum."[7] Having adopted the idea of the *numinosum* from Rudolf Otto, Jung describes it as "a dynamic agency or effect not caused by an arbitrary act of will. On the contrary, it seizes and controls the human subject, who is always rather its victim than its creator. . . . The *numinosum* is either a quality belonging to a visible object or the influence of an invisible presence that causes a peculiar alteration of consciousness."[8]

For Jung, it is an elementary truth that "the God-image corresponds to a definite complex of psychological facts, and is thus a quantity which we can operate with; but what God is in himself remains a question outside the competence of all psychology."[9] Even though Jung is adamant about the fundamental role the psyche plays in religious experience, his agnosticism regarding supernatural realities by definition neither denies nor affirms them.

The Transformative Potential of Psychedelic Experiences

Before turning to my Jungian analysis of psychedelic-related transformation in the next chapter, it will once again be helpful to place Jung's approach to transformation in the context of transpersonal psychology and modern psychedelic research.

Myron Stolaroff expresses a widespread sentiment in the psychedelic community when he says that "psychedelics, used with good motivation, skill, and integrity, can contribute much toward easing the pain and suffering of the world while giving access to wisdom and compassion for spiritual development."[10] Psychedelic substances have been used for religious purposes from time immemorial, explains David Wulff.[11] In modern times, evidence for the transformative potential of psychedelics has been provided by extensive clinical studies in the 1950s and 1960s.[12]

The transformative potential of psychedelic substances is often discussed in relationship to the "transpersonal state." Stanislav Grof describes the transpersonal state as the feeling that one's "consciousness has been expanded beyond the usual ego boundaries and has transcended the limitations of time and space."[13] I use the terms *transpersonal, religious, spiritual,* and *mystical experience* interchangeably to refer to the direct subjective perception of spirit, the divine, or ultimate reality, transcendent or immanent.[14]

Beyond clinical indications, the transformative potential of psychedelics has been reflected in the personal experiences of countless people who have used LSD, mescaline, psilocybin, ayahuasca, and other psychedelic substances. Many maintain, as Dobkin de Rios and Winkelman state, that psychedelics bring about "changes in the individual's awareness of reality, which leads the individual to a perception of a spiritual, mystical, timeless, transcendent reality and of being at one with the universe."[15] Such experiences, say Grinspoon and Bakalar, have left many with the conviction that they understood the nature of mystical experiences described by religious sages.[16]

The transformative potential of a psychedelic experience is usually discussed in terms of psychological or spiritual insights, changes, growth, or development. Even though psychedelic use often leads to experiences that users perceive as spiritual, the significance of such experiences is open to question.[17] Huston Smith makes a valuable distinction between drug-induced religious experiences and drug-inspired religious lives. In his essay "Do Drugs Have Religious Import?," Smith asserts that psychedelics have the potential to induce religious experiences, but those experiences don't inevitably lead to a religious life.[18] This is why I speak of the transformative *potential* of psychedelic experiences. The insights gained during a psychedelic experience count for little if one doesn't integrate them into the concrete reality of one's daily life. Generally, I think of psychedelic-inspired transformation as being a significant and noticeable long-term change in a person's personality, attitudes, worldview, and way of acting.

Christopher Bache emphasizes collective transformation, suggesting that beyond the potential psychedelics have to effect personal healing, psychedelic-inspired transformation in any one person's consciousness can advance transformation in the consciousness of the human species. As suggested by the title of one of his books, *Dark Night, Early Dawn*, Bache envisions transformation as a "dark night of the soul" process. The dark night, Bache writes, "is an arduous stage of spiritual purification in which the aspirant endures a variety of physical and psychological purifications, eventually undergoing a spiritual death and rebirth."[19] Bache maintains that the conscientious use of psychedelics potentially expands the scope of this dark-night process as well as intensifying it. He believes, that is, that the psychedelic-accelerated and intensified dark-night process a person undergoes accelerates the dark-night process that humanity is undergoing. This relationship between the personal and the collective, Bache points out, is consistent with the environmental principle of interconnectedness underlying the deep-ecology thought of Norwegian philosopher Arne Naess.[20]

It is difficult to define conclusively the transformative potential of psychedelics, which are known to evoke a lingering sense of mystery aptly expressed by Grinspoon and Bakalar: Even though most people in the field of psychedelic research no longer see psychedelics as the key to changing the world, many retain a strong sense of possibilities not yet realized, "of something felt as intensely real and not yet explained or explained away."[21]

The Transformative Potential of Psychotic States

The topic of psychosis and transformation is usually discussed in terms of the relationship between psychosis and mystical, spiritual, or religious experience.[22] For example, David Lukoff, who coauthored the *DSM-IV's* transpersonally-inspired category Religious or Spiritual Problem, speaks of mystical experiences and spiritual emergencies with psychotic features.[23] As many have pointed out, mainstream psychiatry tends to ignore or pathologize religious and spiritual experiences.[24] Psychiatry's narrow focus on biological factors, and its historical bias against religion in general and against religious experiences in particular, make it difficult for mainstream practitioners to provide sympathetic and insightful treatment to those struggling with religious and spiritual problems. In such an atmosphere, relatively few people are looking at the transformative potential of psychosis.[25]

Stanislav Grof and Christina Grof give an overview of this emerging school of thought in their anthology *Spiritual Emergency: When Personal Transformation Becomes a Crisis*. The authors represented in this collection challenge traditional psychiatry's blanket diagnosis and treatment of all unusual psychological experiences as simply mental illness. Some of these experiences are "crises of personal transformation," they maintain.[26] The Grofs trace the origin of alternative views of psychosis to C. G. Jung, among others (including William James, Roberto Assagioli, and Abraham Maslow); and they appreciate Jung's interest in spirituality, which was a rare exception among depth psychologists of his time.[27] For Jung, psychological transformation is inherently fraught with psychotic potential because the archetypes of the collective unconscious, which one inevitably encounters during the individuation process, are "so strange that their irruption into consciousness often amounts to a psychosis."[28]

But, as we will see, Jung also appreciated the transformative potential of such irruptions. He writes, for instance, that the unconscious psyche contains its own "'myth-forming' structural elements," or archetypes, which lend "a certain hidden coherence" to even irrational and generally unintelligible psychotic fantasies.[29] Margot Cutner's report in the next chapter illustrates well the transformative potential of the archetypal contents of the collective unconscious. In the case she describes, her psychotic patient was struggling with an LSD-induced vision of being trapped at the bottom of a rubbish pit. Cutner recognized this image as a symbolic manifestation of her patient's descent into the archetypal depths of the unconscious. When Cutner was able to encourage her to stop fighting, the woman encountered a series of healing archetypal images. As Cutner reports, the pit turned from a place of humiliation into "an archetypal 'womb'"— images that Cutner was subsequently able to help her patient understand and integrate in a gradual process that eventually allowed the woman to overcome her psychotic tendencies.[30]

Jungian analyst John Weir Perry became a leading advocate in the 1970s for the transformative potential of acute psychotic episodes. He asserted that, with proper attention, even the apparently scattered images expressed by a person suffering acute psychic upheaval may take on coherent form and may reveal a meaningful psychological process.[31] In a number of books, Perry advanced Jung's approach to psychosis and the transformative potential of psychotic states.[32]

More recently, Isabel Clarke has assembled a collection of essays in *Psychosis and Spirituality* that attempts to link spirituality and psychosis, "the *highest* realms of human consciousness and the *depths* of madness."[33] Clarke asserts that in the minds of many of those exploring the frontiers of human consciousness, the customary polarization into two incommensurable states of consciousness, suggested by reference to "heights" and "depths," conceals an essential commonality between spiritual and psychotic experience. The whole idea of two incomparable states of consciousness is contradicted by the ambiguity and relativity of the two words "heights" and "depths," suggests Clarke.[34] As Richard Tarnas puts it, one could easily say "the deepest realms of human consciousness and the heights of madness."[35] Jung's personal confrontation with the unconscious, Sean Kelly notes, shows that "going 'down' is equivalent to going 'in,'" which suggests that for Jung the "heights" are in the "depths."[36]

Less nuanced arguments than Isabel Clarke's meet criticism, however, even among those who generally agree that conventional views of psychosis are regrettably limited. As I have shown, psychiatrist John Nelson carefully compares religious experience and psychosis from a transpersonal perspective in his book, *Healing the Split: Integrating Spirit Into Our*

Understanding of the Mentally Ill. The relationship between the two, he argues, is a complex one. Opposing schools in psychiatry need to take that complexity into account when discussing this issue and, more importantly, when making a diagnosis. The failure to adequately discriminate between benign and pathological psychotic states, Nelson asserts, "bedevils both mainstream psychiatry and alternative schools of thought. Each errs in its own characteristic way by failing to recognize that various psychotic states of consciousness—although apparently similar—differ from each other in important ways."[37]

The Transformative Potential of Psychedelic-Induced Psychotic States

There is a great deal of literature on the relationship between psychedelics and psychosis, on the one hand, and between psychedelics and transformation on the other. But relatively few people have looked at the transformative potential of psychedelic-induced psychotic states.

Although he is open to criticism for romanticizing psychosis, R. D. Laing views psychosis as "a harrowing but revelatory and potentially restorative mental journey with some of the same virtues as an LSD experience."[38] In his paper "Transcendental Experience in Relation to Religion and Psychosis," Laing writes that "madness need not be all break*down*. It is also break*through*. It is potentially liberation and renewal, as well as enslavement and existential death."[39] Laing describes especially well how things can go wrong when entering the otherness of a psychedelic-induced reality:

> Many people enter it—unfortunately without guides, confusing outer with inner realities, and inner with outer—and generally lose their capacity to function competently in ordinary relations.
>
> This need not be so. The process of entering into *the other* world from this world, and returning to *this* world from the other world, is as "natural" as death and childbirth or being born. But in our present world, [which] is so terrified and so unconscious of the other world, it is not surprising that, when "reality," the fabric of this world, bursts, and a person enters the other world, he is completely lost and terrified, and meets only incomprehension in others.[40]

David Lukoff appreciates John Weir Perry's positive view of acute psychosis "as a renewal process in which the psyche is seeking to reorganize itself fundamentally."[41] Lukoff writes of his own "hallucinogen-induced psychotic disorder," which began in 1971 when he was 23 years old.[42] He describes his "shamanistic initiatory crisis" and the long process through which he was able "to integrate [his] psychotic episode as a transformative transpersonal experience."[43] Lukoff went on to develop new and valuable forms of transpersonal psychotherapy for psychotic disorders and spiritual emergencies with psychotic features.[44]

Ralph Metzner and Richard Alpert (also known as Ram Dass), have both dedicated their lives to realizing the transformative potential of the psychedelic experience following their controversial groundbreaking work in the early 1960s with Timothy Leary at Harvard University. Both view psychotic states as a common element in psychedelic experience. As Metzner puts it, the potential for psychedelic substances to "trigger hellish, psychotic-like trips is so well known that they were first referred to as psychotomimetic."[45] He explains, nevertheless, that when a person who is experiencing a psychedelic-triggered psychosis recognizes—and can yield to the recognition—that he or she is involved in a temporary process, a transitional stage that has a definite purpose or "end," the person can come to regard such experiences "as a necessary purgation, accepted—even welcomed—for their transformative power."[46]

Richard Alpert, speaking to therapists at the Menninger Clinic in the early 1970s about an alternative framework for understanding psychosis, and alluding to insights gained from psychedelic experiences, explains that "the journey of consciousness is to go to the place where you see that all [the different realities] are really relative ... [, are] merely perceptual vantage points for looking at it all."[47] The point, he explains, is that "you have to be able to go in and out of all of them, that any one you get stuck in is the wrong one."[48]

The person whose work most thoroughly relates to all three elements—psychedelics, psychosis, and transformation—is transpersonal psychiatrist Stanislav Grof, who is widely considered the world's foremost researcher on psychedelics and psychedelic-enhanced therapy.[49] (Albert Hofmann, who is often called the father of LSD, has referred to Grof as LSD's godfather.) In *Spiritual Emergency: When Personal Transformation Becomes a Crisis*, Grof writes that "clinical research of nonordinary states of consciousness induced by psychedelics ... has many implications for an alternative understanding of psychosis."[50] Grof is a member of the school of thought that "emphasize[s] the positive value in the psychotic process. In this view, many unusual states of consciousness traditionally considered psychotic ... are seen as radical attempts at problem-solving."[51] If properly understood, Grof asserts, the psychotic process can result in personal transformation. From this theoretical perspective, Grof maintains that it is even appropriate to use psychedelics to "intensify and accelerate the [transformation] process and bring it to a positive resolution."[52] Grof also maintains that substantial empirical evidence shows that many people considered psychotic are undergoing "an extraordinary and potentially healing process of self-discovery."[53]

I close this section on the transformative potential of psychedelic-induced psychosis with an especially pertinent, and Jungian-compatible, passage from Grof's *Beyond the Brain: Birth, Death and Transcendence in Psychotherapy*:

> Many aspects of the phenomenology of psychosis seem to have their origins in the transpersonal realms of the human psyche. These domains contribute to schizophrenic symptomatology the interest in ontological and cosmological problems; an abundance of archetypal themes and mythological sequences; encounters with deities and demons of different cultures; ancestral, phylogenetic, and past incarnation memories; elements of the racial and the collective unconscious. . . .
>
> In spite of the revolutionary developments in modern psychology represented by the contributions of Jung, Assagioli, and Maslow, all these experiences are still automatically considered symptomatic of psychosis by traditional psychiatry. In the light of LSD psychotherapy and other powerful experiential approaches, the concept of psychosis will have to be dramatically revised and reevaluated. The matrices for perinatal and transpersonal experiences seem to be normal and natural components of the human psyche, and the experiences themselves have a distinct healing potential if approached with understanding. It is therefore absurd to diagnose psychosis on the basis of the content of the individual's experience. In the future, what is pathological and what is healing may have to emphasize the attitude toward the experience, the style of dealing with it, and the ability to integrate it into everyday life.[54]

CHAPTER 10

A Jungian Approach to the Transformative Potential of Difficult Psychedelic Experiences

Jung on the Healing Potential of Psychotic Experiences

Even though Jung always regarded schizophrenia as a mental disorder, he was the first to recognize it as the psyche's effort to heal itself and as a pathology amenable to psychotherapy. Jung recognized the healing potential of acute psychotic episodes as early as 1914, and traces of this insight can be seen as early as 1911.[1] In his essay "The Importance of the Unconscious in Psychotherapy," Jung describes the compensating function of the unconscious, a balancing of conscious tendencies that plays out in so-called normal and mentally-ill people alike. "In normal people the principal function of the unconscious is to effect a compensation and to produce a balance," he writes.[2] "[Such] manifestations of the unconscious in actually insane patients are just as clear, but are not so well recognized."[3] The borderline between "normal" and "abnormal" people is further blurred by the delusions and hallucinations healthy people experience. These unconscious, corrective manifestations aren't so readily recognized in the psychotic person because they typically present themselves in a form that the conscious mind, in doctor and patient alike, finds unacceptably disturbing. The unfortunate result of such disturbing manifestations is the obstruction of what should be "the beginning of the healing process."[4]

We must recognize, Jung says, that "the symptomatology of an illness is at the same time a natural attempt at healing."[5] If the therapist can engage in an authentic, caring way with the patient and the patient's inner world, says John Weir Perry, she may be able to see a deeply meaningful process in what at first appears to be only a fragmented barrage of strange ideas. With the support of an enlightened and engaged therapist, the patient may be able to make the critical turn from projecting this process onto the external world to recognizing it as an expression of his own unconscious self. If this is possible, Perry concludes, healing can begin.[6]

We can see the genesis of Jung's open-minded approach to psychosis in his early essay "Two Kinds of Thinking," where he writes that "the dream is a series of images which are apparently contradictory and meaningless, but . . . it contains material which yields a clear meaning when properly translated."[7] This view of dreams—and by extension, psychotic visions—is also apparent in Jung's late essay, "Approaching the Unconscious," in which he observes that the psyche's symbol-producing function bridges modern, differentiated consciousness with the primitive psychic energy of the early mind from which the modern psyche has become alienated. It is, Jung says, as if the unconscious seeks through dreams and visions to bring consciousness back to those "old things from which the mind freed itself as it evolved—illusions, fantasies, archaic thought forms, fundamental instincts, and so on."[8] Such relict contents are so highly charged that they frighten us, he explains; but the more they are repressed, the more they haunt the personality. Dreams and psychotic visions bring these primitive images back to consciousness, and this accounts for their healing potential.[9] Jung validates the non-rational, receptive mode of interpreting the symbolic content of the unconscious, says Perry. This form of "nondirected thinking" leads one into the imagery, symbolism, and metaphor of the deep, archaic unconscious with respect for its subjective value.[10]

Reading through Jung's essay "On Psychological Understanding" in *The Psychogenesis of Mental Disease*, one can appreciate the creative intelligence of Jung's "synthetic-constructive" approach to psychosis. For Jung, this method does more justice than the analytical-reductive approach to "the almost overpowering profusion of fantastic symbolization" manifested in schizophrenia.[11] Rather than seeking to understand how and why the psyche has come to its current condition, Jung's synthetic-constructive method seeks to understand how the psyche might be trying to heal. "The constructive standpoint asks how, out of this present psyche, a bridge can be built into its own future,"[12] Jung explains. "The question is: What is the goal the patient tried to reach through the creation of his [delusional] system?"[13] Jung encourages us, that is, to appreciate that, through her delusions, the patient is unconsciously attempting to bring something to completion. Jung distinguishes the content of the patient's delusions from her confusion of that content with external reality; and Jung maintains that such delusions are valid and justifiable within subjective limits. The synthetic-constructive method, Jung suggests, "must follow the clues laid down by the delusional system itself."[14] Working with highly complex material, this approach traces the person's psychological development and builds towards an as yet unknown goal.[15]

Perry points out that Jung's approach to the unconscious laid the way for what would become known as the "growth" or "developmental crisis" model, a model that views the psyche's tumultuous activation of nonrational, unconscious material as a sign of psychological reorganization.[16] In his essay "On Psychic Energy," Jung hypothesized that, seen subjectively, the symbols of the unconscious are agents for transforming the tension between consciousness and the unconscious. This hypothesis led to Jung's idea of the regressive process, in which the psyche adapts to the person's inner world—and thereby yields to the vital demands of the individuation process. We might call this "regression in the service of the Self," says Perry.[17]

In his essay "The Transcendent Function," Jung presents a theoretical foundation for integrating activated unconscious images, which essentially involves bringing them into a constructive relationship to consciousness, a process usually mediated by the analyst for the patient but which one can undertake oneself (as Jung did). By bringing consciousness to unconscious content, by synthesizing the opposites, as Jung would say, the unconscious is allowed to compensate for the one-sided tendencies of consciousness, thereby creating an awareness that embraces, and transcends, both.[18] Perry attributes Jung's brilliance to his openness to the unknown, to his willingness to engage with what he didn't understand, and to his inclination to validate subjective experience. "He let his empathetic participation in the subjective experience of persons and historical eras speak their own meanings to him," Perry says.[19]

The Painful Passage through the Shadow towards Wholeness

Only by coming to terms with the darkness in ourselves can we approach the psychological wholeness of which Jung speaks. The shadow plays a vital role in Jungian psychology, explains Joseph Henderson, not just because it represents the personality's rejected aspects but because the tension between ego and shadow lies at the heart of what Jung characterized as "the battle for deliverance," a person's struggle to overcome unconsciousness.[20] This process is portrayed symbolically as the mythical hero's struggle against evil powers. Hero myths often represent a confrontation with a destructive force that must be faced, just as the ego must encounter and integrate the unconscious shadow for the personality to approach wholeness.[21] "There is, in fact, no access to the unconscious and to our own reality but through the shadow," says Jungian analyst Edward Whitmont. "It is not until we have truly been shocked into seeing ourselves as we really are ... that we can take the first step toward individual reality."[22]

Recalling Donald Kalsched's discussion of the personal spirit's archetypal defenses against trauma, we come now to the transformative potential of those mysteriously ambivalent figures like the Devil, which represent the paradoxical potential of the Self's dark side to heal as well as destroy. We can think of these dark archetypal figures as representing what I call diabolical forces of transformation.

We can better understand the paradoxical nature of the psyche's dark aspects by considering Jung's observation that repressed unconscious tendencies, and the psychic energies associated with them, form the potentially destructive shadow side of our personality. "Even tendencies that might in some circumstances be able to exert a beneficial influence are transformed into demons when they are repressed," Jung explains.[23] It follows that bringing such tendencies to consciousness could transform their destructive nature. Consider, for instance, the value of becoming aware of repressed anger. As we have seen, unconscious complexes represent the unlived, split-off parts of ourselves; and to be heard they create distress, they rebel against the established order.[24] But the internal tension caused by unconscious complexes is essential to psychological development, Lionel Corbett explains. The goal of therapy concerning the shadow, he says, is to become aware of it because a shadow complex's destructive power is reduced by consciousness.[25]

The confrontational dynamics of unconscious complexes are personified mythologically as Satan the rebel, who challenges the established order, and as Lucifer, the bringer of light, says Corbett.[26] Marie-Louise von Franz characterizes the shadow as the "devilish element" in the individuation process because the shadow is comprised of emotions and drives that disrupt the superficial unity of the personality.[27] Similarly, Jungian analyst and scholar Rivkah Schärf Kluger explains that, psychologically, Satan is the disturber of worldly peace and comfort, and thus the foe of unconsciousness. Suffering and misery drive one inward, she adds, "into the 'other world,'" into the world of God.[28] In the book of Job, Edward Edinger notes, Yahweh and Satan can be interpreted as representing two aspects of the Self; and in this light, Satan's provocation can be understood psychologically as the impelling force that leads to insight and development through a crisis involving liberation as well as destruction.[29] "When we recognize the devil as an aspect of ourselves, this deity can function as teacher and initiator," says Ralph Metzner. "He shows us our own unknown face, providing us with the greatest gift of all—self-understanding. The conflict of opposites is resolved into a *coincidentia oppositorum*," Jung's term for "the 'coming together of opposites,' the acceptance and reconciliation of antagonistic aspects of our nature."[30]

For Jungians, the biblical book of Revelation is another symbolic account of a person's confrontation with the archetypal Self, or the psyche in its totality. In Jung's assessment, the book of Revelation arises out of the one-sided consciousness of the author of the Epistles of John, who saw only light and love in God's nature. "Under these circumstances a counterposition is bound to grow up in the unconscious, which can then irrupt into consciousness in the form of a revelation," explains Jung.[31] In *Archetype of the Apocalypse: A Jungian Study of the Book of Revelation,* Edinger discusses how the apocalypse symbolizes the Self's emergence into consciousness, a "shattering of the world as it has been, followed by its reconstitution."[32] Although inherently disruptive, an expanded relationship to the psyche's transpersonal dimension, in the form of the conscious mind's encounter with the Self, is potentially transformative.[33]

The apocalypse archetype represents the individuation process, which is symbolized by the archetype's four characteristic aspects: Revelation, Judgment, Destruction and Punishment, and the New World. As transpersonal images emerge from the unconscious, the person experiences shattering insights that can result in a new relationship to the Self. In the process, however, one can encounter a destructively judgmental awareness of one's shadow. The image of the Last Judgment, suggests Edinger, represents "a decisive encounter with the Self that requires specifically a thorough assimilation of the shadow."[34]

When used responsibly, psychedelics can drive one into the other world, and into a conscious submission to a transpersonal reality. Given the archetypal, numinous core of negative shadow complexes, says Corbett, therapeutic engagement with one's rage, destructiveness, and terror is as much a spiritual practice as attending to the positive aspects of the *numinosum*.[35] The question is, what would such an engagement look like? To start to answer that question, I now consider Jung's approach to healing the profoundly disturbing effects of trauma.

Treating Trauma: Integration Versus Abreaction in Jung's Psychology

In addition to his criticism of using psychedelics to enhance psychotherapy, Jung opposed using abreaction to treat trauma. Abreaction, you may recall, is the discharge of emotion and pent-up physical energy associated with repressed trauma. Abreaction often involves reliving the original trauma and dramatically acting out associated emotions and energies through body movement and vocal expression (through, you could say, thrashing and screaming). In contrast to Jung, Stanislav Grof highly values abreaction as an important component in the psychedelic-enhanced treatment of trauma.

Grof's prominent standing in the psychedelic community suggests that many other psychedelic therapists probably share his view of abreaction.

The widespread appreciation for the abreactive properties of psychedelics is also indicted by Rick Strassman's observation that people who use psychedelics for personal growth often prefer to "blast through" their personal problems.[36] These people, Strassman suggests, are attracted to "the purifying and relieving value of catharsis" and prefer "earth-shattering" emotional experiences over verbal analysis of their conflicts.[37] (Strassman thinks both approaches to working through emotional blocks are necessary.) Given the value that the psychedelic community seems to place on abreaction, it is worth considering why Jung objects to it and why he puts so much emphasis on integration in treating trauma.

As we have seen, Jung proposed that trauma-induced unconscious images, when translated into the language of consciousness, can advance psychological growth and healing. We will now look more closely at Jung's approach to treating trauma to get a clearer idea of what he means when he speaks of translating unconscious content into the language of consciousness.

Jung's Definitions of Trauma and Abreaction

Jung defines trauma as "either a single, definite, violent impact, or a complex of ideas and emotions which may be likened to a psychic wound."[38] And, he adds, "everything that touches this complex, however slightly, excites a vehement reaction, a regular emotional explosion. Hence one could easily represent the trauma as a complex with a high emotional charge."[39] (In the light of Kalsched's work with trauma victims, we can see how a complex or set of complexes arises from a trauma.) Because the complex's emotional charge seems to be the cause of the pathological disturbance, Jung says, it seems logical that we would prescribe a therapy that aims to completely release this charge. He means a therapy that relies on abreaction, which Jung defines as dramatically reenacting the emotions associated with a trauma to completely release the emotional charge at the core of the complex. Such a release is understood to depotentiate the emotions associated with the trauma and thereby dissipate their disturbing influence. Before considering Jung's critique of abreaction and his alternative approach to treating trauma, it will help to look at Grof's view of abreaction.

Grof's View of Abreaction

Because abreaction has been so earnestly questioned within the field of psychiatry, Grof is careful to explain that he values abreaction as one of many elements within a structured and supportive therapeutic program.

He nonetheless puts considerable emphasis on the value of abreaction, which he describes as the discharge of emotions and physical energies associated with an unconscious experience, especially the repressed memories and feelings associated with a trauma.[40] Based on his extensive experience with psychedelic therapy, Grof attributes the reported failures of abreaction to its limited and unsystematic use, or as he says, to it not having been "encouraged or allowed to go to the experiential extremes that usually lead to successful resolution."[41]

Grof also addresses the issue of retraumatization. Because abreaction often involves the extremely painful reliving of a traumatic experience, Grof explains, many people question its therapeutic value. It seems to these people that such intense reliving of a trauma would carry a high risk of retraumatizing the patient. Grof says that the best response to this concern is provided by Ivor Browne, an Irish psychiatrist, who suggests that "we are not dealing here with an exact replay or repetition of the original traumatic situation, but with the first full experience of the appropriate emotional and physical reaction to it. This means that, at the time when they happen, the traumatic events are recorded in the organism, but not fully consciously experienced, processed, and integrated."[42] That is, the person reexperiencing the trauma is no longer the helpless victim she was at the time of the original event. The nonordinary state of consciousness induced by powerful experiential forms of psychotherapy, including psychedelic therapy, allows the person to experience again all the emotions and physical pain of the original trauma while at the same time analyzing and evaluating the experience from the safe distance of the therapeutic environment and "from a mature adult perspective."[43] Grof also stresses the importance of the therapist's or attendant's committed presence during the entire session. "An atmosphere of security, privacy, and full commitment is absolutely necessary for a successful psychedelic session," he adds.[44]

Given Grof's assessment that even the correct use of abreaction does not always lead to a successful resolution, we should at least consider Jung's method as an adjunct or alternative to Grof's. And although both Jung and Grof trust the wisdom of the unconscious to guide the healing process, and even though both warn against imposing theoretical ideas on the process, Grof is more radical than Jung in this regard. Grof maintains that therapies emphasizing verbal exchange to treat serious problems are generally disappointing because they "are unable to reach the deeper roots of the conditions they are attempting to heal."[45] And, he adds, the therapist, not the patient, is usually regarded as "the active agent and the source of knowledge necessary for a successful outcome."[46] In contrast to verbally-oriented psychotherapy, Grof employs nonordinary states of consciousness to activate, intensify, and resolve symptoms. The therapist or guide only supports a spontaneous process that unfolds within the patient.[47] Grof's pessimistic view of verbal therapies stands in sharp contrast, then, to Jung's emphasis on integrating dissociated psychic elements through one-on-one verbal therapy, to which I will return shortly. We shouldn't forget, however, that Jung's therapy also relied on more experientially-oriented techniques such as dream work and active imagination. Still, the emphasis in Jungian therapy is on verbal analysis.

To fully appreciate the value that Grof places on the experiential qualities of abreaction, we need to recognize the crucial somatic component in his approach to healing. "There is," says Grof, "no emotional distress or disturbing and incomplete psychological gestalt that does not show specific somatic manifestations."[48] Effective physical intervention, Grof maintains, can release blocked energy from the body that is associated with trauma, and can thereby release repressed memories and emotions so they can be integrated.[49] Cultural historian Richard Tarnas, who has worked closely with Grof for over three decades, points out that Jung's practice predates knowledge of the somatic element in trauma and that Jung therefore did not appreciate the extent to which the body contains collective and personal memories of trauma at the cellular level that need to be worked through physically.[50]

Jung's Critique of Abreaction

Whereas Grof advocates abreaction as one element in a comprehensive therapeutic program, Jung's criticism of abreaction seems to be aimed at its more or less exclusive use. But Jung's criticism is useful nevertheless because it leads to different implications for psychedelic-enhanced therapy and for treating psychedelic-induced trauma. In "The Therapeutic Value of Abreaction," Jung criticizes the supposition that a disturbing trauma-induced complex can be relieved by the complete release of its emotional charge. He asserts, to the contrary, that "in quite a large number of cases abreaction is not only useless but actually harmful."[51] Responding to the argument that every method has cases that aren't resolved successfully, Jung suggests that by examining those cases that resist treatment, we can discover the method's limitations. While such examination doesn't necessarily disprove the method's effectiveness, he concludes, it can lead to improvements in its use.[52]

The essential factor in trauma, Jung maintains, "is the dissociation of the psyche and not the existence of a highly charged affect. The main therapeutic problem is not abreaction but how to integrate the dissociation [because] a traumatic complex brings about dissociation of the psyche."[53] Given the powerful autonomy of split-off trauma-induced complexes and their tyrannical invasion of the conscious mind, says Jung, abreaction appears to be "an attempt to reintegrate the autonomous complex, to incorporate it gradually into the conscious mind as an accepted content, by living the traumatic situation over again."[54] Jung questions the assumption that reliving the experience is healing, and he suggests that other measures are necessary—especially the intervention of an understanding, sympathetic, and trusted doctor. "No longer does [the patient] stand alone in his battle with these elemental powers. . . . [but rather] the integrative powers of his conscious mind are reinforced."[55] Jung concludes his criticism of abreaction by asserting the primacy of conscious integration: "The rehearsal of the traumatic moment is able to reintegrate the neurotic dissociation only when the conscious personality of the patient is so far reinforced by his relationship to the doctor that he can consciously bring the autonomous complex under the control of his will."[56]

I don't want to misrepresent Grof's methods here. As I have said, Grof's approach to psychedelic therapy incorporates other elements besides abreaction. These include the person's conscious perspective during the session, a supportive therapeutic environment, and post-session integration of the experience. Still, Jung's critique of abreaction, with his careful analysis of the dissociative nature of trauma-induced complexes and his systematic emphasis on the person's conscious integration, provides a valuable perspective on psychedelic-enhanced therapy and treating psychedelic-induced trauma. To appreciate the value of Jung's psychology for psychedelic treatment, we need only consider the ubiquitous references in the psychedelic literature to the importance of integrating psychedelic experiences, on the one hand, and the striking lack of discussion of what is meant by integrating psychedelic experiences, on the other.

Jung concludes his essay on abreaction by assessing the transference in the psychotherapeutic relationship.[57] In contrast to Freud's focus on transference and the personal origins of the patient's neurosis, Jung emphasizes (as does Grof) that the creative nature of the patient's emerging unconscious images helps her move out of the disorder. The patient must also have the opportunity to form a relationship to the therapist as an equal. Any process involving a patient's fear and resistance, Jung maintains, demands that the therapist as well as the patient be engaged in her own movement toward wholeness.[58] As opposed to "the slavish and humanly degrading bondage of the transference" asserts Jung, a relationship between equals fosters in patients the discovery of their own unique personalities, their own worth, and their ability to adapt themselves to the demands of life.[59]

The building of such a relationship, concludes Jung, demands much more of the therapist than the "mere application of routine technique."[60]

Drawing from Both Grof and Jung

Even though I am highlighting the differences between Jung's and Grof's approaches to treating trauma, it is not my intention to set one against the other. I am convinced that both approaches help us understand psychedelic experiences and the treatment of trauma. A knowledge of Grof's work would help Jungian analysts understand adverse reactions to psychedelic experiences. Jungian methods for integrating unconscious images and emotions would complement a Grofian approach to psychedelic-enhanced therapy. In cases where Grof's more experientially aggressive approach to treating trauma seems inappropriate or proves unproductive, Jung's integrative methods could provide a valuable alternative.

In justifying his own method of psychotherapy, Jung suggests the balance I am looking for when he explains that his particular approach to psychotherapy "is certainly not meant to condemn the existing methods as incorrect, superfluous, or obsolete. The more deeply we penetrate the nature of the psyche, the more the conviction grows upon us that the diversity, the multidimensionality of human nature requires the greatest variety of standpoints and methods in order to satisfy the variety of psychic dispositions."[61]

Before we more carefully examine Jung's method of integration, I would like to highlight two case studies that illustrate psychedelic-enhanced therapy's potential to transform trauma, the shadow, and psychosis.

The Transformative Potential of Psychedelic-Enhanced Psychotherapy: Two Case Studies

Dr. Rick Strassman's Report

One of the volunteers in Rick Strassman's DMT study was a woman, Andrea, who as a child had "sleep paralysis," a condition in which one sees frightening scenes while sleeping and cannot move.[62] Strassman reports that, as a child, Andrea had been told by her mother that Satan was coming to torture her during her sleep and that she needed to pray to Jesus for protection. Andrea was apprehensive about the DMT sessions, even though she had taken psychedelics over one hundred times. Given her chronic inability to fall asleep comfortably, she feared she wouldn't be able to relax into the rush of effects. She was afraid she might have a near-death experience, and she worried that she wouldn't be able to let go. Describing one of Andrea's high-dose sessions, Strassman reports,

She sighed deeply a time or two while the flush was going in.
She then bellowed, *NO! NO! NO!*
For the next minute, she cried, *No! No! No!*

Andrea's legs kicked and flailed. Her husband rested his hand on her leg, gently patting and massaging her. I placed my hand on her other foot.[63]

Her sobbing lasted five minutes. She gradually settled down, and she asked if she had screamed. Strassman told her she had screamed a few times.

> *I thought so. It was hard to let go.*
> "There's a lot of feelings in there."
> She laughed quietly. . . .
> *I never really left my body. I fought it all the way. I thought I was going to die. I didn't want to die. I was afraid. I realized that I had a body for a reason and that I have work to do in this body.*
>
> Andrea now turned her fear into a challenge, rather than a defeat.
>
> *When I was coming down, I wasn't sure if I ever wanted to do this again, but now I think I do. I don't think it will be as scary next time. It was death. I saw myself in that void, the void. It was just black, just too much. I've never had anything like that happen before. . . . I was just totally unprepared and startled and scared.*[64]

Preparing Andrea for her last series of high-dose sessions a month later, Strassman spoke to Andrea about her fear and encouraged her to let go. At the start of the session,

> she let out a brief muffled cry as the first 0.3 mg/kg dose went in. However, anticipating this, her husband, Laura [an assistant], and I quickly responded by placing our hands on her arms and legs. She calmed quickly, and throughout the morning she worked on developing the theme that had emerged on her first high dose: fear of death related to the fear of how to live her life fully.
>
> As was the case with so many of our tolerance study volunteers, Andrea broke through into an ecstatic resolution of her anxiety and confusion during her fourth session.
>
> Eighteen minutes into this session, she said,
> *That was a real gift, this last one. . . .*
> *There was literally a flood of beings saying, "Okay, remember when you were young and idealistic and wanted to learn how to do body work?" There's no reason I can't do that now.*[65]

When Strassman spoke to Andrea during a follow-up call, she expressed gratitude for the experience. "I really wanted to blow things out. It's changed my perspective. It's helped me focus on my interest in healing work. There is so much I want to do. . . ."[66]

Strassman explains that "Andrea could have continued fighting against painful and frightening feelings, making a bad situation worse. We knew she might have difficulty letting go after she told us about her mother's comparing her sleep-related symptoms to demonic attacks. Nevertheless, with her husband's and our support, she continued on through her fear and found the sadness and confusion that lay behind it. Facing her anxiety and fears, giving up resistance, she emerged with a clearer sense of who she was, what she desired, and plans for carrying our her goals."[67]

Dr. Margot Cutner's Report

Discussing her patient who suffered from severe depression and paranoid tendencies (see chapters 5 and 6), Margot Cutner describes the progress the woman made during LSD psychotherapy, which was supplemented by ongoing therapeutic analysis outside her LSD sessions. Before presenting Cutner's report, let me explain that when Cutner reminds her patient of the story of Joseph, who was thrown into a pit, she is no doubt referring to the biblical story of Joseph (Genesis 37:24), who was thrown into a pit by his brothers. For Jungians, the story, like stories of being swallowed by a whale or a monster, represents the myth of the perilous descent, which symbolizes the conscious mind's descent into the unconscious. This descent involves "a diminution or extinction of consciousness, an *abaissement du niveau mental*," which is often accompanied by a terrifying sense of subjugation.[68]

Cutner begins her report by quoting her patient:

"I began to feel that I was lying at the bottom of a pit. I felt that rubbish was being thrown in on top of me and I had to fight my way out."

I suggested that she should stop fighting and I reminded her of the story of Joseph, thrown into a pit. She then relaxed and again experienced a feeling of growing small. Then she heard the ringing of a sawmill saw, and then remembered that she was born near a sawmill. "As I lay, I had the growing conviction that I was going to be born and that it was absolutely essential that Dr. C. should be with me." She then felt that she was "attached to something by a cord, and [Cutner's patient continues] I could feel my limbs beginning to swell, then I began to feel that life was flowing into me and that I was fed by this cord. I was not actually born, but the feeling I had was that, if I could retain this feeling, I could ultimately break away from my mother . . . and that people would have to accept me and my ideas instead of my always trying to conform to theirs."[69]

Cutner continues with her patient's report on another occasion when the transference helped transform a horrifying experience into "one of *integration during the LSD session*."[70] (Cutner's italics)

> "I felt I must run away and kill myself. . . . I felt I wanted to jump off a cliff . . . then I wanted to smash my way out through the window, and Sister [the nurse] locked the shutters. I begged Sister to leave me and lock me in so that I could bash myself to death. I felt inferior, inadequate, and felt that there was nothing worth living for, and there also came a fear of men. I remember Dr. C. coming and telling me to lie down and just let things come. While she was with me, I felt that something was coming from her into my body and that it was giving me strength. . . . When my eyes were closed I felt that there was a room inside me, with red plush carpets and dark red velvet cushions and something inside me went into this room and rested for a while."

As the pit had turned from a place of utter humiliation into an archetypal "womb," so her inner storm center had turned into a center of stillness. In both these instances the presence of the analyst as the "good" and "nourishing" mother had still been necessary; later it was the process of introversion, with or without the actual presence of the analyst, which provided the "womb" inside which rebirth experiences could take place.

In this way a pattern, frequently repeated under LSD, had evolved for this patient. She used to start the day [the LSD session] in a panic, with frightening pictures projected onto the walls, the furniture or the people around her, and moods of paranoid aggression or abject depression. If then she succeeded in letting go—and by remembering experiences like that of the changed character of the pit—adopted an attitude of "giving up fighting" (which under LSD she could do much more easily than at other times), these moods were usually followed by images similar to that of the "inner room." There were inner gardens of great beauty, caves into which a light was shining, fountains inside herself, or experiences of "God coming into her," these last usually connected with perceptions of golden light or with sudden feelings of "a great love" taking hold of her.[71]

After discussing the progression of this case, Cutner concludes that "LSD, by reinforcing introversion (initiated through analysis anyway), brought her up not only against her own, previously unconscious, aggression, hate, and jealousy (stemming from childhood experiences); but it also evolved archetypal (healing) symbolism through which her psychotic tendencies could be overcome."[72]

PART 3

Jung's Psychology and Psychedelic-Enhanced Psychotherapy

Through the assimilation of unconscious contents, the momentary life of consciousness can once more be brought into harmony with the law of nature from which it all too easily departs, and the patient is led back to the natural law of his own being.

C. G. Jung
"The Practical Use of Dream-Analysis"[1]

CHAPTER 11

The Transcendent Function: Jung's Approach to Integration

The term *integration* indicates an interaction between the psyche's parts, between, for example, consciousness and the unconscious, or ego and the shadow. In this sense, integration is the opposite of dissociation. This interaction constitutes the work required by a person to approach psychological wholeness, or individuation. Jung also used the term *integration* to indicate an optimal stage of development in which, ideally, a balanced relationship is reached between the psyche's opposing parts.[1]

To look more closely at what he means by integration, I now turn to Jung's essay "The Transcendent Function," which presents a theoretical foundation and method for integrating activated unconscious material that has manifested in dreams, fantasies, and other symbolic products of the unconscious. Jung spoke of integration as bringing activated unconscious material into a constructive or synthetic relationship to consciousness. In doing this, the psyche creates an awareness that embraces, and thus transcends, both its conscious and unconscious aspects. Jung prefaces "The Transcendent Function" by noting that he is attempting to elucidate the process involved in analytic treatment, a task he states in the form of a question: "How does one come to terms in practice with the unconscious?"[2] Implicitly, this is "the fundamental question, in practice, of all religions and all philosophies," Jung suggests. "For the unconscious is not this thing or that; it is the Unknown as it immediately affects us."[3] Moreover, he adds, the meaning and value of unconscious contents "are revealed only through their integration into the personality as a whole."[4] Elsewhere, Jung asserts that "coming to terms with the contents of the collective unconscious. . . . is *the* great task of the integration process."[5]

Jung also prefaces his essay by explaining that the method of "active imagination" he describes here is the most useful technique for bringing unconscious content to consciousness. He cautions, however, that this method has certain "dangers," two of which are especially relevant to psychedelic-enhanced psychotherapy. One risk is that the patient shows only an "aesthetic interest" in the contents produced and therefore "remains stuck in an all-enveloping phantasmagoria."[6] In this case, nothing is integrated into the personality, an act that involves confronting the "moral demands" of what is revealed.[7] Jung's method also risks releasing unconscious content that may "overpower the conscious mind and take possession of the personality," leading to a "psychotic interval."[8] You may recall that Jung objected to psychedelic-enhanced therapy because, even though it yields results similar to those achieved with active imagination (that is, access to the unconscious), he maintained that psychedelic therapy doesn't lend itself to the therapeutic techniques that his method employs to advance integration and avoid psychotic reactions.[9]

Jung opens "The Transcendent Function" by stating that "there is nothing mysterious or metaphysical about the term 'transcendent function.'"[10] It refers rather to a psychological function that "arises from the union of conscious and unconscious contents."[11] We shouldn't interpret the word *union* here literally. Jung is referring to a uniting of consciousness and the unconscious in the sense of bringing them together through an interaction that can lead to a balanced relationship between the two, which he characterizes as psychological wholeness.

Jung continues by reviewing the compensatory and complementary relationship between consciousness and the unconscious, noting the varying degrees to which consciousness is affected by the unconscious in different people. In contrast to the relatively healthy person, the partition between consciousness and the unconscious in the neurotic is more permeable. The psychotic is even more directly and intensely influenced by the unconscious.[12] As should be obvious by now, despite these variations between people, the basic dynamic relationship between consciousness and the unconscious is, for Jung, the same in all of us—whether we be healthy, neurotic, psychotic, or affected by a psychedelic substance.

Many wonder if Jung would have eventually warmed to the therapeutic potential of psychedelic substances when used appropriately, following rigorous safety guidelines. There are good reasons to suspect that he might have. He points out, for example, that the stability of consciousness and the rigidity of its defense mechanisms tend to exclude psychological elements that under certain conditions could beneficially enrich the conscious mind.[13] He also warns that the concentrated consciousness of civilized life seriously increases the risk of a dangerous disunity, a separation of the conscious mind from the unconscious that can lead to a fatal irruption of unconscious content into consciousness.[14] The responsible use of psychedelics can certainly counter these tendencies. But there is also good reason to suspect that Jung would have maintained his opposition to psychedelics on the grounds that they too easily and quickly open us to the deepest realms of the unconscious, for which we are inevitably unprepared. "How," he might ask, "will you integrate the material that the drug uncovers for you?".

As if addressing these matters, Jung poses a fundamental therapeutic question: "What kind of mental and moral attitude is it necessary to have towards the disturbing influences of the unconscious, and how might they be conveyed to the patient?"[15] The answer, Jung says, is that we must understand that consciousness and the unconscious each plays a vital role in achieving psychological balance and health. When we grasp this fundamental fact, we will appreciate the way disturbances arising from the unconscious help to overcome the limits of the conscious mind. We must recognize, that is, that the disturbing images and feelings arising from the unconscious offer consciousness the very medicine it needs.

Jung's approach to treatment presupposes the analyst's acquaintance with these insights to begin with, and it assumes that these insights can be realized by her patient.[16] The analyst who has experienced the integrative process herself might be able to help her client "bring conscious and unconscious together and so arrive at a new attitude."[17] Recalling that the synthetic-constructive method looks for psychological meaning in unconscious content, Jung explains that his therapy is based on evaluating symbols from the unconscious. As I showed in chapter 3, he sees symbols manifested in dream and fantasy images as "the best possible expression for a complex fact not yet clearly apprehended by consciousness."[18] Yet, for reasons to which I will return shortly, Jung cautions that mere intellectual analysis of the symbol is not a reliable approach to the unconscious. One must start with one's emotional state and become as aware as possible of one's mood, sinking into it unreservedly and noting all possible images and associations that come to mind. One must take care, however, not to let one's associations stray beyond one's emotions and thereby displace them. Out of this kind of attention to affect, or "feeling-toned content," and related images comes a picture of unconscious material and tendencies related to one's condition. This whole procedure enriches and clarifies the emotional content and thereby makes it more understandable.[19] Such work "creates a new situation, since the previously unrelated affect has become a more or less clear and articulate idea thanks to the assistance and cooperation of the conscious mind. This is the beginning of the transcendent function, i.e., of the collaboration of conscious and unconscious data."[20]

At one point, Jung digresses from his description of active imagination to address a possible doubt in his reader's mind: "Does one have to drag the unconscious to the surface by force?" Given that Jung asked essentially the same question about the therapeutic application of psychedelic substances, I find his answer particularly intriguing. Acknowledging that his methods may appear "novel, unusual, and perhaps even rather weird," Jung explains that it is important to bring to light unconscious content that can secretly influence our lives with unpleasant or even catastrophic consequences.[21] That is, when the compensating function of the unconscious is overly suppressed by the strength of the conscious mind, the unconscious eventually loses its capacity to function healthfully.[22]

When the patient cannot generate unconscious content through his own fantasies, concludes Jung, "we have to resort to artificial aid;" and he reviews various methods for encouraging the release of unconscious material, including painting, sculpting, body movement, and spontaneous writing.[23] Having established this foundation for the transcendent function, Jung poses another fundamental question: What are we to do with the unconscious material once we obtain it through one of these methods? When consciousness confronts the contents of the unconscious, Jung sees two tendencies: "creative formulation" and "understanding." Creative formulation is dominated by artistic concerns; understanding emphasizes an intense effort to grasp the meaning of unconscious content.[24]

Jung finds, not surprisingly, advantages and disadvantages to each approach. The first may become sidetracked by purely artistic concerns. The second may overvalue intellectual analysis and interpretation and miss the unconscious material's "symbolic character."[25] As we have seen, a symbol arising from the unconscious is an expression of complex unconscious facts that are to some degree beyond conscious comprehension. So Jung is cautioning us here to avoid overanalyzing a symbol that is pointing us in directions that we cannot fully grasp intellectually. In general, Jung suggests, creative formulation and the understanding of meaning supplement each other in the transcendent function.[26] Ideally, one exists beside the other in "an alternation of creation and understanding," in which unconscious content is first given shape freely and then interpreted.[27]

In either case, the conscious means of expression must serve the unconscious content without influencing it unduly. "In giving the content form," Jung explains, "the lead must be left as far as possible to the chance ideas and associations thrown up by the unconscious."[28] Despite the exceptional value of such content, its unexpected and irrational nature can be disturbing, and people understandably avoid these challenges until they face a psychological crisis.[29] But once the contents of the unconscious have been given form and their meaning is understood, the next stage of the process has been reached: now the ego takes the lead. But, Jung asks, how will the ego relate to this reality, to this meeting with its opposite? Will it be able to transcend its limited position?[30]

I would like to pause here for a moment to suggest how this process might unfold when attempting to come to terms with and integrate a traumatic psychedelic experience. As I have shown, during an LSD trip at the age of nineteen, I was overwhelmed by content from the unconscious, which took the form of a terrifying vision, a delusion that I was in the wrong world and must kill myself to get out. Working years later to come to terms with that trauma in an MDMA-enhanced therapy session, the same unconscious content emerged in the form of reliving that vision. I suddenly saw everyone around me as evil, and I was convinced, as I have been at least momentarily convinced during uncountable flashback experiences over the years, that I must free myself from this world by retracing my way back to the bridge where it all started. When I tell the people supporting me in the session that I now realize I am in Hell again and that they are the Devil's helpers, my therapist asks me, "How does it feel to be in Hell?" Putting this in Jungian terms, my therapist had suggested, perhaps intuitively, that I must start with my emotional state and become as aware as possible of my mood by sinking into it unreservedly. With the support of my therapist and his assistant, I struggled throughout the night to deal with bizarre images, terrifying feelings, and delusional visions. I then worked for months to understand this overwhelming unconscious material by attempting, as Jung puts it, "to bring conscious and unconscious together and so arrive at a new attitude."[31]

For the psyche to heal and transform itself, Jung suggests, ego-consciousness must face and integrate a reality that is entirely contrary to its nature. How can the ego relate to such an alien world, to a reality that transcends its own limited perspective, to a meeting with its opposite? Jung explains that as one opens oneself to the depths of the unconscious, one must value both the ego and the unconscious; and he issues a warning that has significance for the use of psychedelics in general, and for attempts to integrate disturbing unconscious material released during a previous psychedelic experience. Just as the conscious mind has a restrictive effect on the unconscious, he cautions, "so the rediscovered unconscious often has a really dangerous effect on the ego.... A liberated unconscious can thrust the ego aside and overwhelm it."[32] If the ego cannot defend itself from the emotionally disturbing powers of the unconscious, a schizophrenic-like condition arises. This danger would be less acute if the ego's encounter with the unconscious could be divested of its overwhelming emotional force, which is what happens when, through active imagination, unconscious content is given artistic form and given meaning through interpretation.

But, Jung adds, the ego's confrontation with the unconscious, and the psyche's consequent transcendent function, "is not a partial process running a conditioned course."[33] It is rather, "a total and integral event in which all aspects are, or should be, included. The affect must therefore be deployed in its full strength."[34] That is, even though working with unconscious material through creative expression and intellectual effort is useful when the unconscious threatens to overwhelm consciousness, these means should not be used to avoid facing painful emotions. Such a total and integral event involves a renewal of the whole personality, which penetrates every aspect of one's life. For this to happen, the unconscious must be taken seriously (which, Jung points out, doesn't mean that it be taken *literally*), so that it can cooperate with consciousness—instead of disturbing it.[35] Jung draws a beautiful analogy here, describing this process in terms of two people who conduct a dialogue over their different views with mutual respect for the validity of the other's argument. Each of them "considers it worth-while to modify the conflicting standpoints by means of thorough comparison and discussion."[36]

The transcendent function becomes a kind of constructive confrontation, then. It is a process that "generates a tension charged with energy and creates a living, third thing," Jung suggests, "a movement out of the suspension between opposites, a living birth that leads to a new level of being."[37] Because as long as consciousness and the unconscious "are kept apart—naturally for the purpose of avoiding conflict—they do not function and remain inert."[38] But "consciousness is continually widened through the confrontation with previously unconscious contents, or—to be more accurate—could be widened if it took the trouble to integrate them," concludes Jung.[39] With sufficient guidance and with intelligence, self-confidence, and willpower, the transcendent function offers one "a way of attaining liberation by one's own efforts and of finding the courage to be oneself."[40]

* * * *

I close this chapter by drawing from my own experience to illustrate Jung's method of combining creative expression and the understanding of meaning to integrate disturbing symbolic content that has emerged from the unconscious. My attempt to understand and artistically express such content followed a flashback experience I struggled with in the early 1990s during a hike with a friend around Angel Island in the San Francisco Bay. At the onset of that spontaneous recurrence, I was overwhelmed, as I had been many times before, by a terrifying sense that I was either insane or was being told by some silent voice that I must return to the bridge where it all started. The implicit message is always clear (at least for a moment): I must end my life in this world. The extensive notes I made after that experience contain a wide range of spontaneous associations, from a Primo Levi quote on the image of the Devil, to the image of a tide as "a pulling," or "a calling."

Before closing with the poem that developed out of those notes, I will quote some excerpts from them. In retrospect, this work marked the beginning of a new stage, an especially fruitful period, of my ongoing attempt to understand and come to terms with my LSD experiences. The poem I wrote led to conversations with two good friends about my past experiences. My friends were generous enough to suggest that we drive back to the bridge together to take a fresh look. These events led to more writing about my LSD trips, reading about psychedelic drugs, and returning to graduate school to learn everything I could about the nature of psychedelic experiences. As challenging as this work has been, and as bleak as the process may appear, I have over these years become increasingly grateful for the beauty underlying it all.

The angels are laughing maliciously

Walking there in time, my friend laughs good-naturedly and I hear the angels warning again. They've spoken before, told me how pathetic I am, how cowardly to go on living in this world, to accept its absurdity.

When the angels speak we feel terror

It's as if my ears are ringing, separated from my friend

it's as if someone is shouting at me, mocking

mocking angels

They always sneak up on me, often at times of laughing, when tromping freely on fragile plants

It's ugly somehow, because these angels are cruel and brutal while at the same time the vision they bestow is immensely truthful: the self/ we are so pathetically small and forgetful, forgetful of the heavens, or of hell, of all that lies beyond the obvious.

So the angels reveal themselves subtly, like paintings of St. Jerome reveal his temptation in his cave by the devil to be a frightening affair. Just at the hem of the beautiful seductress, one catches, with a startled jerk, the scratchy black tongs of some hideous creature.

Allen laughed, and suddenly, for a long instant, there was silence, then I could hear Allen's voice again in my head, his laughing voice, and I looked at him and wondered if he was only a messenger trying to tell me, like others/the universe has tried to tell me so many times: YOU ARE THE ONE RESPONSIBLE FOR THE WORLD'S MADNESS, if you didn't go along with it, it wouldn't be that way. The universe was shouting: YOU'RE DOING IT AGAIN, YOU'RE FORGETTING THAT LIFE IS A SACRED GIFT.

And for a moment I started to plan my way back to the canyon where years ago I had come out into the wrong world.

There are, it seems, times when our idea of angels and devils, as two opposing forces pulling at our thoughts, our conscience, isn't adequate. I think of a time when I was certain I was being talked to by God. But at that time I was being told I should kill myself, that if I trusted God I would kill myself. Now, looking back on it, I see something both divine and evil about this. It seems clearly true that one should put an end to one's self in some way, that the self has to die in some metaphorical sense. But it also seems clear that the voice telling me to kill myself was malevolent. How can these two manifest themselves as one? They can't in our normal view of things.

As I read these lines again after twenty years, particularly the lines in capital letters, I am struck by one of Jung's most profound insights into the risks inherent in a psychedelic experience: the burden of moral responsibility. Sometimes it seems that if the madness psychedelics can bring doesn't break you, the weight of responsibility will. As Jung puts it, speaking of the effects of a psychedelic experience: "I only know there is no point in wishing to *know* more of the collective unconscious than one gets through dreams and intuition. The more you know of it, the greater and heavier becomes your moral burden, because the unconscious contents transform themselves into your individual tasks and duties as soon as they begin to become conscious. . . . Do you want to find more and more complications and increasing responsibilities?"[41]

Angel Island at Low Tide

Was it because we, deciding at the last minute, took off
drove south talking of car wrecks, San Quentin and those
tacky bank calendars my mother sends me for Christmas?

And the ferry. The way the crew unfurled rope (so calmly)
and lay the gangplank, as if they expected us late—and
waited. There's no reason we should have caught that boat.

Was it that feeling, disarming even, two friends get
hiking around an island, searching old buildings and
bunkers, leaping down steep hills, climbing forbidden

fences, and making ambush on pretended enemies? Or,
is it that we, like some jaded tourists, faced with
what is not in their book, faced with the great

heaviness of a bay, talked so as not to be crushed by it,
talked of what we knew: oil tankers, currents, and cold-
water swimming, talked to shore ourselves up, as if, like a

boat full of holes, we were about to sink in the vastness?
Or, risen up from it, was it that black volcanic rock,
putrid and sulfur sharp, those starfish waiting out low tide in

a world they can't survive, or the thread of root (so easily
broken) holding that kelp to rock? Or was it the memory, held
so tenuously in a headstone, of a detention camp, its

malevolent past rising faintly through new paint and
plaster, the way rust seeps up from old nails to spoil the
perfect facade? It had to be all this. And the way

I spoke so seriously of the self, spoke too seriously,
as if I knew what I meant. How, otherwise, when you laughed,
made fun of me, did I hear not your voice but

something else, something telling me once again I was not,
not at all, who I thought I was, and telling me I could, indeed,
telling me I should, if I dared, end it.

CHAPTER 12

Jungian Psychotherapy

Beyond criticizing the therapeutic application of psychedelic substances in several personal letters, Jung doesn't discuss the relationship between psychedelics and psychotherapy. Nevertheless, Jung's approach to psychotherapy in general is quite relevant to psychedelic-enhanced psychotherapy and provides valuable insights into its practice. And Jung's approach to treating neurosis, trauma, and psychosis is inevitably relevant to treating the adverse effects of a psychedelic experience. This chapter initiates my discussion of the implications of Jung's psychology for psychedelic-related treatment, a discussion that becomes more specific in the next chapter.

The Method and Purpose of Psychotherapy

Jung's therapeutic method involves two general stages. First, one gains access to unconscious content and thereby becomes aware of it. Then one comes to terms with and integrates the released unconscious content. I don't mean to suggest that Jungian therapy is a discrete, linear, or necessarily even a logical process. However, this two-stage scheme provides a useful means for examining psychotherapy as Jung conceives it.

Gaining Access to the Unconscious

Reading through Jung's writings, I often come upon statements that recall Timothy Leary, Ralph Metzner, and Richard Alpert's characterization of Carl Jung as a man who had committed himself "to the inner vision and to the wisdom and superior reality of internal perceptions."[1] I find this, for example, in Jung's statement describing the observation of intrapsychic activity. The first aim in psychotherapy, he writes, "is to observe the sporadic emergence, whether in the form of images or feelings, of those dim representations which detach themselves in the darkness from the invisible realms of the unconscious and move as shadows before the inturned gaze."[2] Those dark and invisible realms of the unconscious cannot be circumscribed; they must be approached as "something boundless: infinite and infinitesimal."[3] Jung's depiction of the extraordinary breadth and depth of the unconscious recalls the vast cartography of the psyche that Stanislav Grof created to account for the seemingly infinite range of phenomena opened to us by psychedelic substances.[4]

For Jung, the focus of psychotherapy is not the neurosis but "the distorted totality of the human being."[5] Through integrating unconscious contents, he says, "the momentary life of consciousness can once more be brought into harmony with the [instinctual] law of nature from which it all too easily departs, and the patient is led back to the natural law of his own being."[6] Psychotherapy should lead far beyond the patient's immediate needs "to that distant goal which may perhaps have been the first urge to life: the complete actualization of the whole human being, that is, individuation."[7] Jung's conception of individuation, as we have seen, entails nothing less then the personality's transformative engagement with the archetype of psychological wholeness, or the Self, the experience of which engenders a sense of timelessness and eternity.

Coming to Terms with the Unconscious

Joan Chodorow points out that the expression "coming to terms with the unconscious" is the usual translation of Jung's use of the German word *auseinandersetzung*, which implies a dialectical relationship between consciousness and the unconscious. This dialectic has the effect of differentiating one from the other while honoring both as complementary psychic elements.[8] Jung's own conscious engagement with the unconscious, his "confrontation with the unconscious," illustrates this dialectical process. In Jung's account we can see him striving for a balanced relationship between the psyche's two aspects.[9]

Chodorow explains that Jung used many names to describe his therapeutic method, including *the dialectical process, the transcendent function, active imagination, active fantasy, the picture method, differentiation, introspection*, and *descent*. This multiplicity of names suggests the development of Jung's thinking about an inevitably complex process. This multiplicity also indicates that, as one would expect, Jung's fundamental therapeutic method found expression in many different forms, some more meditative, others more intellectual, intuitive, artistic, dramatic, physical, or playful. Contrasting Jung's use of the terms *transcendent function* and *active imagination*, Chodorow identifies common elements in all these various forms of Jung's therapeutic method. "The term 'transcendent function' encompasses both a *method* and an inborn *function* of the psyche.

In contrast, the term 'active imagination' refers to the method alone. But, obviously, the *method* (active imagination) is based on the image-producing *function* of the psyche, that is, imagination. Both the transcendent function and the dynamic function of the imagination are complex psychic functions made up of other functions. Both combine conscious and unconscious elements. Both are creative, integrative functions that shape and transform the living symbol."[10]

When Chodorow speaks of creative, integrative functions, she is alluding to Jung's emphasis on the dynamic quality of active imagination. Jung distinguishes between active and passive imagination. Active imagination (which Jung often calls *active fantasy*) is initiated when one turns attention toward unconscious content with an attitude of expectation. The ego's engagement, or "positive participation," with unconscious content invests energy into that material that potentially transforms its relationship to consciousness. When that unconscious content is consciously associated with analogous images, such as mythological symbols (through the technique of amplification), it becomes even more clearly formed in consciousness.[11] Passive imagination, on the other hand, "is an irruption of unconscious contents into consciousness."[12] Passive fantasies require no conscious investment to take shape. They appear "as a result of a relative dissociation of the psyche, since they presuppose a withdrawal of energy from conscious control and a corresponding activation of unconscious material."[13]

Jung considered active imagination an especially advanced form of psychological activity because "the conscious and the unconscious personality of the subject flow together into a common product in which both are united."[14] Because passive imagination is marked by a separation of consciousness and the unconscious, "the fantasy that irrupts into consciousness from such a state can never be the perfect expression of a unified individuality, but will represent mainly the standpoint of the unconscious personality."[15]

The distinction Jung makes between active and passive forms of imagination is central to Michael Fordham's criticism of psychedelic-enhanced psychotherapy. Fordham's complaint, as you may recall, is based on his assertion that psychedelic psychotherapy is a relatively passive process. He cautions that the passive process of LSD-enhanced psychotherapy, in which the substance produces unconscious imagery "by involuntary biochemical means," must be distinguished from "the patient's deliberate activity" during conventional Jungian psychotherapy.[16] Fordham believes that psychedelic psychotherapy diminishes the capacity of the person's conscious mind to actively engage in the therapeutic process; and he therefore takes issue with Margot Cutner's suggestion that unconscious images brought into consciousness by LSD are comparable to images brought into consciousness during active imagination.

Leaving aside for a moment the fact that Cutner compared psychedelic-induced images with images manifested in dreams as well as active imagination, Fordham's criticism of psychedelic therapy ironically suggests an objective way to evaluate its effectiveness in Jungian terms. In his article "Active Imagination and Imaginative Activity," Fordham explains that active imagination is a term developed by Jung to characterize a method whereby images "can be formed by bringing the ego into relationship with the 'inner world' of archetypes."[17] Fordham points out that the term *active imagination* is inappropriate when it is used indiscriminately to describe creative activity in general. Creative activity often involves "imaginative activity," he says, rather than "the active induction of the imagination by the ego."[18] Various forms of creativity, such as painting or fantasying, "may just as well be imaginative activity as active imagination, *the distinction depending upon the activity of the ego*."[19] (my italics)

The distinction Fordham notes here—determining whether a creative activity is psychologically passive or active based on the ego's participation—suggests a way to objectively evaluate psychedelic-enhanced therapy.[20] Contrary to Fordham's assessment, I don't think the critical issue should be whether the psychedelic-released content is an irruption into consciousness (that is, a psychological event in which the ego is passive). As Fordham's distinction between imaginative activity and active imagination suggests, we must take into account how ego-consciousness relates to the released unconscious content. If the ego relates actively to unconscious material that initially emerged without conscious intention or participation, that is a valid integrative process.

The soundness of this approach becomes evident by comparing how we integrate unconscious content that comes to consciousness in a psychedelic experience to how we integrate unconscious content that comes to consciousness in a dream. Jungians, of course, place great weight on interpreting unconscious content released into consciousness during a dream. Yet, for Jung, dreams are "nothing but passive fantasies."[21] Even if we accept that ego-consciousness is always passive when unconscious material is released during a psychedelic experience, we shouldn't evaluate psychedelic-enhanced therapy on this basis any more than we evaluate conventional analysis on the basis of the ego's passivity during a dream. As I show in chapter 13, psychedelic-enhanced psychotherapy usually involves integrating released unconscious images after the psychedelic session. But, according to Margot Cutner and Ronald Sandison, as we will see, patients can form an active, conscious relationship to unconscious material as it emerges during a psychedelic experience.

The Relationship between Analyst and Patient

The Analyst

Unlike physical diseases, which generally call for specific treatments, the only valid principle when treating mental illness, Jung maintains, is that its treatment must be psychological. Despite all the methods and approaches, "the remarkable thing is that any given therapeutic procedure in any given neurosis can have the desired result."[22] All skillful psychotherapists will consciously or unconsciously draw from theories beyond their own school, Jung points out. Ultimately, all therapists not only have their own method, they *are* that method. "The great healing factor in psychotherapy is the doctor's personality," he says.[23] And he repeatedly cautions against relying on theoretical suppositions. "As far as possible I let pure experience decide the therapeutic aims. This may perhaps seem strange. . . . But in psychotherapy it seems to me positively advisable for the doctor not to have too fixed an aim. He can hardly know better than the nature and will to live of the patient. The great decisions in human life usually have far more to do with the instincts and other mysterious unconscious factors than with conscious will and well-meaning reasonableness."[24]

But therapists must undergo analysis themselves before treating others. Therapists who have not undergone analysis have a tendency to project their own unconscious characteristics onto the patient, or to not see those characteristics in the patient.[25] It also seems evident that therapists who have done deep inner work themselves will more likely be able to appreciate and deal with irrational images and projections emerging from their patients' unconscious. This would be especially true for therapists practicing psychedelic psychotherapy. Clearly, they should have an intimate, first-hand knowledge of psychedelic experience.

When therapeutic progress proves unsatisfactory through rational treatment, Jung notes, therapists should let themselves be guided by "the patient's own irrationalities" and thereby allow their patient's latent creative potential to develop. Jung finds dream interpretation a useful guide to the unconscious in such cases. For those who have found no meaning or satisfaction in the rational domain of life, Jung suggests, "it is enormously important to be able to enter a sphere of irrational experience."[26]

The Dialectical Relationship

Besides characterizing the intrapsychic integration of consciousness and the unconscious as a dialectical process, Jung views the ideal relationship between analyst and patient as a dialectical one. "Treatment is an individual, *dialectical* process, in which the doctor, as a person, participates just as much as the patient," Jung advises. "Difficult cases, therefore, are a veritable ordeal for both patient and doctor."[27] Therapists must have as much insight into their own psyches as they expect from their patients. Only when they have healed themselves can they hope to heal their patients. "If I wish to treat another individual psychologically at all," Jung maintains, "I must for better or worse give up all pretensions of superior knowledge, all authority and desire to influence. I must perforce adopt a dialectical procedure consisting in a comparison of our mutual findings."[28] Such a therapeutic relationship supports the individuation process, presumably in patient and analyst alike.[29]

The Transference

Projection seems to be a ubiquitous characteristic of psychological life, and, not surprisingly, projections are a prominent feature of psychedelic experiences.[30] Grof describes the "exteriorization of the process" and "excessive use of the mechanism of projection" as primary characteristics of the psychotic style in confronting one's psyche.[31] As I discussed in "Resistance to and Projection of the Shadow" (chapter 6), Jungians regard projection as a universal psychological tendency that becomes especially persistent when a person encounters images from the collective unconscious. Jungian therapists understandably consider projection, in the form of transference, central to the relationship between patient and analyst. It follows that transference can also play a central role in psychedelic-enhanced psychotherapy. (Thus, the practice of having the patient use eyeshades to keep the process internal.)

Transference is defined generally as the projection of unconscious images onto the therapist by the patient.[32] Transference is usually understood more specifically as the projection of unconscious parental images onto the therapist. Jung identifies the roots of the transference phenomenon in the Western psyche's patriarchal and hierarchical orientation. This deep-seated psychic orientation, Jung suggests, causes people to unconsciously seek parental qualities in the analyst; and a patient's successful therapy often involves recognizing and withdrawing these projections.[33]

The nature of the transference corresponds more or less to the relation between parent and child. "The patient falls into a sort of childish dependence from which he cannot defend himself even by rational insight," Jung observes.[34] However, Jung emphasized the purpose of the transference, and he saw that in recognizing and resolving his projections, the patient creates a bridge to reality and moves toward psychological wholeness.

That is, by interpreting the transference for the patient and explaining what he is projecting, the therapist brings unconscious material to the patient's awareness.[35] This process is potentially dangerous, Jung explains, because, when the patient can no longer project the parental image onto the therapist, that image may shift back to the unconscious, where it originated. Such unconscious images, which "are charged with all the energy they originally possessed in childhood, . . . now appear in dreams and fantasies [as] impersonal, collective contents which are the very material from which certain schizophrenic psychoses are constructed."[36] In this condition, the ego can become "dissolved in contents of the collective unconscious."[37]

Yet working through the transference can be ultimately transformative. The opportunity for psychological transformation occurs during the ego's dangerous dissolution in the collective unconscious. At this point, reports Jung, "a healthful compensatory operation comes into play which each time seems to me like a miracle. Struggling against that dangerous trend towards disintegration, there arises out of this same collective unconscious a counteraction, characterized by symbols which point unmistakably to a process of centering. This process creates nothing less than a new personality, which the symbols show from the first to be superordinate to the ego."[38] Margot Cutner, as we saw in chapter 10, observed such transformative archetypal imagery emerge during one of her patient's psychedelic-induced confrontations with the unconscious.

Sandison confirms that transference phenomena occur just as often in LSD treatment as in conventional analysis.[39] The transference in psychedelic psychotherapy is potentially more complicated and intense, however. The session may be complicated by psychedelic-induced illusions or paranoid feelings that patients have about, for instance, the drugs that the therapist is administering to them. Sandison notes that some patients are convinced at first that they will be cured by merely taking LSD. This illusion, he points out, can potentially reduce their psychological commitment to the session and thereby diminish its effectiveness.[40] We can also recall the case of the psychiatrist who was the subject in his own mescaline experiment and who experienced the paranoid feeling that his colleague had given him a poisoned glass of water during his session. Given the intensity of psychedelic-induced unconscious images, especially when archetypal images are released, it's understandable that people make, as Sandison puts it, "violent psychological projections on to the analyst."[41] In spite of the complications and intensity of the transference during psychedelic treatment, Sandison maintains that the transference is nevertheless susceptible to analysis and interpretation by the patient with the guidance of the therapist.[42]

Dreams and Their Interpretation

Dreams make up the greatest part of the psychic content interpreted in Jungian analysis because they are the most prevalent manifestation of the unconscious. Given the significant parallels that Jung identifies between dreams, schizophrenia, and by implication psychedelic experience, Jung's approach to dreams and their interpretation provides an excellent basis for applying his psychology to psychedelic-related treatment.[43] You may recall that Jung characterized dreams as hallucinatory representations of unconscious material, or "the hallucinations of normal life."[44]

The Sphere of the Irrational

As we've seen, Jung places great importance on the ability "to enter a sphere of irrational experience" through dream work or active imagination. In so doing, "the habitual and the commonplace come to wear an altered countenance, and can even acquire a new glamour."[45] Those who know the brilliant clarity that even a mild psychedelic state can bring to the ordinary should understand the altered countenance and new glamour that Jung refers to here. In the sphere of the irrational, Jung says, common things also take on new meaning. Here, too, the parallel to psychedelic experience, during which ordinary things can become saturated with meaning, is striking.

Considering Jung's emphasis on the dangers of psychedelic therapy, it's notable that he mentions the dangers of subjecting oneself to the irrational through dream work and active imagination. "I do not think I underestimate the risk of this undertaking. It is as if one began to build a bridge out into space."[46] Yet Jung does not hesitate to encourage engagement in imagination, or fantasy, through dream work and active imagination. "Truth to tell, I have no small opinion of fantasy. To me, it is the maternally creative side of the masculine mind. When all is said and done, we can never rise above fantasy. . . . All the works of man have their origin in creative imagination."[47]

Jung describes dreams as fragments of spontaneous psychic activity that are just conscious enough to be recalled in the waking state.[48] Showing again remarkable parallels to psychedelic experience, Jung observes that the combination of ideas in dreams "is essentially *fantastic*; they are linked together in a sequence which is as a rule quite foreign to our 'reality thinking,' and in striking contrast to the logical sequence of ideas which we consider to be a special characteristic of conscious mental processes."[49] The dream appears to have "a minimum of that logical coherence and that hierarchy of values shown by the other contents of consciousness, and is therefore less transparent and understandable. . . . Usually a dream is a strange and disconcerting product distinguished by many 'bad qualities,' such as lack of logic, questionable morality, uncouth form, and apparent absurdity and nonsense. People are therefore only too glad to dismiss it as stupid, meaningless, and worthless."[50]

The Purpose and Value of Dreams

Despite the apparent senselessness of dreams, Jung asserts that it is "we who lack the sense and ingenuity to read the enigmatic message from the nocturnal realm of the psyche."[51] When we judge dreams to be meaningless, we are projecting our lack of understanding onto them; but that doesn't prevent dreams from having their own inherent meaning.[52]

Questions concerning the purpose and effects of dreams are applicable to every form of psychic activity, Jung says. "Everywhere the question of the 'why' and the 'wherefore' may be raised, because every organic structure is a network of purposive functions."[53] Anyone who appreciates the critical role that the unconscious plays in the causes and origins of psychopathology "will attribute a high practical importance to dreams as direct expressions of the unconscious."[54] The aim of dream analysis, and by extension, I suggest, psychedelic-enhanced psychotherapy, is to uncover and understand unconscious content that can help elucidate and treat the pathology.

The Compensating Function of Dreams

When we interpret a dream, Jung advises, it is always useful to consider what conscious attitude the dream is compensating. The compensatory significance of dreams is often not readily apparent, and at times it can be quite remote. But Jung maintains that all dreams compensate consciousness in one way or another. The dream reflects those unconscious contents that complement the current conscious situation. That is, the dream provides consciousness with a completely different view, which can give one a balanced perspective on the current situation. The contrast can be especially striking when the conscious viewpoint threatens a person's vital needs. The more one-sided the conscious attitude, the greater is the possibility that especially intense dreams with contrasting, purposeful content will arise as manifestations of the psyche's self-regulation.[55] "The unconscious is quite capable of bringing about all kinds of unwelcome disturbances," Jung notes. "These disturbances are due to lack of harmony between conscious and unconscious."[56] To appreciate the compensatory nature of dreams, consider how disturbing dream images of ourselves reveal shadow qualities we consciously deny.[57]

Compensation usually helps establish psychological balance, says Jung. But in some cases (with, for instance, a latent psychotic), compensation may lead to destructive action and even suicide.[58] Such extreme consequences would seem rare with dreams, but this phenomenon may account to some extent for the risk of suicide during psychedelic sessions, when unconscious content is too rapidly and too forcefully released into the conscious mind of someone already vulnerable to an overpowering influx from the unconscious.

Dreams (and by extension, psychedelic visions) containing archetypal content may represent more than a personal compensation. Archetypal themes sometimes "express an eternal human problem that repeats itself endlessly, and not just a disturbance of personal balance," Jung points out.[59] Jung finds especially significant the shift in the collective psyche that has accompanied modern civilization's loss of contact with those mythological symbols on which all religion is based. Those symbols form a bridge to the archetypal depths of the unconscious, Jung maintains. But such bridges are currently in a state of collapse, and no individual is personally responsible for this disaster. At the same time, we need to appreciate that the individual's unconscious will try to rebuild those broken connections. We need to understand, that is, "the attempts at restitution and cure which nature herself is making."[60]

Jung describes this restitution process in his essay "Principles of Practical Psychotherapy." "The psychic development of the individual produces something that looks very like the archaic world of fable," he says.

> The individual path looks like a regression to man's prehistory, and . . . consequently it seems as if something very untoward is happening which the therapist ought to arrest. We can in fact observe similar things in psychotic illnesses, especially in the paranoid forms of schizophrenia, which often swarm with mythological images. The fear instantly arises that we are dealing with some misdevelopment leading to a world of chaotic or morbid fantasy. . . .
>
> Now, it would seem that the recuperative process mobilizes these powers for its own ends. Mythological ideas with their extraordinary symbolism evidently reach far into the human psyche and touch the historical foundations where reason, will, and good intentions never penetrate; for these ideas are born of the same depths and speak a language which strikes an answering chord in the inner man, although our reason may not understand it. Hence, the process that at first sight looks like an alarming regression is rather a *reculer pour mieux sauter*, an amassing and integration of powers that will develop into a new order.[61]

CHAPTER 13

Implications for Psychedelic-Enhanced Psychotherapy

It is beyond the scope of this inquiry to propose a comprehensive set of Jungian guidelines for psychedelic-related treatment. My intention, therefore, is to outline here only the most significant treatment implications suggested by Jung's psychology. These are general implications for the practice of psychedelic-enhanced psychotherapy and for treating adverse reactions to a psychedelic experience.

Subject Readiness

The complexity inherent in a Jungian interpretation of psychedelic experience has become apparent throughout this inquiry. This complexity becomes especially evident when examining the different views of psychedelic experience represented by Jung and Fordham, on the one hand, and by Sandison and Cutner, on the other. And nowhere are the issues more apparent than when considering the controversial question of a person's readiness for psychedelic-enhanced therapy.

This issue strikes at the core of Jung's criticism of psychedelic therapy. The psychedelic substance, Jung asserts, "uncovers such psychic facts at any time and place when and where it is by no means certain that the individual is mature enough to integrate them."[1] Jung feared that the overwhelming nature of the psychedelic experience could even release a latent psychosis in some people. Seen in the context of his many papers on psychotherapy, Jung's criticism of psychedelic psychotherapy is clearly a specific instance of his concern for the risks inherent in psychotherapy in general. As one moves toward psychological wholeness, the unconscious can potentially overwhelm consciousness and bring about a psychotic reaction. "A development of this kind may be dangerous with a person whose social personality has not found its feet," Jung warns. "Moreover, any psychotherapeutic intervention may occasionally run into a latent psychosis and bring it to full flower. For this reason to dabble in psychotherapy is to play with fire, against which amateurs should be stringently cautioned. It is particularly dangerous when the mythological layer of the psyche is uncovered."[2]

Jung's warning is consistent with the standard suggestion that only people with a strong ego should undergo psychedelic-enhanced therapy.[3] Yet some experienced psychedelic therapists have found that, under certain circumstances, this precaution may be too restrictive. While Stanislav Grof acknowledges that it takes much less time to prepare a psychologically stable person for psychedelic psychotherapy, he maintains that "under optimal circumstances, which involve a specially structured treatment facility and an experienced therapeutic team, LSD psychotherapy can be experimentally conducted with any psychiatric patient whose condition is clearly not of an organic nature."[4] Ronald Sandison reports that his analytically-oriented LSD clinic (which fulfilled Grof's standards) intentionally selected individuals for treatment who had psychiatric problems that were untreatable by orthodox methods. "They were all in danger of becoming permanent mental invalids, life-long neurotics or of ending their lives by suicide."[5]

Both Grof and Sandison acknowledge that transient psychotic symptoms, aggressive behavior, and suicidal tendencies can arise in patients undergoing psychedelic treatment, especially mentally ill patients. They both maintain, however, that these adverse reactions can be successfully managed in a therapeutic environment. This requires a "situation where no limits are placed on the number of sessions," Grof explains. "Experienced therapists, trained nurses, and the supportive atmosphere of a therapeutic community are necessary prerequisites for such an endeavor."[6]

Grof and Sandison no doubt developed their LSD therapy programs with mentally-ill patients in response to these patients' extreme resistance to facing unconscious images and feelings in conventional therapy. Jung addresses this problem: "It is not always possible to bring the patients close enough to the unconscious for them to perceive the shadows. On the contrary, many of them . . . are so firmly anchored in consciousness that nothing can pry them loose. They develop the most violent resistances to any attempt to push consciousness aside."[7]

In the early 1950s, there was no theoretical basis for supposing that psychedelics could be used as a practical tool in combination with psychotherapy, recalls Sandison. Reviewing earlier LSD research, Sandison understood that the drug "produced a loosening of mental associations, that it facilitated the transference, and that forgotten and sometimes painful memories could be released."[8] Two years after initiating an LSD treatment program for mentally ill patients at Powick Hospital in 1952, Sandison concluded that LSD treatment offered hope to patients who could not be helped by conventional psychiatric methods. For many of these patients, analytical treatment would have been the best solution, Sandison observes. Yet the time and expense required for analysis was prohibitive for the vast majority of them. Moreover, adds Sandison, "in so many cases the rigid conscious barriers and resistances offered by the patient are too great to overcome. LSD gives these people some real and tangible experience of their own unconscious and re-kindles their faith in their own spirit at a comparatively early stage of treatment, and helps it to proceed more readily."[9] Sandison found that after LSD treatment had enabled his patients to observe the contents of their unconscious, they could then assimilate the released material in conventional therapy sessions.

In 1963, looking back on the practice of psycholytic therapy with LSD, Sandison addressed the issue of using LSD for "breaking down the mind's natural barriers between the external ego and the unconscious."

> The attitude of LSD therapists has undergone an interesting change through the years. It was at first thought that the principal dangers of treatment would reside in breaking down resistances too quickly, and this view must to some extent still be sustained. . . . It may be dangerous to break down resistances in the absence of suitable home conditions or in the presence of an inadequate, insecure, rigid and hostile hospital environment, suicide and psychosis being the principal results. On the other hand it cannot be stressed too much that, on the whole, more disservice is done to patients by overcaution dictated by an unsatisfactory environment than has resulted from the vigorous prosecution of treatment in a carefully designed therapeutic situation.[10]

Margot Cutner agrees that psycholytic therapy—when properly integrated into the analytic process as a whole—may be necessary when treatment is urgent or when a person is not considered treatable by conventional means. She acknowledges, nevertheless, that any analyst who practices psychedelic-enhanced therapy must remain alert to a number of issues. "Should not resistances be worked through in patient analytical work: is there perhaps an obstacle in the transference situation which prevents the progress of the analysis; or are there perhaps times of seeming barrenness which in truth may be periods of incubation or assimilation in the unconscious, the rhythm of which should not be disturbed by violent action? Or is it perhaps a simple insufficiency on the part of the analyst that causes the analysis to come to a standstill?"[11] However, she concludes that, for many patients, one cannot deny that auxiliary means such as LSD-enhanced psychotherapy can be helpful. She has also found that the risks of harming patients with psychedelic-enhanced psychotherapy are exaggerated, "as long as the analyst is present during the crucial experiences and can represent the integrating ego-function for the patient."[12]

As we have seen, Sandison has acknowledged that, in the early 1950s, he and his colleagues lacked the means to reliably distinguish between patients who would benefit from LSD-enhanced psychotherapy and those who would be better served by conventional therapy. Nevertheless, Sandison contends that, given the realities of available healthcare, through which only a very small proportion of patients have the opportunity to undergo long-term psychotherapy, it would be irresponsible to not take advantage of LSD treatment if it was available.[13] Ultimately, then, Jungian-oriented therapists Sandison and Cutner (like Grof, Cohen, and many other psychedelic therapists) maintain that, when patients are treated with appropriate therapeutic support, the benefits outweigh the risks.

Sandison and Whitelaw reported in 1957 that they were successfully able to treat patients with obsessional neuroses and psychopathic personalities through LSD-enhanced therapy. They also reported that LSD treatment failed to help patients diagnosed with an actual or latent psychosis or with "inadequate personality," the latter of which they noted was notoriously difficult to assess.[14] These early treatment results, in addition to the overall complexity of issues concerning subject readiness, clearly suggest the need for further study of the relationship between personality traits, subject readiness, and successful psychedelic-enhanced therapy.

Similar questions arise, of course, when using psychedelic-enhanced therapy to treat people for adverse reactions to a past psychedelic experience. When treatment for such adverse effects does not involve psychedelic substances, we should judge the patient's readiness by criteria used for conventional PTSD treatment.

Another seemingly obvious implication is the likelihood that a person who had an adverse reaction to a psychedelic experience wasn't ready for the experience in the first place. Yet here, too, the issue is complex. Other factors certainly contribute to and perhaps even largely account for an adverse reaction. Lack of preparation and the wrong setting are the most obvious answers. I have been struck repeatedly by reports of difficult psychedelic experiences that could have triggered a psychotic reaction—yet didn't do so.[15] Most people, including people who are *not* psychologically mature, appear to benefit from difficult psychedelic experiences when they are in the right setting with skilled and committed interpersonal support.

The Therapist and the Dialectical Relationship

As we have seen, the dialectical relationship between analyst and patient is important for Jung. And I have emphasized the critical role that interpersonal support plays in successful psychedelic-enhanced therapy. It follows, then, that the relationship between the patient and therapist in psychedelic treatment is crucial.

Jung's imperative that all analysts must have undergone analysis corresponds to the prevalent expectation that psychedelic therapists should, in addition to their therapeutic training, be personally familiar with the psychedelic experience.[16] How can therapists who have not experienced the trials and transformations of a psychedelic experience understand and support others during psychedelic therapy? This doesn't mean that therapists who have had many psychedelic experiences have the interpersonal sensitivity needed to be an effective psychedelic therapist. That is, therapeutic training and psychedelic experience are necessary but not sufficient requirements for a psychedelic therapist. Should therapists practicing conventional psychotherapy be psychedelically experienced before treating someone for an adverse reaction? Such experience could help establish rapport with a patient trying to come to terms with a difficult psychedelic experience. But it shouldn't be required. Although any skilled and sensitive therapist would be qualified to help such a person, I clearly think a Jungian analyst would bring an especially useful perspective to this work.

Considering the significant similarities between psychedelic experience and non-drug experiences of the unconscious, it is worth asking whether a psychedelically *inexperienced* analyst who is familiar with the archetypal realities of the unconscious would be qualified to conduct a psychedelic therapy session. There are no doubt such therapists who could provide skillful and sensitive support during a psychedelic session. Some may even be more qualified than the average psychedelically experienced therapist. Still, all other things being equal, I think it is always best that anyone conducting a psychedelic session have personal knowledge of the profound shifts in reality one can encounter during a psychedelic experience.

The relationship between analyst and patient, as Jung characterizes it, has several notable implications for psychedelic-enhanced psychotherapy. To begin with, the psychedelic therapist should exercise self-criticism, especially when a patient's resistance may be warranted. "The view that the patient's resistances are in no circumstances justified is completely fallacious," Jung maintains. "The resistance might very well prove that the treatment rests on false assumptions."[17] This speaks to the complex matter of using psychedelics to overcome a person's resistance, as I discussed above. Jung writes more about this issue in "The Aims of Psychotherapy":

> The resistances of the patient may be valuable signposts. I am inclined to take deep-seated resistances seriously at first, paradoxical as this

may sound, for I am convinced that the doctor does not necessarily know better than the patient's own psychic condition, of which the patient himself may be quite unconscious. This modesty on the part of the doctor is altogether becoming in view of the fact that there is not only no generally valid psychology today but rather an untold variety of temperaments and of more or less individual psyches that refuse to fit into any scheme.[18]

In reference to dream interpretation, Jung points out that analysts can reach a point where they don't understand their patients' dreams. Rather than projecting their own confusion onto their patients, and accusing them of resistance, therapists would do well to admit their lack of understanding. When the patient puts too much reliance on her therapist's understanding, she "loses all sense of reality, falls into a stubborn transference, and retards the cure."[19] For Jung, the individuality of the patient is central, and therefore "every development in the patient is to be regarded as valid."[20] Therapists should provide their patients with the psychological knowledge that allows patients to free themselves from medical authority as quickly as possible, Jung suggests.[21]

Jung's views in this regard are certainly worth bearing in mind when a person's dependence on the therapist is intensified during psychedelic-enhanced work. The relationship between therapist and patient becomes especially susceptible to imbalance when the patient's vulnerability is amplified in a psychedelic state. Jung reminds us that by no means

can the treatment be anything but the product of mutual influence, in which the whole being of the doctor as well as that of his patient plays its part. In the treatment there is an encounter between two irrational factors: that is to say, between two persons who are not fixed and determinable quantities but who bring with them, besides their more or less clearly defined fields of consciousness, an indefinitely extended sphere of non-consciousness. . . . For two personalities to meet is like mixing two different chemical substances: if there is any combination at all, both are transformed. . . . You can exert no influence if you are not susceptible to influence. It is futile for the doctor to shield himself from the influence of the patient and to surround himself with a smokescreen of fatherly and professional authority.[22]

We can see how complex the patient-therapist relationship becomes during psychedelic-enhanced therapy when we consider that, on the one hand, the patient needs to have complete trust in the therapist. But on the other hand, the patient should not have to bestow authority on the therapist. That's a challenging distinction to maintain even in a normal state of consciousness.

The Compensating Function

As far as I know, Margot Cutner's 1959 paper, "Analytic Work with LSD 25," on her use of LSD as an aid to Jungian analysis is the only paper written by a Jungian analyst who has practiced psychedelic-enhanced psychotherapy.[23] During three years of conducting psycholytic therapy with LSD, Cutner observed that the unconscious images emerging during LSD sessions show a clear compensatory relationship to the patient's current psychological needs.[24] The way unconscious images complement consciousness during LSD sessions, Cutner notes, resembles the way images that emerge in dreams, visions, and active imagination complement consciousness in conventional analysis. Indeed, Cutner points out that the psychological phenomena she observed during LSD psychotherapy with many patients over several years seem to confirm—even more clearly than the phenomena observed in conventional analysis—Jung's conception of the psyche as a self-regulating system striving toward wholeness. Looking at this psychedelic-induced content, Cutner explains, "it appears as if something like an autonomous selective process is at work, determining the sequence of the emerging material in a purposive way—as if whatever emerges is just what is 'needed' for any particular patient at any particular time, as a factor complementing the conscious personality."[25] Therapists helping people integrate material that has emerged during a psychedelic session need to consider Jung's advice that it is always useful to ask what conscious attitude the dream is compensating.[26] Because psychedelic experiences, like dreams, are occasions for compensatory unconscious content to emerge into consciousness, this would surely be a fruitful line of inquiry for anyone attempting to understand and integrate a psychedelic experience.

The Significance of the Collective Unconscious

"The most healing, and psychologically the most necessary, experiences are a 'treasure hard to attain,' and its acquisition demands something out of the common," Jung observes. "This something out of the common proves, in practical work with the patient, to be an invasion by archetypal contents."[27] After observing patients undergoing LSD psychotherapy in the early 1950s, Sandison reported that, in addition to experiencing sensory impressions and hallucinations, and reliving forgotten childhood memories, his patients experienced archaic, impersonal images "exactly similar in nature to those experiences of the collective unconscious which patients undergoing deep analysis experience in their dreams, visual impressions, and fantasies. All these images are, moreover, felt with a degree of vividness and a sense of certainty concerning their reality and personal importance which is remarkable and convincing. Furthermore, these more primitive LSD experiences are accompanied by a sense of their agelessness and timeless quality which is the hallmark of the great archetypes of the collective unconscious."[28] Despite the value of coming to terms with personal images and feelings that LSD can release, Sandison maintains that other clues to the patient's disorder can be found in a "conscious relationship to the more universal aspects of psychic life."[29] He gives an example of such treatment with a 25-year-old woman suffering from depression and suicidal tendencies.

Sandison's patient had undergone electroconvulsive therapy and eighteen months of psychotherapy with another therapist before her LSD psychotherapy. She had a history of morbid thoughts about any man with whom she became involved. She was convinced, for instance, that one of her partners was a murderer who meant to harm her. She had tried to counteract these thoughts by participating in church life, but she found that her worst thoughts came to her in church. During her LSD sessions, the young woman had dramatic encounters with archetypal imagery. The most significant of these images was the snake, Sandison notes, which the woman came to recognize as part of herself. "The snake tended to behave autonomously, as the unconscious does when it is not accepted and integrated into consciousness," Sandison explains.[30] He goes on to present the woman's own account:

> I had the sensation as in my first LSD treatment of a snake curling up round me. I felt very sick and dizzy. I then began to see serpents' faces all over the wall—then I saw myself as a fat, pot-bellied snake slithering gaily away to destruction. I felt horrified and thought "whose destruction?" I then realized it was my own destruction—I was destroying myself. . . . [I realized how I was destroying myself] by carrying on this affair with this married man—how all the better side of me was gradually being destroyed through carrying on this affair and I knew it must cease and knew that I must never see him again.[31]

The unconscious is not a demonic monster, says Jung. It is a natural entity that is morally neutral and becomes dangerous only when we have the wrong conscious attitude toward it. "To the degree that we repress it, its danger increases," Jung explains. "But the moment the patient begins to assimilate contents that were previously unconscious, its danger diminishes. The dissociation of personality, the anxious division of the day-time and the night-time sides of the psyche, cease with progressive assimilation."[32]

The patient who saw herself as a snake continues to describe how Sandison helped her consciously relate to her LSD visions by asking her questions that led her to see connections between her visions and her childhood experiences and feelings. Continuing her account of the psychedelic session, she reports,

> I then had the feeling of being back in ancient Egypt lying at the bottom of a well with high walls round and Egyptian faces all round the walls and something hovering over me. I said to the Doctor, "Something terrible is going to happen to me"—I felt as though a huge whitish snake was hovering over the top of me and might drop on me at any minute. Then I had the feeling that I was the Devil—I could see my long, pointed tail curling round the back of the Doctor. I thought, "Poor Doctor, he doesn't know he is sitting with the Devil."[33]

Sandison comments that the young woman's experience of becoming the serpent and the Devil shows how easily one can become possessed by and identify with an archetype.[34] The ease with which a person can fall into unconscious identification with an archetypal complex during a psychedelic experience suggests the important role the therapist plays in representing ego-consciousness for her. Powerful moments of identification with an archetype are characteristic of LSD therapy, Sandison observes. At times like these, "it was all too easy [for the therapist] to enter the patient's mythical world and thus lose one's ability to represent the one stable, sane point in the patient's experience." (I return to this topic in the next section on integration.) Sandison was able to successfully guide his patient to a clear conscious understanding of her difficult experience. "Much had to be integrated which involved several months of psychotherapy," he recalls, "But the process had started."[35]

The woman's progress is also reflected in her own account: "After the Doctor had gone, I had a vision of myself in Hell—of being dragged out by chains—the Doctor and other people were pulling me out and I was very reluctant to come out. I had all sorts of queer dizzy feelings—of patterns and colours all whizzing round in circles and I felt very tired but also a sense of happiness—as though I had sorted out quite a lot of problems under this LSD."[36]

It is critical, Sandison explains, that therapists help patients understand that even though these psychedelic-induced phenomena are illusions, they are also manifestations of something real. Moreover, he adds, therapists must help patients understand that if they are committed to integrating the material that has emerged, their experiences can bear fruit.[37] Clearly, any therapist assisting a person during a psychedelic session or treating a person who has suffered a psychedelic-induced trauma would benefit from an understanding of the collective unconscious and its role in healing. Such knowledge would also help counteract the misunderstanding that bizarre and shocking psychedelic-induced images, and even a psychotic reaction to a psychedelic experience, are merely reflections of a psychological disorder.

Integration and the Role of Ego-Consciousness

Sandison reports that at one point in the LSD treatment of his patient who saw herself as a snake, the young woman wished she could resume the electroconvulsive therapy that she had received some years earlier. Sandison interprets this as "probably a desire to avoid the unconscious, a wish to be made well from outside which is quite contrary to the need for understanding and accepting the unconscious which LSD or analysis demands."[38] Sandison's observation touches on the defenses that can arise when the unconscious is opened by psychedelics. A person can naturally bolt at a terrifying encounter with the archetypal unconscious. Yet, as we've seen, these same defenses can provide the opportunity for psychological development and healing. Cutner suggests that the form and intensity of LSD-induced defenses reveal something about a person's psychopathology. "In fighting the drug, defense mechanisms, which play a part in the patient's make-up anyway, seem usually to become reinforced and thus made more clearly distinguishable for the analyst," she says.[39] If the therapist explains these defenses to the patient, Cutner adds, the patient can perceive them more distinctly, too.

This brings us to the important role the therapist plays in mediating and supporting ego-consciousness on behalf of the patient in psychedelic-enhanced psychotherapy. Cutner points out that some people are clearly aware that their experiences are drug-induced during psychedelic-enhanced therapy. They can maintain the onlooker role within a part of themselves, she notes, similar to the attitude a person takes in active imagination.[40] Sandison confirms that sometimes people are able to consciously relate to images released during the psychedelic experience. The ability to move actively amongst such images, Sandison notes, "is one of the most useful properties that LSD may confer on a patient."[41]

Cutner explains, however, that the closer patients are to a psychotic condition, the more they tend to identify with and become absorbed by their psychedelic-induced visions and hallucinations. When a person is absorbed in such a psychedelic-induced state, someone must be present to keep him from dangerously acting out, she says.[42] Jung's description of the mind's inability to assimilate unconscious content characterizes well the condition occurring in such a psychedelic-induced state: "If the conscious mind proves incapable of assimilating the new contents pouring in from the unconscious, then a dangerous situation arises in which they keep their original, chaotic, and archaic form and consequently disrupt the unity of consciousness. The resultant mental disturbance is therefore advisedly called schizophrenia, since it is a madness due to the splitting of the mind."[43] But the danger that a psychedelic experience will push one from a temporary or a latent psychosis into a chronic psychosis is less than one might expect, Cutner maintains, "as long as the analyst is present during the crucial experiences and can represent the integrating ego-function for the patient."[44] If the therapist can also give the patient the reassurance that he or she so greatly needs at these times, which may include the most elementary comfort, physical touch, Cutner adds, the healing potential of the archetypal images may be realized.[45] Cutner is referring, of course, to what Jung characterizes as the emergence of archetypal content, "the most healing, and psychologically the most necessary," of experiences.[46]

Sandison maintains that even after a successful LSD-induced abreaction of a trauma, the factors that condition a person's psychopathology must be worked out in a conscious relationship to the unconscious. And he raises a fundamental question: How shall the therapist take a person through the "long drawn out process of coming to terms with and assimilating the unconscious?"[47] Sandison's question brings us back to Cutner's statement that the danger involved in psychotic reactions to archetypal content is less than one might expect—"as long as the analyst is present during the crucial experiences and can represent the integrating ego-function for the patient."[48] Because, as Sandison explains, the patient requires "a strong and lively consciousness to absorb his discoveries."[49] If the patient is not able to bring consciousness to the images emerging from the unconscious, the therapist may need to mediate this function.

The psychedelic therapist faces an especially difficult decision at this point. The patient may be able to retain enough consciousness to integrate released content during the LSD session, says Cutner.[50] Sandison confirms this, saying that reliving a traumatic event and associated emotions during LSD-assisted therapy can take place "in a clear setting of consciousness, which can be discussed between patient and therapist at the time and subsequently."[51] Both Cutner and Sandison think, however, that it is generally best not to interrupt or influence the person's inner process by offering interpretations during the psychedelic session. There is always time for interpretation in subsequent interviews, Cutner says. On the other hand, she adds, even during the psychedelic session, "experiences of a predominantly archaic character may persist for a certain length of time; it is, in the main, the task of the analyst to find the right time for breaking the archaic experience and integrating it, by interpretation or action, into the patient's consciousness."[52]

A poignant example of a therapist breaking an overpowering psychedelic-induced experience in an attempt to mediate consciousness for his patient can be found in *Shivitti: A Vision*. The book is Israeli writer Yehiel De-Nur's account of his LSD-enhanced treatment for trauma associated with his internment by the Nazis at the Auschwitz concentration camp.

As De-Nur struggled with tormenting psychedelic-induced images and excruciating pain, his therapist would sometimes attempt to intervene by asking De-Nur to vocalize what he was seeing and feeling. (The following quotes are from various passages in Yehiel De-Nur's account; they did not occur together in the book or in the therapy.)

"Who do you see, Mr. De-Nur? What do you see? Speak, tell me—."

"What are you feeling, Mr. De-Nur? Let me in, Mr. De-Nur."

"Tell us, Mr. De-Nur, what's frightening you?"

"What do you see, Mr. De-Nur? What hurts? What—do—you—see?"

"What is frightening you, Mr. De-Nur? Whom do you see? Whom are you crying to?"

"Who are you screaming at, Mr. De-Nur?"[53]

De-Nur explains that his LSD treatment required a conscious effort on his part to "raise the events from subconscious to memory and from memory to vision and from vision to speech."[54] Dr. Jan Bastiaans, De-Nur's therapist and a specialist in treating Concentration Camp Syndrome, explains in the book's postscript that LSD treatment offers his patients the opportunity of "reliving the inferno of their trauma of decades ago, with a difference: this time they will not go it alone in hell. This time, if they consent to the process, they will have a chance to free themselves from the prison of their memory."[55]

The process Bastiaans refers to clearly entails becoming conscious of the most horrific and painful unconscious images and emotions. "Each image, each fantasy and each feeling is not only important to the patient," Sandison says, "but must be explored by the therapist for it to be understood and integrated by the patient."[56] Sandison describes the integration process in psychedelic-enhanced psychotherapy as a "thrusting to and fro from outer (i.e., normal) consciousness to inner consciousness (the experience of the unconscious during LSD treatment) and back again." This process, he explains, is inherently healing.[57] Jung describes this back and forth movement from outer to inner consciousness as a "mutual penetration of conscious and unconscious, and not a one-sided evaluation, interpretation, and deformation of unconscious contents by the conscious mind."[58]

Sandison also thinks that psychedelic therapists should attempt to guide their patients to the point where they can actively assimilate the images that arise during the LSD session. This allows them to consciously explore their mind and thereby "learn something from the great wisdom of the unconscious."[59] Cutner, as I showed in chapter 10, helped a depressed and paranoid woman learn to consciously relate to psychedelic-induced imagery that initially overwhelmed her. Cutner explains that "as the pit had turned from a place of utter humiliation into an archetypal 'womb,' so her inner storm center had turned into a center of stillness. In both these instances the presence of the analyst as the 'good' and 'nourishing' mother had still been necessary; later it was the process of introversion, with or without the actual presence of the analyst, which provided the 'womb' inside which rebirth experiences could take place."[60] Jung describes the process this way: "The work done by the patient through the progressive assimilation of unconscious contents leads ultimately to the integration of [his or her] personality and hence to the removal of the neurotic dissociation."[61]

Sandison says that resolving the dissociation through psychedelic-enhanced psychotherapy comes only after a period of integration. Integration, he reports, may continue for months or even years after the conclusion of the psychedelic treatment itself.[62] Treating adverse reactions to psychedelic-induced trauma and psychotic states would entail essentially the same integration process. The lengthy integration process Sandison describes is consistent with Jung's advice to his clients to patiently live with and consciously relate to manifestations of unconscious images and feelings during the practice of active imagination.[63]

The ongoing integration that Sandison describes is also consistent with Jung's approach to dream interpretation. In "The Practical Use of Dream-Analysis," Jung writes that dreams provide information about the psyche's hidden inner life and reveal aspects of the personality that underlie a person's symptoms. To effectively treat an individual, "we must bring about a change in and through the unconscious." Yet treatment "can be achieved only by the thorough and conscious assimilation of unconscious contents."[64] To a great extent Sandison and Cutner base their approach to LSD psychotherapy on Jung's approach to interpreting and integrating unconscious images that arise during the dream state. "The material produced under the influence of LSD," Sandison observes, "bears a striking similarity to the dream and fantasy material of patients undergoing deep analysis."[65] And patients undergoing LSD psychotherapy "start to dream, and these dreams frequently reveal material showing continuity with the LSD experience itself."[66]

Sandison presents an account given by one of his patients, a 29-year-old woman who was born in Germany, that illustrates this process. (By my calculations, based on her age and the approximate years of her treatment with Sandison, the woman was a teenager during the rise of fascism in Germany.) The kinds of images described in this woman's account, and portrayed in the paintings she made following her LSD sessions, led Sandison to conclude that LSD opens up the deeper, archetypal levels of the unconscious just as do the dreams of some patients during analysis. "[The images] are not an end in themselves," he says, "but they are indications that individuation is an attainable goal."[67]

The woman's account of her LSD sessions begins with her seeing a face of a one-eyed man with a moustache and a cynical, threatening smile. "I tried to connect him to something which had happened to me a long time ago. It was then that he got mixed up with Hitler and I saw nothing but swastikas. For one brief moment it was my father's face."[68] She then remembers an actual occasion when a German officer took her to his home and seduced her.

In her account, she explains that under LSD she was most disturbed by the realization that she was forced by the officer against her will without showing the slightest resistance. "As I pondered over this, Hitler appeared again and I saw the connection. He too, in a very subtle way, together with his powerful personality, made me do things against my will without my resisting. Then I had a feeling of falling down deeper and deeper and yet I felt detached just as if I was watching it all happen."[69] In subsequent LSD sessions, the woman sees more images of Hitler, hostile faces, skulls and crossbones. "Suddenly," she recalls, "I felt the flesh falling off my bones."[70] Similarly disturbing experiences continued through several LSD sessions, and she became depressed and suicidal. She described her tenth LSD session as follows:

> There is tremendous confusion within me. There is no harmony. The muddled faces had terrific mouths and tried to swallow me up. I feel that they would swallow me up only as long as they were in such a muddle and it was therefore necessary to find order in this confusion. I then found that there was order in this confusion insofar as there were two sides to it, each opposing the other and pulling in two directions. I tried to find out about the two parts and discovered that they must be the good and evil in me.[71]

She then had a dream in which she couldn't make love with her partner. In the dream, she reports, something inside her told her that she couldn't make love because she had "not picked up the five heavy stones from the bottom of the sea."[72] During the next LSD session, Sandison reports, she decided to investigate what she felt was the solution to all her problems. "I felt I must overcome my fear and go to the bottom of the sea," she says. "Then I started going down," she continues,

> but under the water I met alligators who were eating me up and I could feel their teeth in my body. I went down under the water again and as I went deeper the fear grew less. I could see the stones, but now they were only four in number. It was as if the fifth had represented the fear

which was now gone. With this stone gone I had a better view of the others. I came closer and closer and suddenly it was as if I was looking in a mirror. These four stones formed a face. I cannot describe its ugliness and horribleness. At the same time the face was beautiful. I could not say what piece was ugly and what was beautiful, for in it were both extremes completely merging and forming a whole. I felt that these were my anchors and on these I had to build up my personality. I knew too that this was the same in all of us and everything alive. I had a feeling that what I had just seen was part of God.[73]

As Ronald Sandison suggests, the images depicted here are not an end in themselves; but in Jungian terms, while the patient works with them consciously, they reflect a movement toward wholeness.[74]

Conclusion

Our debt to Carl Jung cannot be repaid, suggests Michael Fordham, unless we have studied his work, discovered aspects of it that need to be developed, and built fruitfully on what he left for us.[1] In that spirit, I have suggested that the time is ripe for a critical inquiry into Jung's approach to psychedelic experience and into his views concerning the risks of psychedelic psychotherapy. Like many others who are indebted to Jung for his penetrating insights into the nature of the psyche, I have questioned some of his views and felt impelled to build on his work in ways he perhaps would neither have imagined nor approved. It seems likely, in any case, that Jung would appreciate the inevitable development of divergent views around this aspect of his thought. Remarking on the vitality that divergent interpretations, views, and theories bring to any field of inquiry, Jung asserts that "disagreements are, as always, incentives to a new and deeper questioning."[2]

Concluding his 1963 review of LSD-enhanced psychotherapy, Ronald Sandison observed that despite increasing certainty among therapists that psychedelic-enhanced therapy is a valuable form of treatment, many questions remain unanswered.[3] As a result of widespread irresponsible use of psychedelics, hostile public attitudes fed by sensational media coverage, and, especially, legal restrictions on psychedelic research, many questions still remain unanswered today, half a century after Sandison's assessment. Nonetheless, the recent resurgence of research is reviving the study of psychedelic experience and its potential for psychological healing and transformation.

This book shows that Jungian psychology can contribute to this research, can advance our understanding of adverse reactions to a psychedelic experience, and can improve the practice of psychedelic-enhanced therapy. Jung's fundamental explanation of psychedelic experience as a lowering of the threshold of consciousness, which allows unconscious material to enter consciousness and potentially overwhelm it, provides an excellent foundation for understanding psychedelic experiences in general. The framework I present here builds on Jung's approach to the dynamic relationship between consciousness and the unconscious by showing how Jung's understanding of trauma, the shadow, and psychosis elucidates the nature of adverse reactions to a psychedelic experience and leads to valuable implications for treating them. Jung's idea of the numinous archetypal images that can emerge into consciousness from the collective unconscious, and his explanation of the way in which those images can overwhelm consciousness, provide especially valuable insights into the most challenging adverse reactions, psychedelic-induced psychotic states. Margot Cutner and Ronald Sandison have demonstrated that Jungians can use knowledge about psychedelic experience to shed light on the psyche's fundamental dynamics. As new research expands that body of knowledge, Jungians will have an increasingly rich source of data from which to draw. A more widespread awareness of Jungian insights into psychedelic experiences and their integration could also encourage a deeper respect for psychedelics among those who use them freely. Psychedelic substances are, after all, still widely used recreationally and ritually with only superficial preparation and support.

Perhaps this investigation's most important implication is that Jung's methods of integration provide a uniquely nuanced and thorough way to integrate psychedelic experiences. Cutner and Sandison have shown that Jung's methods can be used at suitable times by skilled therapists to encourage patients to integrate unconscious images and emotions during their psychedelic sessions. Jung's thoughts on the analyst's responsibility and the dialectical relationship between analyst and patient suggest valuable implications for therapists during a psychedelic session, when a patient is especially sensitive to a therapist's attitude and influence.

Over the course of this investigation, I have developed a greater respect for Jung's warning about the dangers inherent in psychedelic experience. My attitude toward Jung's criticism of psychedelic psychotherapy softened when I realized that his concern for its risks reflected his concern for the risks of psychotherapy in general. That is, I realized that Jung's cautions weren't simply a prejudiced reaction to a practice he didn't understand.

It's clear, nonetheless, that Jung's views on psychedelic psychotherapy were prejudiced, and his bias has pushed psychedelic investigation beyond the pale of respectable Jungian inquiry. I find this regrettable because over the course of this investigation I have also gained a greater respect for the knowledge and experience that Jungian analysts embody; and I have no doubt that Jungians could make a valuable contribution to understanding psychedelic experience and to assessing the relative risks and benefits of psychedelic-enhanced psychotherapy.

I'm not implying that Jungians should become proponents of psychedelic psychotherapy. Although this therapy has significant potential, its practice is too complex for anyone to advocate its benefits without acknowledging its risks. But the participation of Jungians in psychedelic research would bring a more eclectic perspective to the work. The critical perspective that Jungians contribute to this work should, however, be more informed and balanced than it has been in the past.

So many issues require objective investigation. Indeed, one of the most important insights I take away from this inquiry is the useful complexity inherent in a Jungian interpretation of psychedelic experience. As I said in the last chapter, this complexity seems most apparent when considering a person's readiness for psychedelic psychotherapy. Yet complexity runs all through this Jungian interpretation of psychedelic experience. It's especially apparent in the destructive versus transformative potential of these experiences. This complexity is also apparent in questions about the passive versus active role of consciousness during psychedelic psychotherapy and about the value of integration versus abreaction in treating trauma.

Toward the end of his paper on the transcendent function, Jung writes that the psyche's integration "is not a partial process running a conditioned course; it is a total and integral event in which all aspects are, or should be, included. *The affect must therefore be deployed in its full strength.*"[4] (my italics) Although I don't think Jung (or Grof, for that matter) would consider this an absolute rule, Jung seems to suggest here that therapeutic integration might even be taken to the same emotional and experiential extremes that Grof thinks are necessary for the successful healing of trauma through abreaction.

This suggests that the two approaches may be more compatible than is initially apparent, thus opening a fruitful line of inquiry into the ways in which therapeutic integration could be combined with psychedelic-induced abreaction. Recalling Margot Cutner's observation that future psychological development can become blocked when material that arises during psychedelic psychotherapy isn't fully integrated into consciousness, and recalling Grof's assertion that the best way to heal trauma is through full experiential engagement with the traumatic event, I can conceive an approach to psychedelic psychotherapy that draws from both Cutner and Grof. Cutner relies on Jung's method of therapeutic integration; she uses LSD as sparingly as possible and emphasizes analysis. Grof relies heavily on the inherent healing potential of LSD-induced abreaction, which he maintains should be carried to emotional and experiential extremes.[5] An approach that draws from Cutner and Grof would offer therapists a broad range of treatment options to match the diverse needs of people undergoing psychedelic psychotherapy or working through psychedelic-induced traumas.

In closing, I would like to return to a passage I quoted earlier, a passage from Jung's *Psychological Commentary on The Tibetan Book of the Great Liberation*. Usually, says Jung,

> the conscious standpoint arbitrarily decides against the unconscious, since anything coming from inside suffers from the prejudice of being regarded as inferior or somehow wrong. But in the cases with which we are here concerned it is tacitly agreed that the apparently incompatible contents shall not be suppressed again, and that the conflict shall be accepted and suffered. At first no solution appears possible, and this fact, too, has to be borne with patience.[6]

This passage takes on new significance, I believe, when we have studied Jung's approach to the terrifying darkness we can encounter in the depths of the unconscious, and when we have come to appreciate Jung's insights into the transformative potential of that confrontation. As I have tried to show, the significance of all this is profoundly relevant to the numinous realms opened to us by psychedelic experience.

Notes

Preface

1. Eliade, 1964, p. 486.
2. Ibid., p. 484.
3. Jung, 1966a, p. 78, para. 119.
4. I use the generic terms psychedelic-enhanced psychotherapy, psychedelic-enhanced therapy, and psychedelic psychotherapy interchangeably throughout this book to refer to the use of psychedelic substances for psychotherapeutic purposes. In chapter 2, I introduce two specific models of psychedelic-enhanced therapy: psychedelic therapy and psycholytic therapy.
5. These further explorations would certainly include what Robert Aziz describes as Jung's synchronistic model of the psyche.

Part 1: Encountering the Unconscious

1. Jung, 1969w, p. 460, para. 746.

Chapter 1: Jung's Confrontation with the Unconscious and Its Relation to Psychedelic Experience

1. Jung, 1963, p. 179.
2. Ibid., p. 181.
3. Ibid., p. 188.
4. Ibid., pp. 188–189.
5. Estevez, 2010.
6. Ibid.
7. Ibid.
8. Ibid.
9. Jung, 1966e, p. 240, para. 406.
10. Ibid.
11. Wulff, 1997, p. 470.
12. Jung, 1966a, p. 119, para. 201.

13. Ibid.
14. Jung, 1963, p. 199.
15. Hofmann, 2005, p. 73.
16. Huxley, 1999, p. 107. *Hallucinogens and Hallucinogenic*, the terms commonly used within the fields of medicine and law, emphasize the striking potential these substances have to enhance and distort perception. Although these terms are commonly used in psychiatric research, they remain problematic for many in the field. By emphasizing perceptual distortions and delusions, and by implying inherently deleterious effects, these terms, like *psychotomimetic*, carry more limiting and negative connotations than *psychedelic*. The word *psychedelic* is burdened by its own problematic associations—associations with the counterculture excesses of the 1960s, in particular. The word *psychedelic* also emphasizes the mental aspects of the experience. Many in the field therefore prefer terms such as *psychoactive substances, psychoactive sacraments, entheogens,* or *sacred medicines*. The question of their relative merit is nonetheless currently an open question in the field. I sympathize with the various arguments for preferring one term over another, and for this reason, depending on the context of the discussion, I tend to use most of them. I think, nevertheless, that the terms *psychedelic* and *psycholytic* convey the most straightforward and neutral attitude toward the nature of the experience itself. I use the word *psychedelic*, rather than *psycholytic*, for this book because it is widely understood.
17. Grinspoon & Bakalar, 1997, p. 9.
18. Grof, 2001a, p. 309.
19. Grof, 2001b, p. 32.
20. Huxley, 1963, p. 26.
21. Huxley, 1999, p. 29.
22. I prefer the term *psychedelic substances* over *psychedelic drugs* because the group includes plants, mushrooms, and other natural substances that aren't adequately subsumed within the general concept of a drug.
23. Cohen, 1985, pp. 294, 295. See also Cohen, 1960, 1967.
24. Cohen, 1966, p. 186. See also, Cohen & Ditman, 1963, p. 480.
25. Smith & Seymour, 1985, p. 298. David Smith invited Timothy Leary to a conference on psychedelics in San Francisco in the late 1960s. Smith enjoyed his bright and personable guest, but when Smith invited him to visit the Haight Ashbury Clinic, Leary wasn't interested. (Smith, personal communication, April 23, 2013)
26. Stevens, 1987, pp. 370–371.
27. From the National Survey on Drug Use and Health, 2009. The 2008 National Survey on Drug Use and Health reported that in 2006 over

twenty-three million people had used LSD in their lifetime. Government statistics on the use of psychedelic, or hallucinogenic, substances vary from source to source. Some of the surveys include drugs such as MDMA (or "Ecstasy") and PCP, which many experts would not consider psychedelic substances. In any case, the numbers of uninformed and unsupported users of classic psychedelics—teenagers, for the most part—are striking.
28. Sessa, 2011; Corbyn, 2013.
29. Studies are in development or have been completed in the United States at Harvard Medical School, Johns Hopkins University, Purdue University, Harbor-UCLA Medical Center, University of California, San Francisco, among others; and in Europe at Norwegian University of Science and Technology, University of Maastricht, the Netherlands, The KEY Institute for Brain-Mind Research at Zurich, and the Swiss Medical Society for Psycholytic Therapy; University College, and The Imperial College of Science, Technology and Medicine, London; University of Heidelberg, Hanover Medical School, and University of Ulm, Germany; among other research centers around the world. The expansion of government-approved research is developing so quickly that any list I include here will soon be out of date. The Multidisciplinary Association for Psychedelic Studies (MAPS) documents research it sponsors at http://www.maps.org/research/mdma/ and documents international advances in psychedelic research at http://www.maps.org/research/ (Retrieved July 6, 2013)
30. Griffiths et al., 2006.
31. Griffiths et al., 2008, p. 631.
32. Johnson et al., 2008.
33. Richards, 2009, p. 141. See also Richards, 2003.
34. Jung, 1969k, p. 510, para. 833.
35. Leary, Metzner, & Alpert, 1995, p. 23.
36. Jung, 1969o, p. 489, para. 780.
37. Ibid., para. 779.
38. I discuss Jung's concepts of the conscious mind, or "consciousness," and the unconscious mind, or "the unconscious," in chapter 3, "Basic Jungian Concepts and Principles." Very briefly, however, we can say that Jung classifies the contents and functions of the psyche into their conscious and unconscious aspects. The conscious aspect includes all ideas, emotions, perceptions, and other psychological elements that a person recognizes or has awareness of. The ego, or what is also known as the self (always with a lower case *s*), is for Jung the center or subject of consciousness, and therefore the center of a person's identity. The unconscious, for Jung, consists of all psychological "contents and processes

that are not conscious, i.e., not related to the ego in any perceptible way." (Jung, 1976, p. 483, para. 837) Jung classifies the unconscious into the *personal* and the *collective* unconscious. The personal unconscious contains sensations, perceptions, ideas, images, and emotions that are derived from personal experience but which one has forgotten, repressed, or didn't consciously notice in the first place. The collective unconscious consists of the psychological content that each of us has inherited from our evolutionary past and therefore shares with all other human beings. Jung often discusses the universal nature of this content in terms of archetypes, psychological images that have been expressed through the ages in such mythological motifs as birth, death, the mother, the hero, or the evil demon. The archetypal nature of the collective unconscious lends a numinous, or strange and fascinating, quality to psychological experience, a quality that engages our emotions and is difficult to comprehend intellectually. In his description of his own descent into the collective unconscious, his "confrontation with the unconscious," Jung attempts to convey the numinous quality of this archetypal world.
39. Jung, 1969o, p. 489, para. 780.
40. Jung, 1969k, p. 521, para. 849. Regarding the use of the term *self* vs. *Self*, see note 58 for chap. 3.
41. Shulgin, 2001, p. 200.
42. Metzner, 1998b, chap. 6.
43. Grof, 1985, pp. 187–192; see also pp. 131, 140–141, 379.
44. I know of three possible exceptions to this omission in the Jungian literature: Most notably, Jungian analyst and author Ian Baker's *LSD 25 and Analytical Psychology* was published in 1970 by the Clinic and Research Center for Jungian Psychology in Zurich. Despite my extensive preliminary research, I learned of this apparently obscure but no doubt valuable work by word of mouth only days before submitting my final manuscript for publication. I regret that I am not able to discuss Baker's work here, but I look forward to doing so in the future. In *Anatomy of the Psyche: Alchemical Symbolism in Psychotherapy*, Edward Edinger includes a very brief account of a woman's LSD experience, an "important experience," he says, one of the kind of experiences that "bear witness to the reality of the psyche." (1994, pp. 130, 131, n. 20) Donald Lee Williams' *Border Crossings: A Psychological Perspective on Carlos Castaneda's Path of Knowledge* is a Jungian analysis of Castaneda's shamanic apprenticeship as portrayed in his don Juan novels. Williams analyzes Castaneda's psychedelic-based spiritual practice, but his treatment of psychedelic experience *per se* is subordinate to his analysis of Castaneda's psychospiritual development.
45. See Singer, 1994, pp. 408–410; von Franz, 1993, pp. 297–305.

46. Jung, 1975b, p. 222.
47. Ibid., p. 224.
48. Jung, 1975a, p. 173.
49. Samuels, 2008.

Chapter 2: Psychedelic Psychotherapy

1. See Grof, 2001a, pp. 116–117; Passie, 1997, pp. 14–15.
2. There are no clear-cut boundaries between what are considered low, medium, and high dosages. Dose ranges are typically given for LSD, the prototypical psychedelic substance; and although these ranges vary somewhat from source to source, the amounts I give here represent the general range. Note also that one microgram equals one millionth of a gram.
3. Sandison, 1997, p. 65; Grof, 2001a, p. 35.
4. See endnote 38 in chapter 1 for a very brief description of these and related terms. See "Consciousness and the Unconscious" in chapter 3 for a more extensive discussion of these terms.
5. Grof, 2001a, pp. 35–36; Grob, 2002d, pp. 273–274. Sandison and Cutner's Jungian-oriented practice was a notable exception to the prevalent Freudian orientation.
6. Stolaroff, 2002, p. 100.
7. Ibid., pp. 100–101.
8. Hoffer, 1970, p. 360.
9. Grof notes that amounts of LSD beyond 400 to 500 micrograms don't appear to have a significant additional effect. (2001a, p. 137)
10. Grof, 2001a, p. 37.
11. Grof, 2001a, pp. 37, 118.
12. Grinspoon & Bakalar, 1997, pp. 194–195; Grof, 2001a, pp. 39, 121; Passie, 1997, p. 13.
13. Grof, 2001a, pp. 118, 121; Passie, 1997, p. 17.
14. Hoffer, 1970, p. 360.
15. Personal communication, October 4, 2009. See also Sandison, 1959, p. 499.
16. Grof, 2001a, p. 116.
17. Grinspoon & Bakalar, 1997, p. 196.
18. Grof, 2001a, pp. 116–117. See also Di Leo, 1975–76; Yensen, 1985, pp. 274–275.
19. Masters & Houston, 1970, pp. 323–324; Buckman, 1967, p. 99; Ditman & Bailey, 1967, p. 75.
20. Buckman, 1967, p. 99. See Blair's comment in the discussion of Buckman's conference paper.

21. Caldwell, 1969, p. 122.
22. See, for example, Winkelman & Roberts, 2007.
23. Merkur, 2007, pp. 197–198.
24. Grof, 1975, p. 20. Grof explains that he "developed, independently of several other European therapists, the concept of a therapeutic series of LSD sessions, usually referred to as *psycholytic therapy.*"
25. Grof, 2001a,, p. 116.
26. Grof, 1985, p. 92, chap. 2. See also Grof, 2000, chap. 2.
27. Grof, 2001a.
28. Winkelman, 2007a, p. 145. See also Schultes, R., & Hofmann, A., 1992.
29. Winkelman, 2007a, p. 148.
30. Ibid., p. 161.
31. Marsden & Lukoff, 2007, p. 287; Metzner, 1998a.
32. Metzner, 1999, pp. 40–42.
33. Marsden & Lukoff, 2007, p. 287.
34. Metzner, 1999, pp. 40–42.
35. Sandison, 1954, p. 514.
36. Sandison, 2001, p. 39.
37. Sandison, 1954, p. 508; Sandison & Whitelaw, 1957, p. 338.
38. Fordham, 1963, p. 125.
39. Ibid., p. 129. Fordham specified the patient's relationship to the therapist through "the transference." Transference can be understood generally as the patient's tendency to identify the therapist with an unconscious image. A patient may see the therapist as, for instance, his father.
40. Sandison, 1954, p. 514.
41. Sandison, 1954, p. 512. Margot Cutner provides an excellent example of this process in her paper "Analytic Work with LSD-25." (Cutner, 1959) See also "Dr. Margot Cutner's Report," in chapter 10.
42. Fordham, 1963, p. 125.
43. Sandison, 2001, pp. 38–39.
44. Personal communication, April 8, 2009.
45. Cutner, 1959, p. 717.
46. Ibid.
47. Ibid., p. 716.

Chapter 3: Basic Jungian Concepts and Principles

1. Jung, 1975e, p. 70.
2. Samuels et al., 1986, p. 2. See also Rowland, 2006.
3. Singer, J., 1994, p. xiii.
4. Jung, 1976, p. 483, para. 837.

5. Ibid., p. 463, para. 797. Jung generally uses the term *psychic* as synonymous with *psychological*, not as synonymous with *paranormal*.
6. Jung, 1969t, p. 200, para. 397.
7. Jung, 1969d, p. 307, para. 582.
8. Jung, 1976, p. 421, para. 700.
9. Jung, 1940, p. 3.
10. Samuels et al., 1986, pp. 36–37.
11. Jung, 1976, p. 425, para. 706.
12. Jacobi, 1973, p. 7.
13. Jung, 1969n, p. 283, para. 506.
14. Samuels et al., 1986, p. 51.
15. James, W., 1982, pp. 231, 232.
16. Jung, 1976, p. 483, para. 837.
17. Jung, 1969n, pp. 275–276, para. 490.
18. Jung, 1969i, p. 349, para. 673.
19. Jung, 1976, p. 485, para. 842.
20. Jung, 1969i, p. 349, para. 673.
21. Jung, 1969t, p. 148, para. 311. When Jung says that the collective unconscious "has nothing to do with our personal experience," he certainly doesn't mean that the collective unconscious has no influence on personal experience.
22. Jung, 1966a, p. 66, para. 103.
23. Henderson, 1964, p. 107.
24. Jung, 1969i, p. 349, para. 673.
25. Ibid., p. 350, para. 674.
26. Jung, 1969g, p. 158, para. 342.
27. Kirsch, 2000, p. 256.
28. Williams, M., 1963.
29. Henderson, 1990, p. 69.
30. Williams, M., 1963, p. 45.
31. Jung, 1976, p. 419, para. 694.
32. Ibid.
33. Ibid. See also Jung, 1966h, p. 153, para. 330; Samuels et al., 1986, p. 32.
34. Jung, 1969n, p. 278, para. 495; see also pp. 277ff., paras. 493, 494, 497.
35. Ibid., p. 282, para. 505; see also pp. 278, 279, 282, paras. 495, 496, 497, 504.
36. Quoted in Miller, 2004, p. 65. Originally from Jung, Nietzsche's Zarathustra: Notes of the Seminar Given in 1934–1939, 1988, p. 975.
37. I use the word *face* here in the same way Samuels et al. characterize working upon [or working through] as reflecting upon and relating to

unconscious material. (Samuels et al.,1986, p. 146) All these terms are shorthand for the complex therapeutic process of becoming conscious of the unconscious, which I discuss in chapter 11, "The Transcendent Function: Jung's Approach to Integration."
38. Jung, 1969n, p. 275, para. 490.
39. Jung, 1976, p. 450, para. 762.
40. Jung, 1940, pp. 26, 27; 1969n, p. 289, para. 524. See also Jung, 1969s, p. 289, para. 548.
41. Jung, 1969t, pp. 223–224, para. 430.
42. Samuels et al., 1986, p. 26. See also Jung, 1969c, p. 133, para. 270, n.7; Edinger, 1955, p. 624.
43. Jung, 1966b, p. 69, para. 109.
44. Jung, 1969f, pp. 53–54, para. 100.
45. Jung, 1963, p. 352. See also Jung, 1969h, p. 38, para. 80; 1969w, p. 452, para. 735.
46. Jung, 1969m, p. 15, para. 24.
47. Jung, 1969n, p. 286, para. 517.
48. Jung, 1966b, p. 70, paras. 109, 110.
49. Jung, 1969n, p. 287, para. 519.
50. Jung, 1969t, p. 212, para. 415.
51. Ibid.
52. Jung, 1966b, p. 71, para. 110.
53. Jung, 1969r, p. 157; para. 233. See also Jung, 1969m, p. 59, para. 102.
54. Jung, 1969r, p. 152, para. 225. This passage reflects Jung's indebtedness to Nietzsche, from whose *Ecce Homo* Jung is quoting almost word for word without attribution. (Richard Tarnas, personal communication, May 14, 2009)
55. Edinger, 1992, p. 3.
56. Jung, 1977, p. 694, para. 1567.
57. Edinger, 1987, p. 26.
58. Jung, 1970, p. 546, para. 778. The term *Self* (as in archetype of the Self) is not capitalized in the English translations of Jung's writings in *The Collected Works of C. G. Jung*, even though the German equivalent of *Self*, *das Selbst*, is always capitalized, as all nouns in German are. Many writers capitalize the term in English, however, to distinguish Jung's usage from theorists who don't associate the term with archetypal, collective or transpersonal dimensions of the psyche. I have adopted this convention, and I also follow the convention of using *self* (that is, with a lowercase *s*) as synonymous with *ego*.
59. Jung, 1969n, p. 144, para. 300.
60. Jung, 1969a, p. 263, para. 505.
61. Whitmont, 1991, p. 20.

62. Quoted in Miller, 2004, p. 65. Originally from Jung, 1988, Nietzsche's Zarathustra: Notes of the Seminar Given in 1934–1939, p. 975.
63. Jung, 1964, p. 20.
64. Ibid., p. 21.
65. Ibid.
66. Jung, 1976, p. 479, para. 825; 1969b, p. 75, para. 148.
67. Samuels et al., 1986, pp. 32, 145; Whitmont, 1991, p. 37.
68. Jung, 1969n, p. 289, para. 524.
69. Sandison, 2001, p. 41. I return to this case at the end of chapter 13.
70. Jung, 1972b, p. 148, para. 308.
71. Jung, 1969d, p. 306, para. 580.
72. Jung, 1969q, p. 226, para. 344.
73. Jung, 1967, p. 7, para. 6.
74. Jung, 1969p, p. 155, para. 263.
75. Diamond, 1996, p. 101.
76. Jung, 1969x, p. 306, para. 460.
77. Ibid.

Chapter 4: Jung's Explanation of Psychedelic Experience

1. Jung, 1975b, p. 222.
2. Jung, 1963, p. 3.
3. Ibid., p. 199.
4. Ibid.
5. Ibid., p. 176.
6. Ibid., p. 178.
7. Ibid., p. 189.
8. Jung, 1972h, p. 238, para. 516. See also Jung, 1972i, p. 251, para. 544; Jung, 1972h, p. 234, para. 505.
9. Jung, 1969p, p. 155, para. 263.
10. Jung, 1976, p. 451, para. 765.
11. Jung, 1969y, p. 446, para. 856.
12. Ibid, pp. 436–437, para. 841.
13. Ibid.
14. Jung, 1972j, p. 262, para. 566.
15. Ibid., p. 263, para. 569.
16. Grof, 2001a, pp. 11, 32.
17. As we will see in "The Compensating Function" in chapter 13, this view is supported by Jungian analyst Margot Cutner's observation that "it appears as if something like an autonomous selective process is at work, determining the sequence of the emerging material in a purposive way" during an LSD session. (Cutner, 1959, p. 720)

18. Jung, 1972j, p. 263, para. 569.
19. See, for instance, Jung, 1969b, p. 71, para. 139.
20. Jung, 1963, pp. 176–177.
21. Ibid., p. 187.
22. Ibid., p. 189.
23. Jung, 1975c, p. 300.
24. Jung, 1975d, p. 382.
25. Sandison, 1963, p. 34.
26. Ibid., p. 35. Sandison cites the 1960 study by Sidney Cohen that I referred to in chapter 1.
27. Sandison, 1997, pp. 71, 82. See also Sandison, 1959, pp. 499–500; Cutner, 1959, p. 725.
28. Fordham, 1963, p. 129.
29. Sandison, 2001, p. 36.
30. Ibid., pp. 36–37.
31. Sandison, 1997, pp. 69–71.
32. Jung, 1975a, p. 172.
33. Sandison, 1997, p. 82.
34. Sandison, 1963.

Part 2: Jungian Insights into Difficult Psychedelic Experiences

1. Jung, 1972c, p. 178, para. 387.

Chapter 5: Psychedelic Experience and Trauma

1. Strassman, 1984, p. 581.
2. Grof, 2001a, p. 158.
3. Brian Richards, PsyD, who is a member of the Johns Hopkins team investigating high-dose psilocybin-induced states of consciousness, articulates a number of other specific elements of set and setting worth considering. He suggests that set includes a person's ability to trust and form a meaningful therapeutic relationship with openness, sincerity, curiosity, self-compassion; willingness to "take a leap of faith;" and the courage to let go of control, and to go beyond understanding, thinking, and discussing. Setting, he points out, includes physical safety and an aesthetically supportive environment as well as interpersonal empathy, respect, genuineness, and the ability of all involved to be focused and present. (Source: Brian Richards' presentation, "Managing High Dose Psychedelic Sessions: Insights from Johns Hopkins," at the Psychedelic Science 2013 conference in Oakland, California, April

18–23.) Dr. Richards' presentation can be viewed at http://www.maps.org/conference/ps13cosimanorichards/ (Retrieved August 20, 2013)
4. Ungerleider, 1968, p. 61.
5. Fadiman, 2011; Frecska, 2007, pp. 86–87; Goldsmith, 2007, pp. 117–125; Goldsmith, 2011, Appendix 2; Grof, 2001a, p. 151, chap. 4; Johnson et al., 2008.
6. Grof, 2001a, p. 144; see also pp. 129, 309–318; Bravo & Grob, 1996a, p. 340.
7. Di Leo, 1975–76, pp. 329–330.
8. See, for instance, Mojeiko, 2007, p. 15.
9. Littlefield & Martin, 2002.
10. Grof, 2001a, p. 309; see also pp. 151, 160, 308–311; Blewett & Chwelos, 1959; Cohen, 1967, pp. 266–277.
11. American Psychiatric Association, 1994, pp. 424–429. See also Frances, First, & Pincus, 1995, *DSM-IV Guidebook*.
12. Frances et al., 1995. The authors say there is "a very characteristic human pattern of response to an extreme stressor." (p. 258)
13. American Psychiatric Association, 1994, pp. 424, 428.
14. Frances et al., 1995, p. 262. These PTSD characteristics raise questions about the possibility of retraumatizing a patient during psychedelic psychotherapy, an issue I return to in chapter 10.
15. Grinspoon & Bakalar, 1997, p. 159. See also Fadiman, 2011, pp. 99–100.
16. Grinspoon & Bakalar, 1997, p. 159.
17. American Psychiatric Association, 1994, pp. 428–429.
18. Frances et al., 1995, p. 261.
19. Cohen, 1967, p. 208ff.; Frecska, 2007; Grof, 2001a, pp. 151–154; Johnson et al., 2008. Regarding the physical safety of psychedelics, Cohen's survey of investigators who had tested the effects of LSD and mescaline revealed no serious physical complications even when the drugs had been given to chronic alcoholics who were in very poor health.
20. Bastiaans, 1983; Grob, 2002d, p. 273.
21. Grof, 2001a, pp. 30, 36, 74, 105, 207, 250, 282, 285.
22. Grof, 2001a, pp. 156, 282. See also Grof, 1985, pp. 381–382.
23. Kalsched, 1996, p. 1.
24. Kohut, quoted in Kalsched, 1996, p. 34.
25. Kalsched, 2003, p. 203.
26. Kelly, 1993, p. 53.
27. Kalsched, 1996, p. 7.
28. Perry, 1999, pp. 4–5.

29. Kalsched, 1996, pp. 1–2, 11.
30. Ibid., pp. 1–3.
31. Ibid., p. 3.
32. See chapter 6, "Psychedelic Experience and the Shadow."
33. Jung, 1968a, p. 69, para. 88.
34. Kalsched, 1996, pp. 16–17.
35. Ibid., pp. 3–4.
36. Ibid., p. 216.
37. Ibid., pp. 4–5.
38. Ibid., p. 5.
39. Ibid., p. 12.
40. Ibid., p. 13.
41. Jung, 1969d; Jung, 1969l, p. 121, para. 253; Kalsched, 1996, pp. 12–13.
42. Jung, 1966d, pp. 131–132, para. 267.
43. Jung, 1973a, pp. 406–407, para. 861.
44. Kalsched, 1996, pp. 14, 16.
45. Grof, 2001a, pp. 74, 100.
46. Sandison, 1954, p. 512.
47. Ibid.
48. Cutner, 1959, p. 740.
49. Ibid., p. 741.
50. Leuner, 1983, p. 180.
51. Jung, 1968a, p. 69, para. 88.
52. *American Heritage Dictionary of the English Language* (3rd ed.). (1996). Boston: Houghton Mifflin, p. 497. (See *demon*.)
53. In his book *Anger, Madness, and the Daimonic: The Psychological Genesis of Violence, Evil, and Creativity*, clinical psychologist Stephen Diamond quotes Rollo May's apt description of the daimonic: "The daimonic can be either creative or destructive and is normally both. When this power goes awry, and one element usurps control over the total personality, we have 'daimon possession,' the traditional name through history for psychosis. The daimonic is obviously not an entity but refers to a fundamental, archetypal function of human experience—an existential reality." See Diamond, 1996, p. 65.
54. Kalsched, 1996, pp. 27–28.
55. Ibid., pp. 38–39.
56. Ibid., p. 68. See also Ellenberger, 1970.
57. Kalsched, 1996, pp. 69–70.
58. Jung, quoted in Kalsched, p. 71. Kalsched's review of Freud's developing thought on trauma (in relation to Jung's thinking and object-relations theory) is intriguing in its own right. Although Freud's early trauma theory focused on milder forms of trauma and reduced its

psychic defense mechanisms to repression (as opposed to dissociation), he was later forced to address the complexities of severe trauma. His consequent theoretical speculations "beyond the pleasure principle" led him to deeper and more complex notions of resistance, such as the repetition compulsion, negative therapeutic reactions, the death instinct, and the severe superego—ideas that coincide to a surprising extent with Jung's thought on the archaic and daimonic functions of the deeper psyche. (Kalsched, 1996, pp. 79–83)

59. Kalsched, 1996, pp. 70–72. See also Samuels et al., 1986, pp. 33–35.
60. Jung, 1972b, p. 41, para. 84.
61. Jung, 1969j, p. 98, para. 204.
62. Kalsched, 1996, pp. 72–78. See also Jung, 1972j, pp. 264–265, paras. 571–572, where Jung presents the case of the incest victim in his paper "Schizophrenia."
63. Mogenson, quoted in Kalsched, 1996, p. 77. See also Mogenson, 2005.
64. Kalsched, 1996, p. 78.
65. Jung, 1972b, p. 38, para. 78.
66. Jung, 1973b, p. 599, para. 1350; Jung, 1972b, p. 40, para. 82.
67. Kalsched, 1996, p. 89.
68. Ibid., pp. 89–90.
69. Jung, 1969e, p. 330, para. 628.
70. Jung, 1973b, p. 602, para. 1354; see also p. 601, para. 1352.
71. Ibid., p. 602, para. 1353; see also p. 601, para. 1352.
72. Jung, 1969d, p. 311, para. 590.
73. Ibid., p. 314., para. 594.
74. Ibid., pp. 314–315, paras. 594–596.
75. Kalsched, 1996, p. 91.
76. Ibid.
77. Ibid., p. 13. I do not mean to suggest that Kalsched's theory provides *the* answer to understanding my difficult psychedelic experiences or to trauma in general, any more than Jung's theories do. I see his work, like Jung's, as one of many useful contributions to an ongoing process of inquiry, discovery, and integration.

Chapter 6: Psychedelic Experience and the Shadow

1. Liliane Frey-Rohn, quoted in Zweig & Abrams, 1991, p. 3.
2. Zweig & Abrams, 1991, pp. 3–4.
3. Whitmont, 1991, p. 12.
4. Jung, 1966a, p. 66, para. 103, n. 5.
5. Jung, 1969v, p. 267, para. 423.
6. Jung, 1969u, pp. 8–10, paras. 13–19.

7. Jung, 1969u, p. 8, para. 13.
8. Henderson, 1990, p. 69.
9. Jung, 1969u, p. 10, para. 19.
10. Jung, 1969, p. 266, para. 422.
11. Diamond, 1996, pp. 96–97.
12. Jung, 1969u, p. 10, para. 19.
13. This is apparently the only reference Jung makes to *absolute evil*. It is the only mention of absolute evil in the *General Index to the Collected Works of C. G. Jung*. (Jung, 1979, p. 257)
14. Henderson, 1990, p. 66.
15. Kelly, 1993, pp. 26–27, 30. Kelly notes that a *complexio oppositorum*, as "the total union of opposites," was one of Jung's favorite definitions of the Self. See also Jung, 1969w, p. 443, para. 716.
16. Kalsched, 1996, p. 97.
17. Jung, 1969w, p. 369, para. 567.
18. Jung, 1969r, p. 152, para. 225.
19. Otto, R., 1958, p. 80.
20. Jung, quoted in Edinger, 1992, p. 49. See also Edinger, 1987, p. 26.
21. Edinger, 1992, p. 48.
22. Jung, 1969h, p. 21, para. 45.
23. Ibid.
24. Zweig & Abrams, 1991, p. 3.
25. Jung, 1966e, p. 163, para. 254.
26. Kalsched, 1996, pp. 27, 28.
27. von Franz, 1980, p. 19.
28. Corbett, 1996, pp. 29–30.
29. Ibid., pp. 21–22.
30. Ibid., pp. 31–32.
31. Ibid., p. 30.
32. Jung, 1969u, p. 9, para. 16.
33. Whitmont, 1991, p. 13, 14.
34. Jung, 1969u, p. 9, para. 17.
35. Corbett, 1996, p. 30.
36. Leary, 1995, p. 249.
37. Ibid.
38. Ibid., p. 257.
39. Shulgin, 2001, pp. 200, 203.
40. Ibid., p. 200. Shulgin also emphasizes that "no person can be asked to do the work of confronting his Shadow without being told by his therapist, in advance, that what he will see and feel is not—NOT—the whole truth about who he is, but only one important and essential part." (p. 201)
41. See, for instance, Stephen Diamond's (1996) *Anger, Madness, and the Daimonic: The Psychological Genesis of Violence, Evil, and Creativity*.

42. Sandison, 1954, p. 513.
43. Ibid.
44. Ibid.
45. Cutner, 1959, p. 739.
46. Ibid., p. 740.
47. Ibid.

Chapter 7: Psychedelic Experience and Psychosis

1. American Psychiatric Association, 1994, p. 273. See also Lukoff, 1985, p. 156.
2. American Psychiatric Association, 1994, p. 273.
3. Ibid.
4. Ibid.
5. Ibid.
6. Nelson, 1994, p. 3.
7. Ibid., p. 4.
8. Grof, 1985, p. 303.
9. Ibid.
10. Nelson, 1994, p. 266; see also pp. 4–7, 14; Lukoff, 1985, p. 164.
11. Hastings, 1999, p. 198.
12. Walsh & Vaughan, 1993, p. 13.
13. Those members of the transpersonal psychology community who have been profoundly affected by their own psychedelic experiences include Ralph Metzner, David Lukoff, Frances Vaughan, James Fadiman, Charles Tart, and two of the field's founders, Stanislav Grof and Anthony Sutich.
14. Nelson, 1994, p. xix.
15. Ibid., p. 312.
16. Ibid. Nelson draws from, and to some degree tries to reconcile, the transpersonal theories of Michael Washburn and Ken Wilber, as well as contributing his own insights.
17. The whole question of Jung's metaphysical views and their implication for interpreting his psychology, and for interpreting psychedelic experience in the light of his psychology, is an intriguingly complex one that is beyond the scope of this book. I look forward, however, to extending my investigation in this direction in the future, especially to Jung's conception of synchronicity.
18. Nelson, 1994, p. xxiii.
19. Ibid., p. xx. See also Lukoff, 1985. The specific criteria Lukoff establishes for distinguishing between mystical experiences with psychotic features, which are essentially religious experiences, and psychotic disorders with mystical features are relevant here, too. Lukoff was

instrumental in psychiatry's official recognition of religious and spiritual issues through the adoption of the transpersonally-inspired diagnostic category Religious or Spiritual Problem in *DSM-IV*. (See American Psychiatric Association, 1994, p. 685; Lukoff & Lu, 1990.)
20. Nelson, 1994, p. 12. See also Washburn, 1995.
21. Nelson, 1994, pp. 13–14.
22. Ibid., p. 16.
23. Ibid., pp. 15–17.
24. Beringer, K. (Ed.). (1927). *Der meskalinrausch*. Berlin: Springer.
25. Stevens, 1987, p. 11.
26. Quoted in Stevens, 1987, p. 11. See also Grinspoon & Bakalar, 1997, pp. 59, 374. For a nuanced and fascinating description of the neurophysiological and biochemical correlates of psychotic states of consciousness, see John Nelson's "The Chemistry of Madness" in his *Healing the Split*, 1994, chap. 6, pp. 117–131.
27. Bravo & Grob, 1996a, p. 335; Grinspoon & Bakalar, 1997, p. 6; Grob, 2002d, p. 268; Grof, 2001a, p. 24.
28. See, for example, Grinspoon & Bakalar, 1997, p. 6; Stevens, 1987, p. 25.
29. Hofmann, 2005, p. 48.
30. Ibid., p. 49.
31. Ibid. Needless to say, as the discoverer of LSD's psychoactive properties, Hofmann had no one to tell him that he was only experiencing the effects of the drug he had ingested, that those effects would wear off, and that he would be fine. But even today those who take a psychedelic drug without the proper preparation and support can experience the terror of finding themselves in another world, another place, another time. Such a shift in reality is simply beyond imagination until one is there.
32. Quoted in Grob, 2002d, p. 271.
33. Grinspoon & Bakalar, 1997, pp. 245–246.
34. The *DSM* no longer classifies schizophrenia in terms of *acute* and *chronic*. The *DSM-IV* classifies short-term schizophrenia as Brief Psychotic Disorder when episodes last at least one day but less than one month and as Schizophreniform Disorder when episodes last at least one month but less than six months. The *DSM-IV* also uses classifications such as Substance- and Hallucinogen-Induced Psychotic Disorder that specifically describe psychedelic-induced psychotic states. (American Psychiatric Association, 1994, pp. 290, 304, 310–311. See also Frances et al., 1995, pp. 152–154.)
35. Grinspoon & Bakalar, 1997, p. 245.
36. Bravo & Grob, 1996b, p. 183; Stevens, 1987, pp. 273–274.

37. Grinspoon & Bakalar, 1997, p. 248.
38. Ibid.
39. Ibid.
40. Grof, 2001a, p. 11.
41. Grinspoon & Bakalar, 1997, p. 248.
42. Hollister, 1968, p. 122. See also Bravo & Grob, 1996a, pp. 335–336; Grinspoon & Bakalar, pp. 6, 248–249; Grof, 2001a, p. 25.
43. Grinspoon & Bakalar, 1997, pp. 248–249.
44. Grob's paraphrase in Grob, 2002d, p. 271.
45. Grob, 2002d, p. 272.
46. Grof, 1985, p. 294.
47. Grob, 2002d, pp. 270, 271; Grof, 2001a, p. 24.
48. Hoffer, 1970, p. 360.
49. Grob, 2002d, pp. 274–275; Grof, 2001a, p. 24.
50. Grof, 2001a, p. 25.
51. Bravo & Grob, 1996a, p. 336. See also Fischman, 1983; Grinspoon & Bakalar, 1997, p. 6.
52. Grof, 2001a, p. 25.
53. Grinspoon & Bakalar, 1997, p. 249.
54. Nelson, 1994, p. 150. Nelson's *better or worse* can briefly be translated as "temporary or permanent, wholesome or morbid, uplifting or destructive." See Nelson, 1994, p. 131.
55. Grinspoon & Bakalar, 1997, p. 249.
56. Ibid., p. 252.
57. Ibid.
58. Nelson, 1994, pp. 149–150.
59. Ibid., pp. 12–14, 150. Nelson maintains that "every major hallucinogenic drug slows the firing of serotonin-rich neurons in the raphe nucleus. In other words, they inhibit an inhibitor and free neurons downstream to fire without constraint." They affect, that is, the limbic system of the brain, which is mediated by dopamine and implicated in psychosis. This very roughly is the biochemical mechanism that regulates the expansions and contractions of self-boundaries. This link between serotonin and dopamine activity also appears to provide a compelling link among psychedelic experiences, dreams, and psychosis. (Nelson, 1994, p. 151)
60. Grof, 1985, p. 303.
61. Ibid.
62. Ibid.
63. Grof, C., & Grof, S., 1990, p. 31.
64. Ibid., p. 61.
65. Ibid., p. 62.

66. Shulgin, 2001, p. 198.
67. Ibid., p. 199.
68. Metzner, 2002b p. 24.
69. Ibid., p. 25.
70. Grob, 2002d, p. 265. See also Harner, 1973.
71. Grob, 2002d, p. 266.
72. Weil & Rosen, 1993, pp. 132–133. See also Weil, 1986.
73. Ibid., p. 133.

Chapter 8: Psychosis in Jung's Psychology

1. Jung, 1972j, p. 261, paras. 563–565; Read, Fordham, Adler, & McGuire, 1972, p. v.
2. Jung, 1969n, p. 287, para. 519. Jung writes specifically here of the anima and animus.
3. Jung, 1969b, p. 68.
4. Jung, 1964, pp. 34, 76. Jung often refers to "normal people." I usually transcribe this into "so-called normal people," a characterization Jung occasionally uses himself.
5. Ibid., pp. 98, 94.
6. Ibid., p. 95. See also Jung, 1972e, p. 209 para. 463.
7. Jung, 1972c, p. 178, para. 387.
8. Perry, 1999, p. 63.
9. Samuels et al., p. 123.
10. See "Dr. Margot Cutner's Report" at the end of chapter 10 and Dr. Sandison's reports in "Integration and the Role of Ego-Consciousness" at the end of chapter 13.
11. Edinger, 1992, pp. 38, 129.
12. Jung, 1972f, p. 213, para. 471.
13. Jung, 1972g, p. 227, para. 497; Jung, 1972j, p. 256, para. 554.
14. Jung, 1972g, pp. 226–227, para. 497.
15. Ibid., pp. 226–227, paras. 497, 498; see also Jung, 1972j, pp. 263–264, para. 570.
16. Jung, 1972j, pp. 263–264, para. 570.
17. Jung, 1972g, p. 227, para. 498.
18. Ibid., pp. 227–229, paras. 498, 500, 501, 503.
19. Jung, 1972j, p. 262, para. 567.
20. Ibid., p. 262, para. 566; see also pp. 258–259, 261, 263, paras. 559, 563, 568–569.
21. Jung, 1972c, p. 178, para. 387.
22. Jung, 1972j, pp. 256–257, para. 555.
23. Ibid., p. 257, para. 557.

24. Ibid.
25. Ibid., p. 263, para. 570. Jung wrote, "The fluid and mobile continuity of mescaline phenomena differs from the abrupt, rigid, halting, and discontinuous behavior of schizophrenic apperception."
26. Ibid., p. 263, para. 569.
27. Jung, 1969j, p. 98, para. 203.
28. Ibid., p. 100, para. 209; see also p. 98, para. 204.
29. Jung, 1972j, p. 258, para. 558.
30. Ibid., pp. 256, 258, paras. 554, 559.
31. Jung, 1972h, pp. 234–236, paras. 506–511.
32. Jung, 1972j, pp. 258–259, para. 559.
33. Jung, 1972h, p. 235, para. 507. See also Jung, 1972j, pp. 256, 258–259, 261, paras. 554, 559, 563.
34. Jung, 1972h, p. 238, para. 516.
35. Ibid., pp. 235–236, para. 508.
36. Perry, 1999, p. 72.
37. Jung, 1972h, p. 238, paras. 516, 517.
38. Jung, 1972j, 268, para. 578.
39. Jung, 1972h, p. 236, para. 511.
40. Jung, 1972j, p. 262, para. 566.
41. Grinspoon & Bakalar, 1997, p. 9.
42. Jung, 1972j, p. 262, para. 566; Jung, 1972g, p. 228, para. 501.
43. Quoted in Leary, 1995, p. 141. Originally published as "Return Trip to Nirvana" in the *Sunday Telegraph* in 1967. In this essay, besides writing about his own psychedelic experiences, Koestler challenged Aldous Huxley's positive view of psychedelic experience.
44. Quoted in Leary, 1995, pp. 140–143.
45. Ibid., p. 147.
46. Ibid., p. 148.
47. Ibid., pp. 148–149.
48. Ten to twenty such cathartic sessions were conducted at intervals of a month or more, interspersed with verbal therapy to integrate the material that had emerged during the psychedelic sessions. See Grinspoon & Bakalar, 1997, p. 197; Grof, 2001a, pp. 43–44.
49. Clark, 1983, p. 73.
50. Ibid., pp. 73–74.
51. Ibid., p. 74.
52. Strassman, 2001, pp. 247–248. Richard Tarnas notes that this question could be clarified through a study administering DMT to a control group in circumstances more conducive to positive responses. (Richard Tarnas, personal communication, May 14, 2009)
53. Strassman, 2001, p. 252.

54. Osmond, 1970, pp. 24–26.
55. Ibid., p. 28.

Chapter 9: Psychedelic Experience and Transformation

1. See, for instance, Grob, 2002b; Grof, 2001a; Lukoff, Lu, & Turner, 1996; Lukoff, Zanger, & Lu, 1990; Roberts, 2001; Stolaroff, 1994; Winkelman & Roberts, 2007.
2. Daniels, 2005, pp. 225, 230.
3. Kelly, 1993, p. 18.
4. Jung, 1969r, p. 200, para. 295.
5. Samuels et al., 1986, p. 151.
6. Corbett, 1996; Edinger, 1992. See also Ferrer, 2002, pp. 44–45; Samuels et al., p. 130.
7. Jung, 1966k, p. 6. See also Jung, 1969m, p. 8, para. 9, for a slightly different translation of Jung's definition of religion.
8. Jung, 1969m, p. 7, para. 6. Otto formed the term *numinous* from the Latin *numen*, divine power. (Otto, 1958, pp. 6–7)
9. Jung, 1969a, p. 279, para. 528.
10. Stolaroff, 2002, p. 103.
11. Wulff, 1997, p. 90. See also Schultes & Hofmann, 1992.
12. Walsh & Grob, 2005.
13. Grof, 1985, p. 129.
14. This usage is consistent with the way transpersonal theorist Jorge Ferrer refers to "transpersonal, spiritual, and mystical phenomena somewhat interchangeably." Given the lack of consensus on defining these complex phenomena, Ferrer suggests that "their relationship is more one of family-resemblance than identity, equivalence, or inclusion." See Ferrer 2002, p. 193.
15. Dobkin de Rios & Winkelman, 1989, p. 4.
16. Grinspoon & Bakalar, 1997, pp. 86–88.
17. See, for example, Roberts, 2001; Smith, H., 2000.
18. Smith, H., 2000, p. 30. See also Doblin, 2001, p. 74. Rick Doblin refers to the criteria we can use to measure the lasting significance of a psychedelic-induced mystical experience as "persisting positive effects."
19. Bache, 2000, p. 15.
20. Ibid., p. 16.
21. Grinspoon & Bakalar, 1997, p. 88.
22. For psychosis and mysticism see Lukoff, 1985; Wapnick, 1969. For psychosis and spirituality, see Clarke, 2001. For psychosis and religious experience, see James, 1982, pp. 21–25; Lukoff, 1985, p. 155.
23. Lukoff, 1985, pp. 155–156; Lukoff, 1996, p. 272. See also Lukoff & Lu, 1990; American Psychiatric Association, 1994, p. 685.

24. Lukoff, Lu, & Turner, 1996, p. 231. See also Clark, I., 2001; Grof, 2000; Grof, S., & Grof, C., 1989; Lukoff, 1985, p. 158.
25. Lukoff, 1985, pp. 156–158; 1996, p. 272; Grof, S., & Grof, C., 1989, p. 238.
26. Grof, S., & Grof, C., 1989, p. x.
27. Ibid., 1989, p. 237. Depth psychology came to include other theorists and therapists open to spiritual concerns. These include John Weir Perry, Edward Edinger, and Lionel Corbett.
28. Jung, 1969n, p. 287, para. 519.
29. Jung, 1969p, pp. 152, 153, paras. 259, 260.
30. See "Dr. Margot Cutner's Report" at the end of chapter 10 and Dr. Sandison's reports in "Integration and the Role of Ego-Consciousness" at the end of chapter 13.
31. Perry, 1999, pp. 4–5.
32. See, for instance, Perry's *The Far Side of Madness, The Self in Psychotic Process, Roots of Renewal in Myth and Madness,* and *Trials of the Visionary Mind: Spiritual Emergency and the Renewal Process.* Other notable critics of conventional attitudes toward psychotic states are Kazimierz Dabrowski (*Positive Disintegration*), Thomas Szasz (*The Myth of Mental Illness*), and R. D. Laing (*The Politics of Experience*).
33. Clarke, 2001, p. 1.
34. Ibid., pp. 1–5.
35. Personal communication, 2007.
36. Kelly, 2002, p. 82.
37. Nelson, 1994, p. 4.
38. Grinspoon & Bakalar, 1997, p. 6.
39. Laing, 1979, p. 115.
40. Ibid., pp. 117–118.
41. Lukoff, 1996, p. 271.
42. Ibid., p. 279.
43. Ibid.; Lukoff, 1991, p. 28.
44. Lukoff, 1991, p. 28; 1996, pp. 278, 279. See also Shorto, 1999, pp. 16–29.
45. Metzner, 1998b, p. 81.
46. Ibid., pp. 81–82.
47. Alpert, 1979, p. 129.
48. Ibid.
49. Walsh & Grob, 2005, pp. 119–120.
50. Grof, S., & Grof, C., 1989, p. 238.
51. Grof, 1985, p. 295.
52. Ibid., p. 296.

53. Ibid.
54. Ibid., p. 315.

Chapter 10: A Jungian Approach to the Transformative Potential of Difficult Psychedelic Experiences

1. Perry, 1999, p. 63; Perry, 1976, pp. 11–12.
2. Jung, 1972e, p. 205, para. 449.
3. Ibid., p. 206, para. 452.
4. Ibid., pp. 206–210, paras. 453, 458, 465.
5. Jung, 1969g, p. 149, para. 312.
6. Perry, 1999, p. 26ff.
7. Jung, 1967, p. 7, para. 6.
8. Jung, 1964, p. 98.
9. Ibid., p. 99.
10. Perry, 1999, pp. 65–66.
11. Jung, 1972d, pp. 179–180, paras. 389–390. See also, Jung, 1966c.
12. Ibid., p. 183, para. 399.
13. Ibid., p. 186, para. 408.
14. Ibid., p. 191, para. 421.
15. Ibid., p. 192, paras. 422–423; see also pp. 186, 187, 191–192, paras. 410, 412, 421.
16. Perry, 1999, p. 67.
17. Ibid., p. 68.
18. Ibid., p. 69.
19. Ibid., p. 71.
20. Jung, quoted in Henderson, 1964, p. 118.
21. Henderson, 1964, pp. 118–121.
22. Whitmont, 1991, p. 16.
23. Jung, 1964, p. 93.
24. It seems more appropriate perhaps to say that complexes only become objects of consciousness when their effects cause distress. This wording removes the suggestion that complexes are willful agents in their own right. Yet Jung repeatedly characterizes complexes as autonomous, willful agents.
25. Corbett, 1996, pp. 197, 200.
26. Ibid., p. 197.
27. von Franz quoted in Zweig & Abrams, 1991, p. xxii.
28. Kluger quoted in Edinger, 1992, p. 93.
29. Edinger, 1992, pp. 80–81.
30. Metzner, 1998b, pp. 135, 114.
31. Jung, 1969w, p. 435, para. 698.

32. Edinger, 1999, p. 5.
33. Ibid., pp. 12–13.
34. Edinger, 1999, pp. 7, 149.
35. Corbett, 1996, p. 30.
36. Strassman, 2001, p. 160.
37. Ibid., p. 354, n. 1 for chapter 11.
38. Jung, 1966d, p. 130, para. 262.
39. Ibid.
40. Grof, 1985, pp. 381–382. See also Grof, 2001a, pp. 30, 282.
41. Grof, 1985, p. 381. The value Grof places on abreaction is also based on years of experience with "holotropic breathwork," a therapeutic technique he developed with Christina Grof that exploits the cathartic energies induced by accelerated breathing, evocative music, and body work. (Grof, 2000, pp. 183–205)
42. Grof, 2000, p. 196.
43. Ibid. See also Grof, 2001a, p. 282.
44. Grof, 2001a, p. 140.
45. Grof, 2000, p. 178.
46. Ibid., p. 179.
47. Ibid., p. 179.
48. Grof, 2001a, p. 144.
49. Grof, 2000, p. 192.
50. Richard Tarnas, personal communication, October 8, 2008. See also Grof, 2000, pp. 32, 191–194.
51. Jung, 1966d, p. 131, para. 263.
52. Ibid., para. 265.
53. Ibid., p. 131, para. 266.
54. Ibid., p. 132, para. 268.
55. Ibid., paras. 269–270.
56. Ibid., pp. 132–133, para. 271.
57. Ibid., pp. 133–138, paras. 275–293.
58. Jung, 1969j, p. 102, para. 213.
59. Jung, 1966d, p. 137, para. 290.
60. Ibid., p. 138, para. 291.
61. Jung, 1966i, p. 9, para. 11. See also Jung, 1966f, p. 36, para. 66.
62. I describe Strassman's DMT study in "Accounts of Psychedelic-Induced Psychotic States" in chapter 8.
63. Strassman, 2001, pp. 254–255.
64. Ibid., p. 255.
65. Ibid., pp. 256–257.
66. Ibid., p. 257.
67. Ibid., p. 257.

68. Jung, 1968b, p. 333, para. 437, fig. 170.
69. Cutner, 1959, pp. 741–742.
70. Ibid., p. 742.
71. Ibid. The frightening pictures projected onto the walls, etc. are the patient's psychological projections.
72. Ibid., pp. 743–744.

Part 3: Jung's Psychology and Psychedelic Psychotherapy

1. Jung, 1966h, p. 160, paras. 351.

Chapter 11: The Transcendent Function: Jung's Approach to Integration

1. Samuels et al., 1986, pp. 83–84.
2. Jung, 1969b, p. 67, Prefatory Note.
3. Ibid., p. 68.
4. Ibid.
5. Jung, 1969h, p. 31, para. 64, n. 35.
6. Jung, 1969b, p. 68, Prefatory Note.
7. Ibid.
8. Ibid.
9. Jung, 1975b, p. 222.
10. Jung, 1969b, p. 69, para. 131.
11. Ibid.
12. Ibid., p. 69, paras. 132–134.
13. Ibid., pp. 70–71, paras. 136–137.
14. Ibid., p. 71, para. 139.
15. Ibid., p. 73, para. 144.
16. Ibid., pp. 73–74, para. 145.
17. Ibid., p. 74, para. 146. Although Jung initially defines the transcendent function as an *attitude*, he ultimately describes it as a *process*. (Ibid., p. 75, para. 147)
18. Ibid., p. 75, para. 148.
19. Ibid., pp. 82, 86, paras. 167, 178.
20. Ibid., p. 82, para. 167.
21. Ibid., pp. 78–79, paras. 157–158.
22. Ibid., pp. 79–81, paras. 160–164.
23. Ibid., p. 81, para. 166; pp. 82–84, paras. 168–171.
24. Ibid., pp. 84–85, paras. 173–176.
25. Ibid., p. 85, para. 176.
26. Ibid., p. 85, para. 177.

27. Ibid., p. 86, para. 179.
28. Ibid., p. 85, para. 178; see also pp. 86–87, para. 180.
29. Ibid., pp. 85–86, para. 178.
30. Ibid., p. 87, para. 181.
31. Ibid., p. 74, para. 146.
32. Ibid., pp. 87–88, para. 183.
33. Ibid., p. 88, para. 183.
34. Ibid.
35. Ibid., p. 88, para. 184.
36. Ibid., p. 89, para. 186.
37. Ibid., p. 90, para. 189.
38. Ibid.
39. Ibid., p. 91, para. 193.
40. Ibid.
41. Jung, 1975a, p. 172.

Chapter 12: Jungian Psychotherapy

1. Leary et al., 1995, p. 23.
2. Jung, 1966g, p. 59, para 134.
3. Jung, 1966n, pp. 90, 91, paras. 203, 206.
4. Grof, 2001a, pp. 66–87. See also Grof, 2000, chap. 2.
5. Jung, 1966n, p. 88–89, para. 199.
6. Jung, 1966h, p. 160, para. 351.
7. Ibid., para. 352.
8. Chodorow, 1997, pp. 10–11.
9. Jung, 1963, chap. 6.
10. Chodorow, 1997, pp. 3–5. See also page 17, where Chodorow briefly summarizes the development of Jung's view of active imagination in relation to dream interpretation, self-knowledge, psychotherapy, and individuation.
11. Amplification, for Jung, is the interpretative technique of making associations between symbolic images that have emerged from one's unconscious and symbols expressed collectively in mythology and religion.
12. Jung, 1976, p. 427, para. 711.
13. Ibid., p. 428, paras. 712, 713; Chodorow, p. 6.
14. Jung, 1976, p. 428, para. 714.
15. Ibid., p. 429, para. 714.
16. Fordham, 1963, p. 125.
17. Fordham, 1956, p. 207.
18. Ibid., p. 208.

19. Ibid.
20. There are other criteria, of course: the readiness of the subject, the knowledge and skill of the therapist, the relationship between subject and therapist. I discuss these in chapter 13.
21. Jung, 1976, p. 429, para. 715.
22. Jung, 1966n, p. 87, para. 198.
23. Ibid., p. 88, para. 198.
24. Jung, 1966f, p. 41, para. 81.
25. Jung, 1966o, p. 115, para. 237.
26. Jung, 1966f, pp. 41, 42, 45, paras. 82, 86, 96.
27. Jung, 1966o, p. 116, para. 239.
28. Jung, 1966i, p. 5, para. 2.
29. Ibid., p. 20, para. 25.
30. Grinspoon & Bakalar, 1997, p. 248.
31. Grof, 1985, p. 303.
32. Jung, 1966a, p. 62, para. 94, n. 13.
33. Jung, 1966l, p. 99, paras. 217, 218.
34. Jung, 1966g, p. 61, para. 139.
35. Jung, 1966g, pp. 62, 63, paras. 141, 144. See also Fordham, 1974, pp. 5–6.
36. Jung, 1966l, p. 101, para. 218.
37. Ibid.
38. Ibid., pp. 101–102, para. 219.
39. Sandison, 1959, p. 500.
40. Sandison, 1954, pp. 513–514.
41. Sandison, 1959, p. 500.
42. Ibid. See also Cutner, 1959, p. 722ff.; Sandison, 1954, p. 514.
43. Jung, 1969s, p. 287, para. 544. See also von Franz, 1993, p. 2.
44. Jung, 1972b, p. 148, para. 308. See also "Dreams and Other Symbolic Products of the Unconscious" in chapter 3, and "Commonalities between Schizophrenia and Other Conditions" in chapter 8.
45. Jung, 1966f, p. 45., para. 96.
46. Ibid., para. 97.
47. Ibid., para. 98.
48. Jung, 1969s, p. 282, para. 532.
49. Jung, 1969a, p. 238, para. 445.
50. Jung, 1969s, p. 282, para. 532.
51. Jung, 1966h, p. 151, para. 325.
52. Jung, 1969a, p. 238, para. 446.
53. Ibid., p. 243, para. 462.
54. Jung, 1966h, p. 139, para. 294.
55. Ibid., p. 153, para. 330; Jung, 1969a, pp. 245, 248–249, 250, 253, paras. 469, 477, 483, 488.

56. Jung, 1969s, p. 288, para. 546.
57. von Franz, 1964, p. 168ff.
58. Jung, 1969s, p. 288, para. 547.
59. Jung, 1969s, p. 292, para. 556.
60. Jung, 1966o, pp. 122–123, paras. 251, 252.
61. Jung, 1966i, pp. 15–16, paras. 18–19.

Chapter 13: Implications for Psychedelic Psychotherapy

1. Jung, 1975b, pp. 222, 224.
2. Jung, 1966i, p. 15, para. 18.
3. Vaughan, 2001, p. 194; See also Johnson, Richards, & Griffiths, 2008; Winkelman & Roberts' (2007) *Psychedelic Medicines*, Volume 2, Part II: "Guidelines for Psychotherapeutic Applications."
4. Grof, 2001a, pp. 124, 153.
5. Sandison, 1963, p. 33; Sandison, 1954, p. 501.
6. Grof, 2001a, p. 153; Sandison, 1963.
7. Jung, 1966g, p. 60, para. 137.
8. Sandison, 2001, p. 38.
9. Sandison, 1954, p. 509.
10. Sandison, 1963, pp. 34–35.
11. Cutner, 1959, pp. 717, 725.
12. Ibid., p. 717.
13. Sandison, personal communication, April 8, 2009.
14. Sandison & Whitelaw, 1957, p. 336.
15. See, for instance Cutner's reports in chapters 6 and 10 or Sandison's report, below.
16. For an example of Jung's views regarding the analyst's training, see his "Fundamental Questions of Psychotherapy." (1966o, p. 115, para. 237)
17. Jung, 1966o, p. 115, para. 237.
18. Jung, 1966f, pp. 39–40, para. 76.
19. Jung, 1966h, pp. 145–146, para. 313.
20. Jung, 1966i, p. 10, para.11.
21. Jung, 1966j, p. 27, para. 43.
22. Jung, 1966g, p. 71, para. 163.
23. Cutner's Jungian-oriented colleague, Dr. Ronald Sandison, was not an analyst. Margot Cutner was elected to membership in the British Society of Analytic Psychology in 1948, having been proposed by Gerhard Adler. Her paper, "Analytic Work with LSD 25," was based on a paper she read at a meeting of the British Society of Analytic Psychology in 1957. (Jungian analyst Ian Baker's thesis, *LSD 25 and Analytical Psychology*, discusses his experimental practice of LSD-enhanced psychotherapy in the late 1960s. See endnote 44 for chap. 1.)

24. Cutner, 1959, p. 720. I have discussed the psyche's compensatory function in "The Relationship between Consciousness and the Unconscious" in chapter 3, and in "The Compensating Function of Dreams" in chapter 12.
25. Cutner, 1959, p. 720.
26. Jung, 1966h, p. 153, para. 330. See also "The Compensating Function of Dreams" in chapter 12 of this book.
27. Jung, 1966m, p. 82, paras. 187, 188.
28. Sandison, 1954, p. 508.
29. Ibid., p. 508.
30. Ibid., p. 509.
31. Ibid., p. 510.
32. Jung, 1966h, p. 152, para. 329.
33. Sandison, 1954, p. 510.
34. Ibid., p. 511. See also Sandison, 2001, p. 45.
35. Sandison, 2001, p. 45.
36. Sandison, 1954, p. 510.
37. Sandison, 1959, p. 500.
38. Sandison, 1954, p. 511.
39. Cutner, 1959, p. 726; see also p. 725.
40. Ibid., p. 718.
41. Sandison, 1954, p. 512.
42. Cutner, 1959, p. 718.
43. Jung, 1967, p. 408, para. 631; quoted in Sandison, 1959, p. 500.
44. Cutner, 1959, p. 717.
45. Ibid., 722; see also p. 744.
46. Jung, 1966m, p. 82, paras. 187–188. Cutner's observations on the value of the therapist's reassurance through physical touch lead to considerations beyond the scope of this book. Her observations are worth noting, however, because they remind us of the complexity of the psychotherapeutic process, and they remind us that my present focus on ego-consciousness and integration inevitably omits other aspects of that complex process. Cutner explains that in a psychedelic-induced state, individuals have a unique opportunity to experience and integrate sense impressions (including touch and sensual experiences) with emotional experiences. "In this way," she says, "a reorientation in [the individual's] object relationships can take place on a level more archaic than that of language." (Cutner, 1959, p. 723) Cutner's observations regarding touch and sense impressions bring to mind the value Grof places on the physical element of psychedelic psychotherapy, which I discussed in "Grof's View of Abreaction" in chapter 10.
47. Sandison, 1954, pp. 508, 509.

48. Cutner, 1959, p. 717; see also p. 723.
49. Sandison, 1959, p. 502.
50. Cutner, 1959, p. 723.
51. Sandison, 1959, p. 499.
52. Cutner, 1959, p. 718.
53. Ka-Tzetnik 135633, 1998, pp. 7, 8, 42, 44, 83, 97. The author's use of the name Ka-Tzetnik 135633 is initially confusing. The author's actual name is Yehiel De-Nur. The name Ka-Tzetnik 135633 combines the Yiddish Ka-Tzetnik, for inmate of a Nazi concentration camp, with the number 135633, De-Nur's identification number at Auschwitz.
54. Ka-Tzetnik 135633, 1998, p. 33.
55. Ibid., pp. 117–118. See also Bastiaans, 1983.
56. Sandison, 2001, p. 39.
57. Sandison, 1959, p. 499.
58. Jung, 1966h, p. 152, para. 327.
59. Sandison, 1954, pp. 512–513.
60. Cutner, 1959, p. 742.
61. Jung, 1966i, p. 20, para. 27.
62. Sandison, 1963, p. 36.
63. Chodorow, 1997, p. 14.
64. Jung, 1966h, pp. 151–152, para. 326.
65. Sandison, 1954, p. 514.
66. Sandison, 1959, p. 499.
67. Sandison, 2001, p. 42.
68. Ibid., p. 40.
69. Ibid.
70. Ibid.
71. Ibid., pp. 40–41.
72. Ibid., p. 41.
73. Ibid., pp. 41–42.
74. Ibid., p. 42.

Conclusion

1. Fordham, 1974, pp. 20–21.
2. Jung, 1966o, p. 119, para. 244.
3. Sandison, 1963, p. 36.
4. Jung, 1969b, p. 88, para. 183.
5. Cutner, 1959, pp. 716, 725; Grof, 1985, p. 381. See also Grof, 2001a, pp. 282, 285.
6. Jung, 1969o, p. 489, para. 780.

Bibliography

Unless otherwise noted, all references to *The Collected Works of C. G. Jung* have the same editors, translator, and publisher: Edited by Herbert Read, Michael Fordham, Gerhard Adler, and William McGuire. Translated by R. F. C. Hull. Bollingen Series XX. Princeton, NJ.: Princeton University Press.

Abramson, H. (Ed.). (1967). *The use of LSD in psychotherapy and alcoholism*. New York: Bobbs-Merrill.

Alpert, R. (1979). Psychosis: A framework for an alternate possibility. In J. Fadiman & D. Kewman (Eds.), *Exploring madness: Experience, theory, and research* (pp. 128–133). Monterey, CA: Brooks/Cole.

American heritage dictionary of the English language (3rd ed.). (1996). Boston: Houghton Mifflin.

American Psychiatric Association. (1994). *Diagnostic and statistical manual of mental disorders* (4th ed.). Washington, D.C.: Author.

Bache, C. (2000). *Dark night, early dawn: Steps to a deep ecology of mind*. Albany: State University of New York Press.

Baker, I. (1970). *LSD 25 and analytical psychology*. Zurich: Clinic and Research Center for Jungian Psychology.

Bastiaans, J. (1983). Mental liberation facilitated by the use of hallucinogenic drugs. In L. Grinspoon & J. Bakalar (Eds.), *Psychedelic reflections* (pp. 143–152). New York: Human Sciences Press.

Blewett, D., & Chwelos, N. (1959). *Handbook for the therapeutic use of lysergic acid diethylamide-25, individual and group procedures*. (n.d.) Retrieved July 6, 2013, from http://www.maps.org/ritesofpassage/lsd-handbook.html

Bravo, G., & Grob, C. (1996a). Psychedelic psychotherapy. In B. Scotton, A. Chinen, & J. Battista (Eds.), *Textbook of transpersonal psychiatry and psychology* (pp. 335–341). New York: Basic Books.

Bravo, G., & Grob, C. (1996b). Psychedelics and transpersonal psychiatry. In B. Scotton, A. Chinen, & J. Battista (Eds.), *Textbook of transpersonal psychiatry and psychology* (pp. 176–185). New York: Basic Books.

Brown, D. (2007/2008). Psychedelic healing? *Scientific American Mind, Dec. /Jan.*, 67–71. Retrieved July 6, 2013, from http://www.sciam.com/article.cfm?id=psychedelic-healing

Buckman, J. (1967). Theoretical aspects of LSD therapy. In H. Abramson (Ed.), *The use of LSD in psychotherapy and alcoholism* (pp. 83–100). New York: Bobbs-Merrill.

Caldwell, W. (1969). *LSD psychotherapy: An exploration of psychedelic and psycholytic therapy.* New York: Grove Press.

Chodorow, J. (1997). Introduction. In J. Chodorow (Ed.), *Jung on active imagination* (pp. 1–20). Princeton: Princeton University Press.

Clark, W. H. (1983). Life begins at sixty. In L. Grinspoon & J. Bakalar (Eds.), *Psychedelic reflections* (pp. 70–77). New York: Human Sciences Press.

Clarke, I. (Ed.). (2001). *Psychosis and spirituality: Exploring the new frontier.* London: Whurr.

Cohen, S. (1960). Lysergic acid diethylamide: Side effects and complications. *Journal of Nervous and Mental Disease, 130*, 30–40.

Cohen, S. (1966). A classification of LSD complications. *Psychosomatics, 7*, 182–186.

Cohen, S. (1967). *The beyond within: The LSD story.* New York: Atheneum.

Cohen, S. (1985). LSD: The varieties of psychotic experience. *Journal of Psychoactive Drugs, 17*(4), 291–296.

Cohen, S., & Ditman, K. (1963). Prolonged adverse reactions to lysergic acid diethylamide. *Archives of General Psychiatry, 8*, 475–480.

Corbett, L. (1996). *The religious function of the psyche.* New York: Brunner-Routledge.

Corbyn, Z. (2013). Psychedelic academe: Research into mind-altering drugs is back. *The Chronicle of Higher Education, June 2.* Retrieved July 8, 2013, from http://chronicle.com/article/Psychedelic-Academe/139509/

Cutner, M. (1959). Analytic work with LSD-25. *Psychiatric Quarterly, 33*(4), 715–757.

Daniels, M. (2005). *Shadow, self, spirit: Essays in transpersonal psychology.* Charlottesville, VA: Imprint Academic.

Diamond, S. (1996). *Anger, madness, and the daimonic: The psychological genesis of violence, evil, and creativity.* Albany: State University of New York Press.

Di Leo, F. (1975–76). The use of psychedelics in psychotherapy. *Journal of Altered States of Consciousness, 2*(4), 325–337.

Ditman, K., & Bailey, J. (1967). Evaluating LSD as a psychotherapeutic agent. In H. Abramson (Ed.), *The use of LSD in psychotherapy and alcoholism* (pp. 74–80). New York: Bobbs-Merrill.

Dobkin de Rios, M., & Winkelman, M. (1989). Shamanism and altered states of consciousness: An introduction. *Journal of Psychoactive Drugs, 21*(1), 1–6.

Doblin, R. (2001). Pahnke's Good Friday experiment: A long-term follow-up and methodological critique. In T. Roberts (Ed.), *Psychoactive sacramentals: Essays on entheogens and religion* (pp. 70–79). San Francisco: Council on Spiritual Practices.

Edinger, E. (1955). The collective unconscious as manifested in psychosis. *American Journal of Psychotherapy, 9*, 624–629.

Edinger, E. (1987). *The Christian archetype: A Jungian commentary on the life of Christ*. Toronto, Canada: Inner City Books.

Edinger, E. (1992). *Ego and archetype: Individuation and the religious function of the psyche*. Boston: Shambhala.

Edinger, E. (1999). *Archetype of the apocalypse: A Jungian study of the book of Revelation*. Chicago: Open Court.

Eliade, Mircea. (1964). *Shamanism: Archaic technology of ecstasy*, translated by Willard R. Trask. Princeton: Princeton University Press.

Ellenberger, H. (1970). *The discovery of the unconscious: The history and evolution of dynamic psychiatry*. New York: BasicBooks.

Estevez, M. (2010). High light: When a psilocybin study leads to spiritual realization. *Scientific American, November 23*. Retrieved July 6, 2013, from http://www.scientificamerican.com/article.cfm?id=psilocybin-book

Fadiman, J. (2008). Review of *Psychedelic medicine: New evidence for hallucinogenic substances as treatments*, by M. Winkelman & T. Roberts (Eds.), *Journal of Transpersonal Psychology, 40*, 125–127.

Fadiman, J. (2011). *The psychedelic explorers guide: Safe, therapeutic, and sacred journeys*. Rochester: VT: Park Street Press.

Ferrer, J. (2002). *Revisioning transpersonal theory: A participatory vision of human spirituality*. Albany: State University of New York Press.

Fischman, L. (1983). Dreams, hallucinogenic drug states, and schizophrenia: A psychological and biological comparison. *Schizophrenia Bulletin, 9*, 73–94.

Fordham, M. (1956). Active imagination and imaginative activity. *Journal of Analytical Psychology, 1*(2), 207–208.

Fordham, M. (1963). Analytic observations on patients using hallucinogenic drugs. In R. Crocket, R. Sandison, & A. Walk (Eds.), *Hallucinogenic drugs and their psychotherapeutic use* (pp. 125–130). Springfield, IL: C. C. Thomas.

Fordham, M. (1974). Jung's conception of transference. *Journal of Analytical Psychology, 19*(1), 1–21.

Frances, A., First, M., & Pincus, H. (1995). *DSM-IV guidebook*. Washington: American Psychiatric Press.

Frecska, E. (2007). Therapeutic guidelines: Dangers and contraindications in therapeutic applications of hallucinogens. In M. Winkelman & T. Roberts (Eds.), *Psychedelic medicines: New evidence for hallucinogenic substances as treatments* (Vol. 1, pp. 69–95). Westport, CT: Praeger.

Goldsmith, N. (2007). The ten lessons of psychedelic psychotherapy, rediscovered. In M. Winkelman & T. Roberts (Eds.), *Psychedelic medicines: New evidence for hallucinogenic substances as treatments* (Vol. 2, pp. 107–141). Westport, CT: Praeger.

Goldsmith, N. (2011). *Psychedelic healing: The promise of entheogens for psychotherapy and spiritual development*. Rochester: VT: Healing Arts Press.

Griffiths, R., Richards, W., Johnson, M., McCann, U., & Jesse, R. (2008). Mystical-type experiences occasioned by psilocybin mediate the attribution of personal meaning and spiritual significance 14 months later. *Journal of Psychopharmacology, 22*(6), 621–632.

Griffiths, R., Richards, W., McCann, U., & Jesse, R. (2006). Psilocybin can occasion mystical-type experiences having substantial and sustained personal meaning and spiritual significance. *Psychopharmacology, 187*, 268–283.

Grinspoon, L., & Bakalar, J. (1997). *Psychedelic drugs reconsidered*. New York: The Lindesmith Center. (Original work published 1979)

Grob, C. (2002a). A conversation with Albert Hofmann. In C. Grob (Ed.), *Hallucinogens: A reader* (pp. 15–22). New York: J. P. Tarcher/Putnam.

Grob, C. (Ed.). (2002b). *Hallucinogens: A reader*. New York: J. P. Tarcher/Putnam.

Grob, C. (2002c). Introduction: Hallucinogens revisited. In C. Grob (Ed.), *Hallucinogens: A reader* (pp. 1–13). New York: J. P. Tarcher/Putnam.

Grob, C. (2002d). Psychiatric research with hallucinogens: What have we learned? In C. Grob (Ed.), *Hallucinogens: A reader* (pp. 263–291). New York: J. P. Tarcher/Putnam.

Grof, C. and Grof, S. (1990). *The stormy search for the self: A guide to personal growth through transformational crisis*. Los Angeles: Jeremy P. Tarcher.

Grof, S. (1975). *Realms of the human unconscious: Observations from LSD research*. New York: Viking Press.

Grof, S. (1985). *Beyond the brain: Birth, death and transcendence in psychotherapy*. Albany: State University of New York Press.

Grof, S. (2000). *Psychology of the future: Lessons from modern consciousness research*. Albany: State University of New York Press.
Grof, S. (2001a). *LSD psychotherapy: Exploring the frontiers of the hidden mind*. Sarasota, FL: Multidisciplinary Association for Psychedelic Studies.
Grof, S. (2001b). The potential of entheogens as catalysts of spiritual development. In T. Roberts (Ed.), *Psychoactive sacramentals: Essays on entheogens and religion* (pp. 27–45). San Francisco: Council on Spiritual Practices.
Grof, S., & Grof, C. (Eds.). (1989). *Spiritual emergency: When personal transformation becomes a crisis*. Los Angles: Jeremy P. Tarcher/Putnam.
Harner, M. (1973). The role of hallucinogenic plants in European witchcraft. In M. Harner (Ed.), *Hallucinogens and shamanism* (pp. 125–150). London: Oxford University.
Hastings, A. (1999). Transpersonal psychology: The forth force. In D. Moss (Ed.), *Humanistic & transpersonal psychology: A historical & biographical sourcebook* (pp. 192–208). Westport, CT: Greenwood Press.
Henderson, J. (1964). Ancient myths and modern man. In C. G. Jung & M. L. von Franz (Eds.), *Man and his symbols* (pp. 104–157). Garden City, NY: Doubleday.
Henderson, J. (1990). *Shadow and self: Selected papers in analytical psychology*. Wilmette, IL: Chiron.
Hoffer, A. (1970). Treatment of alcoholism with psychedelic therapy. In B. Aaronson & H. Osmond (Eds.), *Psychedelics: The uses and implications of hallucinogenic drugs* (pp. 357–366). Garden City, NY: Anchor Books.
Hofmann, A. (2005). *LSD my problem child: Reflections on sacred drugs, mysticism, and science*. Sarasota, FL: Multidisciplinary Association for Psychedelic Studies.
Hollister, K. (1968). *Chemical psychoses*. Springfield, IL: Thomas.
Huxley, A. (1963). *The doors of perception* and *Heaven and hell*. New York: Harper & Row. (Original work published 1954)
Huxley, A. (1999). Letters. In M. Horowitz & C. Palmer (Eds.), *Moksha: Aldous Huxley's classic writings on psychedelics and the visionary experience* (pp. 29–30, 100–116). Rochester, VT: Park Street Press.
Jacobi, J. (1973). *The psychology of C. G. Jung: An introduction with illustrations*. New Haven, CT: Yale University Press. (Original work published 1942)
James, W. (1982). *The varieties of religious experience: A study in human nature*. New York: Penguin Books. (Original work published 1902).

Johnson, M. W., Richards, W. A., & Griffiths, R. A. (2008). Human hallucinogen research: Guidelines for safety. *Journal of Psychopharmacology, 22*(6), 603–620.

Jung, C. G. (1940). The meaning of individuation (S. Dell, Trans.). In *The integration of the personality* (pp. 3–29). London: Routledge & Kegan Paul.

Jung, C. G. (1963). *Memories, dreams, reflections*. Recorded and edited by Aniela Jaffé. Translated by R. & C. Winston. New York: Vintage Books.

Jung, C. G. (1964). Approaching the unconscious. In C. Jung & M. L. von Franz (Eds.), *Man and his symbols* (pp. 18–103). Garden City, NY: Doubleday.

Jung, C. G. (1966a). On the psychology of the unconscious. In *The collected works of C. G. Jung* (Vol. 7, pp. 1–119). (Original work published 1917)

Jung, C. G. (1966b). The personal and collective (or transpersonal) unconscious. In *The collected works of C. G. Jung* (Vol. 7, pp. 64–79). (Original work published 1917)

Jung, C. G. (1966c). The synthetic or constructive method. In *The collected works of C. G. Jung* (Vol. 7, pp. 80–89). (Original work published 1917)

Jung, C. G. (1966d). The therapeutic value of abreaction. In *The collected works of C. G. Jung* (Vol. 16, pp. 129–138). (Original work published 1921)

Jung, C. G. (1966e). The relations between the ego and the unconscious. In *The collected works of C. G. Jung* (Vol. 7, pp. 123–241). (Original work published 1928)

Jung, C. G. (1966f). The aims of psychotherapy. In *The collected works of C. G. Jung* (Vol. 16, pp. 36–52). (Original work published 1929)

Jung, C. G. (1966g). Problems of modern psychotherapy. In *The collected works of C. G. Jung* (Vol. 16, pp. 53–75). (Original work published 1929)

Jung, C. G. (1966h). The practical use of dream-analysis. In *The collected works of C. G. Jung* (Vol. 16, pp. 139–161). (Original work published 1934)

Jung, C. G. (1966i). Principles of practical psychotherapy. In *The collected works of C. G. Jung* (Vol. 16, pp. 3–20). (Original work published 1935)

Jung, C. G. (1966j). What is psychotherapy? In *The collected works of C. G. Jung* (Vol. 16, pp. 21–28). (Original work published 1935)

Jung, C. G. (1966k). *Psychology and religion*. New Haven, CT: Yale University Press. (Original work published 1938)

Jung, C. G. (1966l). Psychotherapy today. In *The collected works of C. G. Jung* (Vol. 16, pp. 94–110). (Original work delivered as a lecture 1941)

Jung, C. G. (1966m). Psychotherapy and a philosophy of life. In *The collected works of C. G. Jung* (Vol. 16, pp. 76–83). (Original work delivered as a lecture 1943)

Jung, C. G. (1966n). Medicine and psychotherapy. In *The collected works of C. G. Jung* (Vol. 16, pp. 84–93). (Original work published 1945)

Jung, C. G. (1966o). Fundamental questions of psychotherapy. In *The collected works of C. G. Jung* (Vol. 16, pp. 111–125). (Original work published 1951)

Jung, C. G. (1967). *The collected works of C. G. Jung: Vol. 5, Symbols of transformation.* (Original work published 1911–1912)

Jung, C. G. (1968a). Individual dream symbolism in relation to alchemy. In *The collected works of C. G. Jung* (Vol. 12, pp. 39–472). (Original work published 1936)

Jung, C. G. (1968b). Religious ideas in alchemy. In *The collected works of C. G. Jung* (Vol. 12, pp. 225–472). (Original work published 1937)

Jung, C. G. (1969a). General aspects of dream psychology. In *The collected works of C. G. Jung* (Vol. 8, pp. 237–280). (Original work published 1916)

Jung, C. G. (1969b). The transcendent function. In *The collected works of C. G. Jung* (Vol. 8., pp. 67–91). (Original work published 1916 and considerably revised 1958)

Jung, C. G. (1969c). Instinct and the unconscious. In *The collected works of C. G. Jung* (Vol. 8, pp. 129–138). (Original work published 1919)

Jung, C. G. (1969d). The psychological foundation of belief in spirits. In *The collected works of C. G. Jung* (Vol. 8, pp. 301–318). (Original work published 1920)

Jung, C. G. (1969e). Spirit and life. In *The collected works of C. G. Jung* (Vol. 8, pp. 319–337). (Original work published 1926)

Jung, C. G. (1969f). On psychic energy. In *The collected works of C. G. Jung* (Vol. 8, pp. 3–66). (Original work published 1928)

Jung, C. G. (1969g). The structure of the psyche. In *The collected works of C. G. Jung* (Vol. 8, pp. 139–158). (Original work published 1931)

Jung, C. G. (1969h). Archetypes of the collective unconscious. In *The collected works of C. G. Jung* (Vol. 9, Part I, pp. 3–41). (Original work published 1934)

Jung, C. G. (1969i). Basic postulates of analytical psychology. In *The collected works of C. G. Jung* (Vol. 8, pp. 338–357). (Original work published 1934)

Jung, C. G. (1969j). A review of the complex theory. In *The collected works of C. G. Jung* (Vol. 8, pp. 92–104). (Original work published 1934)

Jung, C. G. (1969k). Psychological commentary on *The Tibetan book of the dead*. In *The collected works of C. G. Jung* (Vol. 11, pp. 509–526). (Original work published 1935)

Jung, C. G. (1969l). Psychological factors determining human behavior. In *The collected works of C. G. Jung* (Vol. 8, pp. 114–125). (Original work published 1937)

Jung, C. G. (1969m). Psychology and religion. In *The collected works of C. G. Jung* (Vol. 11, pp. 3–105). (Original work published 1938)

Jung, C. G. (1969n). Conscious, unconscious, and individuation. In *The collected works of C. G. Jung* (Vol. 9, Part I, pp. 275–289). (Original work published 1939 as "The Meaning of Individuation")

Jung, C. G. (1969o). Psychological commentary on *The Tibetan book of the great liberation*. In *The collected works of C. G. Jung* (Vol. 11, pp. 475–508). (Original work written 1939)

Jung, C. G. (1969p). The psychology of the child archetype. In *The collected works of C. G. Jung* (Vol. 9, Part I, pp. 151–181). (Original work published 1940)

Jung, C. G. (1969q). Transformation symbolism and the mass. In *The collected works of C. G. Jung* (Vol. 11, pp. 201–296). (Original work published 1940–1941)

Jung, C. G. (1969r). A psychological approach to the dogma of the trinity. In *The collected works of C. G. Jung* (Vol. 11, pp. 107–200). (Original work published 1942)

Jung, C. G. (1969s). On the nature of dreams. In *The collected works of C. G. Jung* (Vol. 8, pp. 281–297). (Original work published 1945)

Jung, C. G. (1969t). On the nature of the psyche. In *The collected works of C. G. Jung* (Vol. 8, pp. 159–234). (Original work published 1947)

Jung, C. G. (1969u). The shadow. In *The collected works of C. G. Jung* (Vol. 9, Part II, pp. 8–10). (Original work published 1948)

Jung, C. G. (1969v). Conclusion. In *The collected works of C. G. Jung* (Vol. 9, Part II, pp. 266–269). (Original work published 1951)

Jung, C. G. (1969w). Answer to Job. In *The collected works of C. G. Jung* (Vol. 11, pp. 355–470). (Original work published 1952)

Jung, C. G. (1969x). Foreword to White's *God and the unconscious*. In *The collected works of C. G. Jung* (Vol. 11, pp. 299–310). (Original work published 1952)

Jung, C. G. (1969y). Synchronicity: An acausal connecting principle. In *The collected works of C. G. Jung* (Vol. 8, pp. 417–519). (Original work published in 1952)

Jung, C. G. (1970). The conjunction. In *The collected works of C. G. Jung* (Vol. 14, pp. 457–553). (Original work published 1955–1956)

Jung, C. G. (1972a). *The collected works of C. G. Jung: Vol. 3, The psychogenesis of mental disease.*

Jung, C. G. (1972b). The psychology of dementia praecox. In *The collected works of C. G. Jung* (Vol. 3, pp. 1–151). (Original work published 1907)

Jung, C. G. (1972c). The content of the psychoses. In *The collected works of C. G. Jung* (Vol. 3, pp. 153–178). (Original work published 1908)

Jung, C. G. (1972d). On psychological understanding. In *The collected works of C. G. Jung* (Vol. 3, pp. 179–193). (Original work published 1914)

Jung, C. G. (1972e). On the importance of the unconscious in psychopathology. In *The collected works of C. G. Jung* (Vol. 3, pp. 203–210). (Original work published 1914)

Jung, C. G. (1972f). On the problem of psychogenesis in mental disease. In *The collected works of C. G. Jung* (Vol. 3, pp. 211–225). (Original work published 1919)

Jung, C. G. (1972g). Mental disease and the psyche. In *The collected works of C. G. Jung* (Vol. 3, pp. 226–230). (Original work published 1928)

Jung, C. G. (1972h). On the psychogenesis of schizophrenia. In *The collected works of C. G. Jung* (Vol. 3, pp. 233–249). (Original work published in 1939)

Jung, C. G. (1972i). Recent thoughts on schizophrenia. In *The collected works of C. G. Jung* (Vol. 3, pp. 250–255). (Original work published 1956)

Jung, C. G. (1972j). Schizophrenia. In *The collected works of C. G. Jung* (Vol. 3, pp. 256–272). (Original work published 1958)

Jung, C. G. (1973a). Association, dream, and hysterical symptom. In *The collected works of C. G. Jung* (Vol. 2, pp. 353–407). (Original work published 1906)

Jung, C. G. (1973b). Appendix four: On the doctrine of complexes. In *The collected works of C. G. Jung* (Vol. 2, pp. 598–604). (Original work published 1913)

Jung, C. G. (1975a). Letter to Fr. V. White, April 10, 1954 (R. Hull, Trans.). In G. Adler & A. Jaffe (Eds.), *C. G. Jung Letters* (Vol. 2, 1951–1961, pp. 163–174). Princeton: Princeton University Press.

Jung, C. G. (1975b). Letter to A. M. Hubbard, February 15, 1955 (R. Hull, Trans.). In G. Adler & A. Jaffe (Eds.), *C. G. Jung Letters* (Vol. 2, 1951–1961, pp. 222–224). Princeton: Princeton University Press.

Jung, C. G. (1975c). Letter to R. Nijinsky, May 12, 1956 (R. Hull, Trans.). In G. Adler & A. Jaffe (Eds.), *C. G. Jung Letters* (Vol. 2, 1951–1961, pp. 299–300). Princeton: Princeton University Press.

Jung, C. G. (1975d). Letter to B. G. Eisner, August 12, 1957 (R. Hull, Trans.). In G. Adler & A. Jaffe (Eds.), *C. G. Jung Letters* (Vol. 2, 1951–1961, pp. 382–383). Princeton: Princeton University Press.

Jung, C. G. (1975e). Letter to R. J. Werblowsky, June 17, 1952 (R. Hull, Trans.). In G. Adler & A. Jaffe (Eds.), *C. G. Jung Letters* (Vol. 2, 1951–1961, pp. 69–70). Princeton: Princeton University Press.

Jung, C. G. (1976). Definitions. In *The collected works of C. G. Jung* (Vol. 6, pp. 408–486). (Original work published 1921)

Jung, C. G. (1977). On resurrection. In *The collected works of C. G. Jung* (Vol. 18, pp. 692–696). (Original work published 1954)

Jung, C. G. (1979). *The collected works of C. G. Jung: Vol. 20, General index to the collected works of C. G. Jung*.

Jung, C. G. (1988). Lecture V, June 3, 1936. In J. L. Barret (Ed.), *Nietzsche's Zarathustra: Notes of the seminar given in 1934–1939* (pp. 965–982). Princeton: Princeton University Press.

Kalsched, D. (1996). *The inner world of trauma: Archetypal defenses of the personal spirit*. New York: Routledge.

Kalsched, D. (2003). Response to James Astor. *Journal of Analytical Psychology*, 48, 201–205.

Ka-Tzetnik 135633. (1998). *Shivitti: A vision*. Nevada City, CA: Gateways/IDHHB.

Kelly, S. (1993). *Individuation and the absolute: Hegel, Jung, and the path toward wholeness*. New York: Paulist Press.

Kelly, S. (2002). Space, time, and spirit: The analogical imagination and the evolution of transpersonal theory: Part one: Contexts—theoretical and historical. *Journal of Transpersonal Psychology*, 34, 73–86.

Kirsch, T. (2000). *The Jungians: A comparative and historical perspective*. London: Routledge.

Laing, R. D. (1967). *The politics of experience*. New York: Pantheon Books.

Laing, R. D. (1979). Transcendental experience in relation to religion and psychosis. In J. Fadiman & D. Kewman (Eds.), *Exploring madness: Experience, theory, and research* (pp. 113–121). Monterey, CA: Brooks/Cole. (Original work published 1965)

Leary, T. (1995). *High priest*. Berkeley, CA: Ronin Publishing.

Leary, T., Metzner, R., & Alpert, R. (1995). *The psychedelic experience: A manual based on the Tibetan book of the dead*. New York: Citadel. (Original work published 1964)

Lee, M., & Shlain, B. (1985). *Acid dreams: The CIA, LSD, and the sixties rebellion*. New York: Grove Press.

Leuner, H. (1983). Psycholytic therapy: Hallucinogens as an aid in psychoanalytically oriented psychotherapy. In L. Grinspoon & J. Bakalar (Eds.), *Psychedelic reflections* (pp. 177–192). New York: Human Sciences Press.

Littlefield, C. (Writer, Director), & Martin, K. (Producer). (2002). *Hofmann's potion: The pioneers of LSD* [Documentary Motion Picture]. National Film Board of Canada.

Lukoff, D. (1985). The diagnosis of mystical experiences with psychotic features. *Journal of Transpersonal Psychology, 17*, 155–181.

Lukoff, D. (1991). Divine madness: Shamanistic initiatory crisis and psychosis. *Shaman's Drum, 22*, 24–29.

Lukoff, D. (1996). Transpersonal psychotherapy with psychotic disorders and spiritual emergencies with psychotic features. In B. Scotton, A. Chinen, & J. Battista (Eds.), *Textbook of transpersonal psychiatry and psychology* (pp. 271–281). New York: Basic Books.

Lukoff, D., & Lu, F. (1990). Toward a more culturally sensitive DSM-IV: Psychoreligious and psychospiritual problems. *Journal of Nervous and Mental Disease, 180*, 673–682.

Lukoff, D., Lu, F., & Turner, R. (1996). Diagnosis: A transpersonal clinical approach to religious and spiritual problems. In B. Scotton, A. Chinen, & J. Battista (Eds.), *Textbook of transpersonal psychiatry and psychology* (pp. 231–249). New York: Basic Books.

Lukoff, D., Zanger, R., & Lu, F. (1990). Transpersonal psychology research review: Psychoactive substances and transpersonal states. *Journal of Transpersonal Psychology, 22*, 107–147.

Marsden, R., & Lukoff, D. (2007). Transpersonal healing with hallucinogens. In M. Winkelman & T. Roberts (Eds.), *Psychedelic medicines: New evidence for hallucinogenic substances as treatments* (Vol. 2, pp. 287–305). Westport, CT: Praeger.

Masters, R., & Houston, J. (1970). Toward an individual psychedelic psychotherapy. In B. Aaronson & H. Osmond (Eds.), *Psychedelics: The uses and implications of hallucinogenic drugs* (pp. 323–342). Garden City, NY: Anchor Books.

Merkur, D. (2007). A psychoanalytic approach to psychedelic psychotherapy. In M. Winkelman & T. Roberts (Eds.), *Psychedelic medicines: New evidence for hallucinogenic substances as treatments* (Vol. 2, pp. 195–211). Westport, CT: Praeger.

Metzner, R. (1998a). Hallucinogenic drugs and plants in psychotherapy and shamanism. *Journal of Psychoactive Drugs, 30*(4), 333–341.

Metzner, R. (1998b). *The unfolding self: Varieties of transformative experience.* Novato, CA: Origin Press.

Metzner, R. (Ed.) (1999). *Ayahuasca: Hallucinogens, consciousness, and the spirit of nature.* New York: Thunder's Mouth Press.

Metzner, R. (2002a). Ritual approaches to working with sacred medicine plants: An interview with Ralph Metzner, Ph.D. In C. Grob (Ed.), *Hallucinogens: A reader* (pp. 164–184). New York: J. P. Tarcher/Putnam.

Metzner, R. (2002b). The role of psychoactive plant medicines. In C. Grob (Ed.), *Hallucinogens: A reader* (pp. 23–37). New York: J. P. Tarcher/Putnam.

Miller, J. (2004). *The transcendent function: Jung's model of psychological growth through dialogue with the unconscious*. Albany: State University of New York Press.

Mithoefer, M. (2007). MDMA-assisted psychotherapy for the treatment of post-traumatic stress disorder. In M. Winkelman & T. Roberts (Eds.), *Psychedelic medicines: New evidence for hallucinogenic substances as treatments* (Vol. 1, pp. 155–176). Westport, CT: Praeger.

Mogenson, G. (2005). *A most accursed religion: When trauma becomes God*. Putnam, CT: Spring.

Mojeiko, V. (2007). Psychedelic emergency services: Report for Burning Man 2007. *MAPS Bulletin, 17*(3), 15–17.

Multidisciplinary Association for Psychedelic Studies. *Psychedelic research around the world.* (n.d.) Retrieved July 6, 2013, from http://www.maps.org/research/

Nelson, J. (1994). *Healing the split: Integrating spirit into our understanding of the mentally ill*. Albany: State University of New York Press.

Osmond, H. (1970). On going mad. In B. Aaronson & H. Osmond (Eds.), *Psychedelics: The uses and implications of hallucinogenic drugs* (pp. 21–28). Garden City, NY: Anchor Books.

Otto, R. (1958). *The idea of the holy*. New York: Oxford University Press.

Passie, T. (1997). *Psycholytic and psychedelic therapy research 1931–1995: A complete international bibliography*. Hannover, Germany: Laurentius.

Perry, J. W. (1974). *The far side of madness*. Englewood Cliffs, NJ: Prentice-Hall.

Perry, J. W. (1976). *Roots of renewal in myth and madness: The meaning of psychotic episodes*. San Francisco: Jossey-Bass.

Perry, J. W. (1987). *The self in psychotic process*. Dallas: Spring.

Perry, J. W. (1999). *Trials of the visionary mind: Spiritual emergency and the renewal process*. Albany: State University of New York Press.

Read, H., Fordham, M., Adler, G., & McGuire, W. (Eds.). (1972). Editorial note. In *The collected works of C. G. Jung* (Vol. 3, pp. v-vi). Princeton: Princeton University Press.

Richards, W. (2003). Entheogens in the study of mystical and archetypal experiences. *Research in the Social Scientific Study of Religion, 3*, 143–155.

Richards, W. (2009). The rebirth of research with entheogens: Lessons from the past and hypotheses for the future. *Journal of Transpersonal Psychology, 41*(2), 139–150.

Roberts, T. (Ed.). (2001). *Psychoactive sacramentals: Essays on entheogens and religion.* San Francisco: Council on Spiritual Practices.

Rowland, S. (2006). Jung, the trickster writer, or what literary research can do for the clinician. *Journal of Analytical Psychology, 51,* 285–299.

Salinger, J. D. (1955). *Raise high the roof beam, carpenters* and *Seymour: An introduction.* Boston: Little, Brown.

Samuels, A. (1986). *Jung and the post-Jungians.* Boston: Routledge & Kegan Paul.

Samuels, A. (2008). New developments in the post-Jungian field. In P. Young-Eisendrath & T. Dawson (Eds.). *The Cambridge companion to Jung.* Cambridge: Cambridge University Press.

Samuels, A., Shorter, B., & Plaut, F. (1986). *A critical dictionary of Jungian analysis.* New York: Routledge.

Sandison, R. (1954). Psychological aspects of the LSD treatment of the neuroses. *Journal of Mental Science, 100,* 508–515.

Sandison, R. (1959). The role of psychotropic drugs in individual therapy. *Bulletin of the World Health Organization, 21,* 495–503.

Sandison, R. (1960). The nature of the psychological response to LSD. In H. Abramson (Ed.), *The use of LSD in psychotherapy: Transactions of a conference on d-lysergic acid diethylamide (LSD-25)* (pp. 81–149). New York: Josiah Macy, Jr. Foundation.

Sandison, R. (1963). Certainty and uncertainty in the LSD treatment of psychoneurosis. In R. Crocket, R. Sandison, & A. Walk (Eds.), *Hallucinogenic drugs and their psychotherapeutic use* (pp. 33–36). Springfield, IL: C. C. Thomas.

Sandison, R. (1997). LSD therapy: A retrospective. In A. Melechi (Ed.), *Psychedelia britannica: Hallucinogenic drugs in Britain* (pp. 53–86). London: Turnaround.

Sandison, R. (2001). *A century of psychiatry, psychotherapy and group analysis: A search for integration.* London: Jessica Kingsley.

Sandison, R., Spenser, A., & Whitelaw, J. (1954). The therapeutic value of lysergic acid diethylamide in mental illness. *Journal of Mental Science, 100,* 491–507.

Sandison, R., & Whitelaw, J. (1957). Further studies in the therapeutic value of lysergic acid diethylamide in mental illness. *Journal of Mental Science, 103,* 332–343.

Schultes, R., & Hofmann, A. (1992). *Plants of the gods: Their sacred, healing and hallucinogenic powers.* Rochester, VT: Healing Arts Press.

Sessa, B. (2005). Can psychedelics have a role in psychiatry once again? *British Journal of Psychiatry, 186,* 457–458.

Sessa, B. (2008). Update from the UK and an interview with pioneering psychedelic psychiatrist Dr. Ronald Sandison. *MAPS Bulletin, 18*(3), 30–33.

Sessa, B. (2012). *The psychedelic renaissance: Reassessing the role of psychedelic drugs in 21st century psychiatry and society.* London: Muswell Hill Press.

Shorto, R. (1999). *Saints and madmen: How pioneering psychiatrists are creating a new science of the soul.* New York: Henry Holt.

Shulgin, A. (2001). The new psychotherapy: MDMA and the shadow. In T. Roberts (Ed.), *Psychoactive sacramentals: Essays on entheogens and religion* (pp. 197–204). San Francisco: Council on Spiritual Practices.

Singer, J. (1994). *Boundaries of the soul.* New York: Anchor Books.

Smith, D., & Seymour, R. (1985). Dream becomes nightmare: Adverse reactions to LSD. *Journal of Psychoactive Drugs, 14*(4) 297–303.

Smith, H. (2000). *Cleansing the doors of perception: The religious significance of entheogenic plants and chemicals.* New York: Tarcher/Putnam.

Stevens, J. (1987). *Storming heaven: LSD and the American dream.* New York: Grove Press.

Stockings, G. (1940). A clinical study of mescaline psychosis, with special reference to the mechanism of the genesis of schizophrenia and other psychotic states. *Journal of Mental Science, 86,* 29–47.

Stolaroff, M. (1994). *Thanatos to eros: Thirty-five years of psychedelic exploration.* Berlin: VWB – Verlag für Wissenschaft und Bildung.

Stolaroff, M. (2002). Using psychedelics wisely. In C. Grob (Ed.), *Hallucinogens: A reader* (pp. 94–103). New York: J. P. Tarcher/Putnam.

Strassman, R. (1984). Adverse reactions to psychedelic drugs: A review of the literature. *Journal of Nervous and Mental Disease, 172*(10), 577–595.

Strassman, R. (2001). *DMT: The spirit molecule: A doctor's revolutionary research into the biology of near-death and mystical experiences.* Rochester, VT: Park Street Press.

Ungerleider, J. (1968). The acute side effects from LSD. In J. Ungerleider (Ed.), The problems and prospects of LSD (pp. 61–68). Springfield, IL: Charles C Thomas.

Vaughan, F. (2001). Transpersonal counseling: Some observations concerning entheogens. In T. Roberts (Ed.), *Psychoactive sacramentals: Essays on entheogens and religion* (pp. 191–195). San Francisco: Council on Spiritual Practices.

von Franz, M.-L. (1964). The process of individuation. In C. G. Jung & M. L. von Franz (Eds.), *Man and his symbols* (pp. 158–229). Garden City, NY: Doubleday.
von Franz, M.-L. (1980). *Projection and re-collection in Jungian psychology: Reflections of the soul*. La Salle, IL: Open Court.
von Franz, M.-L. (1993). *Psychotherapy*. Boston: Shambhala.
Walsh, R., & Grob, C. (Eds.). (2005). *Higher wisdom: eminent elders explore the continuing impact of psychedelics*. Albany: State University of New York Press.
Walsh, R., & Vaughan, F. (Eds.). (1993). *Paths beyond ego: The transpersonal vision*. New York: J. P. Tarcher.
Wapnick, K. (1969). Mysticism and schizophrenia. *Journal of Transpersonal Psychology, 1*, 49–67.
Washburn, M. (1995). *The ego and the dynamic ground: A transpersonal theory of human development*. Albany: State University of New York Press.
Wasson, R. G. (1998). The Wasson road to Eleusis. In R. G. Wasson, A. Hofmann, & C. A. P. Ruck, *The road to eleusis* (pp. 21–34). Los Angeles: William Daily Rare Books.
Weil, A. (1986). *The natural mind: An investigation of drugs and the higher consciousness*. Boston: Houghton Mifflin.
Weil, A., & Rosen, W. (1993). *From chocolate to morphine: Everything you need to know about mind-altering drugs*. New York: Houghton Mifflin.
Whitmont, E. (1991). *The symbolic quest: Basic concepts of analytical psychology*. Princeton: Princeton University Press.
Williams, D. (1981). *Border crossings: A psychological perspective on Carlos Castaneda's path of knowledge*. Toronto: Inner City Books.
Williams, M. (1963). The indivisibility of the personal and collective unconscious. *Journal of Analytical Psychology, 8*, 45–50.
Winkelman, M. (2007a). Shamanic guidelines for psychedelic medicine. In M. Winkelman & T. Roberts (Eds.), *Psychedelic medicines: New evidence for hallucinogenic substances as treatments* (Vol. 2, pp. 143–167). Westport, CT: Praeger.
Winkelman, M. (2007b). Therapeutic bases of psychedelic medicines: Psychointegrative effects. In M. Winkelman & T. Roberts (Eds.), *Psychedelic medicines: New evidence for hallucinogenic substances as treatments* (Vol. 1, pp. 1–19). Westport, CT: Praeger.
Winkelman, M., & Roberts, T. (Eds.). (2007). *Psychedelic medicine: New evidence for hallucinogenic substances as treatments*. Westport, CT: Praeger.

Wulff, D. (1997). *Psychology of religion: Classic and contemporary*. New York: John Wiley & Sons.

Yensen, R. (1985). LSD and psychotherapy. *Journal of Psychoactive Drugs, 17*(4), 267–277.

Zweig, C., & Abrams, J. (Eds.). (1991). *Meeting the shadow: The hidden power of the dark side of human nature*. New York: J. P. Tarcher/Putnam.

Index

abaissement du niveau mental. See lowering the threshold of consciousness
abreaction
  defined, 57, 125, 126, 127
  Jung's vs. Grof's views, 125–30, 175
active imagination, 25, 148–49, 201 n. 10
  creation and understanding in, 140–41, 142
  psychedelic psychotherapy and, 14, 26, 154, 163, 166, 169
  risks, Jung on, 97, 137–38, 154
  vs. passive imagination, 149–50
  See also transcendent function
adverse reactions
  Jung's psychology and, 30, 33–34, 100–1, 147, 157, 165, 173
  management of, 11, 54–55, 57–58, 158, 166–67
  psychotic reactions, 6, 9, 14, 54–55, 106–11
  research on, 9, 53–54, 109
  short- and long-term, 9, 11, 53, 89, 109
  transformative potential of, 33, 40, 54–55
  trauma and, 53–58
  treatment of, 101, 160, 161, 169
  See also LSD: adverse reactions to; psychedelic experiences: flashbacks
Alpert, Richard (Ram Dass), 12, 94, 147
  Psychedelic Experience, The (Leary, Metzner, Alpert), 12
  on psychosis, 119
American Indians, 5, 94. *See also* indigenous peoples
"Analytic Work with LSD 25" (Cutner), 26–27, 182 n. 41, 203 n. 23
anger
  Anger, Madness, and the Daimonic (Diamond), 188 n. 53, 190 n. 41
  psychosis, shadow, trauma, and, 71, 79–81
archetype(s), 6, 18, 35–37, 71–72, 97, 180 n. 38
  in mythological images, 24, 35, 73, 76, 124–25, 156, 169–71
  numinous quality of, 35–36, 37, 45, 66–67, 73–74, 75–76, 100
  in psychedelic experience, 25, 45, 62–63, 74–75, 132–33, 163–65, 169–71
  psychosis and, 36, 74–75, 76, 97, 100, 116, 117
  Self as, 37, 73, 148, 190 n. 15
    dark side of, 60, 66, 73, 75, 76
    symbols of, 36–37, 66, 73, 123–24, 124–25
  shadow and, 66, 73, 74, 75–76
  transformative potential, 33, 36, 117, 132–33, 163–165, 169–171
  trauma and, 58, 61, 66–67, 69
ayahuasca, 5, 8, 11, 23, 24, 43, 93, 115
Aziz, Robert, 177 n. 5

Bache, Christopher, 115–16
bad trips. *See* psychedelic experiences: difficult (bad trips)
Bakalar, James, 7, 8, 21, 56, 88, 89, 91, 92, 105, 115, 116
Baker, Ian
  LSD 25 and Analytical Psychology, 180 n. 44, 203 n. 23
Bergson, Henri, 8
Beringer, Kurt, 5, 87
Bleuler, Eugen, 90, 99
Bleuler, Manfred, 90
Burghölzli Mental Hospital (Zurich), 24–25, 90, 99, 102

Castaneda, Carlos, 180 n. 44
Clark, Walter Houston, 107–9

Cohen, Sidney
   adverse reactions, research on, 9, 187 n. 19
   psychedelic drugs, value of, 9
coincidentia oppositorum, 13, 124
collective unconscious, 18, 31, 32, 35, 180 n. 38
complexio oppositorum, 73, 190 n. 15
consciousness (conscious mind)
   archetypes and, 35, 36, 40
   unconscious invasions of, 36, 40, 44, 80, 101, 104, 166
   unconscious, the, and, 30, 32–34, 47, 137–39, 148, 167 (*see also* lowering the threshold of consciousness)
   See also ego
Corbett, Lionel, 75–76, 77, 124, 125, 197 n. 27
Cutner, Margot
   Adler, Gerhard, and, 203 n. 23
   "Analytic Work with LSD 25," 26, 163, 182 n. 41, 203 n. 23
   on integrating LSD experiences, 27, 117, 133, 159, 166, 167, 168–69, 174
   LSD therapy, accounts of, 80, 62–63, 117, 132–33
   LSD therapy, Jungian-oriented, 14, 25, 26, 98, 163, 174, 175, 181 n. 5, 185 n. 17
   on patient-therapist relationship, 117, 133, 166–67, 168–69
   on problems in psychedelic therapy, 26–27, 159, 166–67
   on touch in psychedelic therapy, 167, 204 n. 46

Daniels, Michael, 113
death-rebirth process, xiv, 22, 55, 94, 98, 108, 115, 133
delusions,
   Jung on, 38, 40, 44, 100, 102, 121, 122
   in psychedelic experience, 53–54, 83, 87, 98, 107, 141, 178 n. 16
   psychosis and, 67, 83, 88
De-Nur, Yehiel, 167–68, 205 n. 53
Devil / devils, 73, 95, 124, 130, 144
   Lucifer (bringer of light), 124
   in psychedelic experience, 64, 65, 79, 95–96, 141, 165
   as symbol, 60, 65, 66, 74, 123
Diagnostic and Statistical Manual of Mental Disorders (DSM-IV) (American Psychiatric Association), 55–56, 57, 83, 116, 191–92 n. 19, 192 n. 34
Diamond, Stephen, 41, 72, 188 n. 53, 190 n. 41
dissociation
   complexes and, 61–62, 66, 102–3
   as ego defense, 58, 60
   Jung's theory of, 59, 61–62, 67
   manifest in daimonic images, 59–60, 61, 62, 63, 64, 67, 103
   psychosis and, 67, 103
   trauma and, 58–61, 128–29
DMT (dimethyltryptamine), 8, 109, 130
Doblin, Rick, 196 n. 18
Doors of Perception, The (Huxley), 8, 49
dreams, 37–38
   compensating function of, 33, 38, 155–56, 163
   interpretation of, 150, 151, 154–56
   meaning in, 38, 40, 59, 102, 122, 155
   psychedelic experiences, similarity, 8, 25, 39–40, 46, 101–2, 154, 163, 169
   reflecting fragmentation, 59, 61, 62
   schizophrenia, similarity, 40, 101, 102, 154
   as symbolic products of the unconscious, 37–38, 59, 156
DSM-IV. See Diagnostic and Statistical Manual of Mental Disorders
DSM-IV Guidebook (Frances, First, Pincus), on PTSD, 56

Edinger, Edward, 37, 74, 99, 124, 125, 180 n. 44, 197 n. 27
ego
   death of (ego death), 19, 37, 54, 56, 76, 93–94
   defenses, 54, 58, 71
   disruption, risk of, 34, 36, 45, 48, 86, 141–42, 153
   integration and, 26, 47, 123, 141, 149
   nature of, 30–31, 34, 85–86, 179 n. 38

INDEX   225

psychedelic experience and, 48, 54, 87, 93, 114–15, 150, 158, 165, 166–67
psychosis and, 83, 98, 100, 103, 104–5, 141–42
Self and, 37, 76
transformation and, 114, 123, 141, 153
trauma and, 61, 62, 67, 68–69
unconscious, the, and, 31, 32–33, 34, 45, 99, 150
   confrontation with, 13, 33, 40, 74
See also consciousness (conscious mind)
Eisner, Betty, Jung's letter to, 48
entheogens, 24, 94, 178 n. 16
Estevez, Maria
   mystical experience of, 4, 11, 19
   Jung's experience, similarity, 4
evil, 65, 66, 144
   absolute evil, 73, 79, 190 n. 13
   archetype of, 60, 73
   experience of, 39, 75, 76, 79, 81, 107, 141, 170
   shadow and, 72–73, 123
   unconsciousness as, 73

Fadiman, James, 191 n. 13
Ferrer, Jorge, 196 n. 14
Fordham, Michael, 157, 173, 182 n. 39
   "Active Imagination and Imaginative Activity," 150
   on active vs. passive imagination, 149–50
   on integrating psychedelic experience, 49
   psychedelic psychotherapy, criticism of, 25, 26, 27, 149
Freud, Sigmund, 38, 44, 129
   Grof's psychedelic theory and, 13, 22
   Jung's shadow theory and, 71
   Kalsched's trauma theory and, 59
   psycholytic therapy, influence on, 18, 22
   trauma theory, 66, 188 n. 58

God
   archetype, 37, 74, 114, 124
      dark side, 73, 76
   experience of, 37, 60
      in psychedelic experience, 19, 74–75, 81, 94, 133, 144, 171
   gods and goddesses, 37, 38
   metaphysical question of, 114
   mythological representation of, 37, 73, 75, 76, 125
God is Trauma (Mogenson), 67
Griffiths, Roland, 11
Grinspoon, Lester, 7, 8, 21, 56, 88, 89, 91, 92, 105, 115, 116
Grob, Charles, 90
Grof, Christina, 93, 116, 199 n. 41
   Spiritual Emergency, 116, 119
Grof, Stanislav
   abreaction, 57–58, 125, 126–28, 129, 130
   consciousness transformation, model of, 22–23
   on difficult psychedelic experiences, 55, 57–58
   on ego death, 10, 54, 93–94
   holotropic breathwork, 199 n. 41
   Jung's psychology and, 4, 8, 13, 84, 116, 120, 148, 175
   low vs. high doses, 19, 181 n. 9
   LSD, 22, 23, 57–58, 120
   LSD Psychotherapy, 23
   psychedelic psychotherapy, 17–18, 19, 21, 158, 175
      Grofian framework, 22–23
      as treatment for trauma, 57–58, 62
   psychedelic psychotic states, 55, 84, 93, 119–20, 152, 158
   psychedelics as catalysts, 8, 46, 89
   somatic component in healing, 128, 204 n. 46
   Spiritual Emergency, 116, 119
   transpersonal state, the, 114–15

hallucinations
   Jung on, 33, 36, 40, 44, 68, 99, 100, 101, 121
   in psychedelic experience, 25, 40, 53, 87, 89, 91, 166
   psychosis and, 83, 88, 89, 90, 91
hallucinogen(s), as medical and legal terms, 178 n. 16
Henderson, Joseph, 31, 32, 72, 73, 123
Hoffer, Abram, 20, 90-91
Hofmann, Albert
   LSD and, 17, 119
   LSD-induced psychosis, personal, 87–88, 192 n. 31

Hubbard, Alfred, Jung's letter to, 14, 43
Huxley, Aldous, 7, 49, 195 n. 43
   Doors of Perception, The, 8, 49
   mescaline, on effects of, 8

ibogaine, 8
indigenous peoples, 10, 11, 23, 91, 94, 95, 108
individuation in Jung's psychology, 34–35, 123, 124, 137
   challenges of, 13, 116
   as goal of psychotherapy, 33, 47, 148
   symbols of, 124, 125, 169–70
integration
   Jung's conception of, 34, 123, 128–29, 137, 141, 148–49, 164
      on psychedelic experience and, 14, 46–48, 49, 138, 139, 157
   psychedelic experience and, 6, 19, 26, 40, 48–49, 115, 129, 141, 150
   during psychedelic sessions, 20, 22, 27, 133, 166, 167–69, 174
   psychosis and, 84, 100, 120
   resistance to, 26–27, 44, 129, 132, 158–59, 161–62, 166
   of shadow, 18, 76, 78, 123–24
   trauma and, 127, 128–29, 130
   See also transcendent function

James, William, 31, 116, 196 n. 22
Job, book of, 73, 74, 75, 76, 124
Johns Hopkins Medical Center, psilocybin investigation, 4, 11–12, 19, 186 n. 3
Jung, C. G.
   analytical method of, 14, 147–49 (*see also* Jung, C.G.: psychotherapy)
   complexes, theory of, 66–69, 100, 101–2, 102–3, 104
   conceptions, hypothetical nature of, 40–41
   confrontation with the unconscious, personal, 3, 4, 5, 43–44, 47–48
   on delusions, 38, 40, 44, 100, 102, 121, 122
   on dissociation, 59, 61–62, 66, 67, 68
   on hallucinations, 33, 36, 40, 44, 68, 99, 100, 101, 121
   on intellect, limits of, 5, 35, 139, 140
   metaphysical conclusions, avoidance of, 85, 113–14, 191 n. 17
   mystical sensibility of, 4, 12, 147–48
   on psychedelic experience, 4, 5, 43, 46–48
      explanation of, 8, 44–46
      moral responsibility and, 144
      schizophrenia and, similarities, 40, 46, 101–2, 104–6, 166
   psychedelic psychotherapy, criticism of, 6, 14–15, 139, 157–58
   on psychosis, 97–106
      personal fear of, 3, 44
      psychedelic experience and, similarities, 40, 46, 97, 101–2, 104–5, 166
      as the psyche's effort to heal, 59, 98, 121–23
      See also psychosis; schizophrenia
   on psychotherapy, 137–42, 147–56
      integration in, primacy of, 129, 169
      purpose and method of, 147–49
      risks inherent in, 157
      therapist-patient relationship, 129, 139, 151–53, 160–62
      transference, 129–30, 152–53, 162
      See also active imagination; integration
   religion, characterization of, 114
   on transformation, 33–35, 114
      regression in, 114, 123, 156
      See also individuation in Jung's psychology
   transpersonal experience, phenomenological descriptions of, 85, 113
   writing style, 29
Jung, C.G., works of
   "Aims of Psychotherapy, The," 161–62
   Answer to Job, 1, 73
   "Approaching the Unconscious," 122
   Archetypes and the Collective Unconscious, The, viii
   "Content of the Psychoses, The," 51
   "Fundamental Questions of Psychotherapy," 203 n. 16
   "Importance of the Unconscious in Psychotherapy, The," 121
   Man and His Symbols, 38
   Memories, Dreams, Reflections, 43, 97
   "On the Nature of the Psyche," 34

"On Psychic Energy," 123
"On Psychological Understanding," 122
"Practical Use of Dream-Analysis, The," 135, 169
"Principles of Practical Psychotherapy," 156
Psychogenesis of Mental Disease, The, 99, 122
"Psychological Approach to the Dogma of the Trinity, A," 37, 113
"Psychological Foundation of Belief in Spirits, The," 69
Psychology and Religion, 114
"Psychology of Dementia Praecox, The," 99
Red Book, The, 5, 43
"Schizophrenia," 99, 100, 189 n. 62
"Shadow, The," 72
"Transcendent Function, The," 123, 137–42
"Therapeutic Value of Abreaction, The," 128
Two Essays on Analytical Psychology, 5
"Two Kinds of Thinking," 122
Jungian analysis / psychotherapy
    psychedelic psychotherapy and
        implications, 157–71, 174
        similarities, 14, 25, 159, 163, 166–67, 169, 174
    See also Jung, C.G.: psychotherapy
Jungians
    psychedelic research and, 6, 14, 50, 173, 174–75

Kalsched, Donald
    archetypal self-care system, 59–61, 67, 69
    daimonic imagery, paradox in, 58–59, 60, 65, 67, 73, 123–24
    on the daimonic vs. demonic, 60, 65, 188 n. 53
    Inner World of Trauma, The, 58
    trauma, theory of, 58–62, 65–66, 69
        relevance to psychedelic experiences, 58
    See also trauma
Kelly, Sean, 113, 117, 190 n. 15
Kirsch, Thomas, 32
Kluger, Rivkah Schärf, 124

Koestler, Arthur, personal psychedelic experience, 106–7, 195 n. 43
Kohut, Heinz, 58, 59

Laing, R. D., 92, 118, 197, n. 32
Leary, Timothy, 7, 12, 13, 55, 147, 178 n. 25
    Psychedelic Experience, The (Leary, Metzner, Alpert), 12
    shadow and psychosis, confrontation with, 77–78
Leuner, Hanscarl, 63
lowering the threshold of consciousness, 44–46
    in psychedelic experience, 30, 45, 48, 173
    schizophrenia, similarity, 40, 44, 46–47, 100, 101, 104, 105
LSD
    adverse reactions to, 9, 48, 87–88, 108, 187 n. 19 (*see also* adverse reactions)
    chemical psychosis model and, 6–7, 87, 91
    Grof on, 19, 22, 23, 57–58, 91, 120
    Jung's ignorance of, 8, 15, 49–50
    Hofmann, Albert, and, 17, 87–88, 119, 192 n. 31
    misuse of, 9, 10, 25
    mystical states and, 19, 91, 115
    research on, 7, 8–10, 17, 50, 90, 178–79 n. 27 (*see also* psychedelic research)
    Sandoz Pharmaceuticals and, 7, 17, 25, 88, 90
    therapy and (*see under* psychedelic psychotherapy)
    See also psychedelic drugs / substances
LSD: My Problem Child (Hofmann), 87
LSD Psychotherapy (Grof), 23
Lukoff, David, 24, 116, 118–19, 191–92 n. 19
lysergic acid diethylamide. *See* LSD

MAPS (Multidisciplinary Association for Psychedelic Studies), 10, 63, 179 n. 29
Marsden, Roger, 24
May, Rollo, 188 n. 53

MDMA-assisted psychotherapy, 11, 64, 78, 94
Meier, Carl, 49
Merkur, Dan, 22
mescaline, 5, 6, 19, 109, 115, 187 n. 19
   chemical psychosis model and, 6, 87, 88, 90
   Jung on
      effects of, 8, 14, 43, 46, 49, 195 n. 25
      psychosis and, 14, 100, 101
   Huxley on effects of, 8
Metzner, Ralph, 12, 124, 147
   hybrid shamanic psychotherapeutic rituals, 24
   Jung's psychology and, 13, 14
   Psychedelic Experience, The (Leary, Metzner, Alpert), 12
   on psychedelic psychosis and transformation, 119
   on psychedelics and cultural attitudes, 94–95
Mogenson, Greg, 67
morning glory seeds, 95
Multidisciplinary Association for Psychedelic Studies (MAPS), 10, 63, 179 n. 29

National Survey on Drug Use and Health LSD use, 10, 178–79 n. 27
Nelson, John, 83
   on benign vs. malignant psychotic states, 84, 85, 86
   Healing the Split, 83, 117, 192 n. 26
   Jung's psychology and, 85
   psychedelic psychosis, explanation of, 86, 93
numinosity, 35, 37, 61, 75–76, 125
   Jung's description, 36, 45, 66–67, 73, 114, 180 n. 38
   Otto, Rudolf, on, 73–74, 196 n. 8
   psychedelic experience and, 14, 43, 100, 106, 176

Osmond, Humphry, 7, 19
   "On Being Mad," 109, 111
   psychedelic psychosis, account of, 109–11
   psychedelic therapy practice, 90–91
Otto, Rudolf, 73–74, 114, 196 n. 8

Perry, John Weir
   on Jung's psychology, 122–23
   psychosis, on meaning in, 59, 117, 118, 121
peyote, 5, 11, 24, 94, 95
possession, psychological, 61, 66, 68–69, 188 n. 53
Posttraumatic Stress Disorder (PTSD)
   psychedelic experience and, 55–57
projection, 76–77
   in psychedelic experience, 81, 89, 93, 107, 152
   in psychedelic psychotherapy, 62–63, 64, 80, 132–33, 151, 153, 169
   psychosis and, 93, 121, 152
   shadow and, 72, 75–77, 79, 81
   as transference, 182 n. 39
   Jung on, 76, 129, 151, 152–53, 162
psilocybin, 4, 5, 10, 11, 24, 95
   mystical experience and, research on, 11–12, 19, 186 n. 3
psyche, 23, 41, 50
   Jung's description, 29, 30, 113, 122, 123, 137
   psyche- in the word psychedelic, 7
   religious function of, 20, 68, 114
   See also consciousness (conscious mind); ego; unconscious, the
psychedelic as a word, 7, 8, 19, 91, 178 n. 16
Psychedelic Drugs Reconsidered (Grinspoon, Bakalar), 7, 8, 88
psychedelic drugs / substances, 7–8
   abreactive properties, 57
   as catalysts, 8, 46, 89, 185 n. 17
   drugs vs. *substances*, 178 n. 22
   indigenous peoples use of, 5, 10, 11, 23, 91, 94, 95, 108
   misuse of, 9, 10, 25, 174, 179 n. 27
   physical safety of, 187 n. 19
   political backlash against, 9–10
   as psychosis-inducing, 87–90
   religious / spiritual use of, 10, 11, 23, 95, 114
   similarities among, 8, 93
   widespread use of, 9, 173, 178–79 n. 27
   See also entries for specific drugs / substances
Psychedelic Experience, The (Leary, Metzner, Alpert), 12

psychedelic experiences
  archetypes manifest in, 25, 45, 62–63, 132, 133, 163–65, 169–71
  complexes and, 100, 101–2
  daimonic images in, 13, 58, 62–63, 69–70, 87, 95–96, 108, 170
    Grof's description, 120
    Jung's explanation, 68–69
  delusions in, 53–54, 83, 87, 98, 107, 141, 178 n. 16
  difficult (bad trips), 53–55
    non-drug factors and, 54
    as opportunities, 54–55, 57–58
    as potentially traumatic, 54, 55
    See also adverse reactions
  dreams, similarity, 8, 25, 39–40, 46, 101–2, 154, 163, 169
  flashbacks (spontaneous recurrences), 56, 61, 63, 70, 99, 141, 143
  hallucinations and, 25, 38, 40, 53, 89, 91, 163, 166
  integration of (*see* integration: psychedelic experience and)
  Jung and, speculation on, 5
  Jung's psychology, relevance of, 5–6, 12, 13, 43, 53, 85, 97, 100–101, 105
  mystical experience and, 11, 17, 18–20, 48, 91, 114–15, 196 n. 18
  projection in, 81, 89, 93, 107, 152 (*see also* psychedelic psychotherapy: projection in)
  psychosis, risk of, 14, 45, 48, 89, 95, 96, 97
  psychosis and, differences, 89–90, 90–91
  psychosis and, similarities, 6–7, 40, 46, 86, 87–89, 91–92, 101–2, 166
  psychotic states, 86, 87–89, 106–11
    cultural factors, 94–96
    transpersonal explanations, 92–96
  safety guidelines, 11–12, 57, 186 n. 3
  shadow and, 13, 18, 78, 79
  suicide, risk of, 48, 54, 81, 87, 133, 156, 159
  transcendent / transpersonal states, 4, 11, 18, 19, 114–15
  transformative potential, 10, 19, 23, 30, 33, 55, 114–16, 118–20
  trauma and, 53–58, 62
  the unconscious manifest in, 23–24, 25, 62–63, 164–65

psychedelic experiences, accounts of
  integration of, 141, 142–45, 164–65, 169–71
  psychotic reactions to , 63–65, 78, 87–88, 106–11
  shadow in, 74–75, 77–78, 79–81, 132–33, 164–65, 169–71
  symbols in, 39, 62–63, 98–99, 164–65, 169–71
  transformation and, 130–33, 164–65, 169–71
  trauma manifest in, 62–65, 69–70, 106–7, 132–33, 169–71
Psychedelic Medicines (Winkelman, Roberts), 22
psychedelic psychotherapy, 17–24
  archetypal imagery manifest in, 45, 62–63, 132–33, 163–65, 169–71
  dose ranges, 17, 19 , 181 n. 2, n. 9
  dream analysis, similarity, 155, 163, 169
  Fordham, Michael, criticism of, 25–27, 149–50
  integration and (*see* integration: psychedelic experience and)
  Jungian analysis and, 14, 24–27, 48–49, 163
  Jung's psychology, relevance of, 12–13, 147, 157–71
  LSD therapy
    Grof on, 19, 23, 57–58 (*see also under* Grof, Stanislav)
    Jungian-oriented (*see under* Cutner, Margot; Sandison, Ronald)
    Jung's opposition to, 14–15
  projection in, 62–63, 64, 80, 132–33, 151, 153, 169, 182 n. 39
  psycholytic therapy model, 17–18, 182 n. 24
  risks, 27, 55, 127, 144, 157–58, 159–60
    psychotic reactions, 48, 158, 159
    suicide, 48, 54, 133, 156, 158, 159
  subject readiness, 157–60
  theoretical frameworks, 21–24
  therapist-patient relationship, 20, 25–26, 26–27, 94, 127–28, 160–62, 166–69, 190 n. 40
  as treatment for disorders, 9, 10–11, 90–91, 167–68

psychedelic research
  on adverse reactions, 9,
    53–54, 109
  history of, 6–12
  Johns Hopkins studies, 4, 11–12, 19,
    186 n. 3
  on mescaline intoxication, 87, 88
  need for, 20, 27, 50, 160
  psychedelic paradigm, 7, 17, 18–20,
    90–91
  psychotomimetic paradigm
    adoption of, 6–7, 87, 88
    criticism and abandonment of, 19,
      90–91
    reconsideration of, 91–92
  renewal of, 10–11, 50, 179 n. 29
  studies in 1950s and 1960s, 8–9, 14,
    18–19, 22, 50, 89, 158
psycholytic as a word, 17–18, 25
psychosis
  Alpert, Richard (Ram Dass), on, 119
  anger and, 79–81
  chemical model of, 87, 91
  complexes and, 68–69, 104
  definitions of, 83
  delusions and, 67, 83, 88
  destructive vs. transformative, 84, 85,
    86, 93, 94
  DSM-IV on, 83, 192 n. 34
  Grof on psychedelic psychosis
    explanation of, 93
    transformative potential of, 55, 84,
      119–20
  hallucinations and, 83, 88, 89, 91, 99
  intrusions from the unconscious and, 12,
    32–33, 36
  Jung on, 97–106
    personal fear of, 3, 44
    psychedelic experience and,
      similarities, 40, 46, 97, 101–2,
      104–6, 166
    as the psyche's effort to heal, 59, 98,
      121–23
  Laing, R. D., on, 118
  latent, 102–3, 104
    risk of releasing, 14, 45, 103, 105,
      156, 157, 166–67
  Lukoff, David, on (*see* Lukoff, David)
  meaning in, 40, 59, 67, 98, 100, 102,
    103, 117, 121–22

Perry, John Weir, on (*see under* Perry,
  John Weir)
projection in, 93, 121, 152
psychedelic experience and, differences,
  89–90, 90–91
psychedelic experience and, similarities,
  6–7, 40, 46, 86, 87–89, 91–92,
  101–2, 166
psychedelic-induced, 86, 87–89, 106–11
  cultural factors, 94–96
  transpersonal explanations, 92–94
psychotic states vs. chronic psychosis,
  88–89
shadow and, 74, 75–76
transformative potential of, 84, 97, 98,
  116–17, 118–20, 122–23
trauma and, 54, 55, 67
See also schizophrenia
PTSD. *See* Posttraumatic Stress Disorder

Ram Dass (Alpert, Richard), 12, 147
  Psychedelic Experience, The (Leary,
    Metzner, Alpert), 12
  on psychosis, 119
rebirth. *See* death-rebirth process
reification, the problem of, 41
Revelation, book of, 124–25
Richards, Brian, 186, n. 3
Richards, William (Bill)
  Johns Hopkins psilocybin study, 12
  collective unconscious, on the value of
    the, 12
Rinkel, Max, 88
Roquet, Salvador, 108

Samuels, Andrew, 15
Sandison, Ronald
  on archetypal images in LSD therapy,
    25, 163–65, 169–71
  establishing LSD therapy in Britain,
    24–25, 49
  on integrating psychedelic experiences,
    49, 159, 165, 167, 168, 169, 174
  Jung, Jungians, and, 49–50, 174
  Jung's and Fordham's criticisms, response
    to, 25, 26, 48–50, 158–59, 160
  LSD therapy, accounts of, 39, 62, 80,
    163–65, 169–71
  LSD therapy, Jungian-oriented, 14, 25,
    48–50, 169, 174

psycholytic therapy and, 17, 20, 25, 159
  on therapist-patient relationship, 26, 49, 153, 165, 167, 168
Sandoz Pharmaceuticals, 7, 8, 17, 25, 88, 90
Satan. *See* Devil / devils
schizophrenia
  acute vs. chronic, 88–89, 192 n. 34
  complexes and, 100, 101–2, 102–3, 104
  dissociation and, 101, 102, 103, 105
  dreams, similarities to, 40, 101, 102, 154
  DSM-IV on, 83, 192 n. 34
  hallucinations and, 88, 89, 90, 91, 99
  intrusions from the unconscious and, 12, 32–33, 36
  Jung on, 97, 99–106
    psychedelic experience and, similarities, 40, 46, 97, 101–2, 104–6, 166
    as the psyche's effort to heal, 59, 98, 121–23
  latent, 102–3, 104
    risk of releasing, 14, 45, 103, 105, 156, 157, 166–67
  meaning in, 40, 59, 67, 98, 100, 102, 103, 117, 121–22
  psychedelic experience and, differences, 89–90, 90–91
  psychedelic experience and, similarities, 6–7, 86, 87–89, 91–92
  See also psychosis
set and setting, 54, 93, 105, 106, 107, 186 n. 3
shadow, 71
  archetypal, 60, 65–66, 73, 74
  archetypal vs. personal, 72–73, 75–76
  evil and, 60, 72–73
  integration of, 18, 76, 78, 123–24
  projection of, 75–77, 78, 79, 81
  psychedelic experience and, 13, 18, 78, 79
  psychotic reactions to, 75–76, 81
  transformative potential of, 123–25
Shulgin, Ann
  "New Psychotherapy: MDMA and the Shadow, The," 94
  psychedelic psychotherapy, 94
  on the shadow, 13, 78–79, 190 n. 40
Smith, David
  Haight Ashbury Free Medical Clinic, 9
  Leary, Timothy, and, 178 n. 25
  LSD misuse observed by, 9
Smith, Huston, xiv, 115
spiritual emergency, 84, 93, 116, 197 n. 32
Spiritual Emergency (Grof, Grof), 116, 119
Stevens, Jay, 10
Storming Heaven: LSD and the American Dream, 10
Stockings, G. T., 87, 91
Stolaroff, Myron
  low- vs. high-dose sessions, 18
  psychedelics and transformation, 114
  shadow work in psychedelic therapy, 18
Strassman, Rick
  on abreaction, 126
  adverse reactions research, 53
  DMT research, case accounts, 109, 130–32
symbols, 37–39
  archetypes manifest in, 24, 35, 37, 58, 73, 122, 124
  interpreting, 98–99, 117, 122, 139, 140, 154, 201 n. 11
  in psychedelic experience, 62–63, 74, 98–99, 132–33, 163–65, 169–71
  transformation and, 59, 67, 153, 156

Tarnas, Richard, 117, 128, 184 n. 54, 195 n. 52
Tibetan Book of the Dead, The, 12, 13
Tibetan Book of the Great Liberation, The, 12, 176
transcendent function, 123, 137–42, 200 n. 17
transformation, 113
  Jung's conception of, 34, 114, 122–23
  manifestations of the unconscious and, 40, 69, 156
  psychedelic experience and, 114–16
  psychedelic psychosis and, 118–20
  psychosis and, 116–18
  in Jung's psychology, 121–23
transpersonal psychology, 20, 84, 93, 113, 114
  altered states as subject of, 84, 191 n. 13
  Journal of Transpersonal Psychology, 12, 84
  Jung as forefather of, 84
  transpersonal state described, 114–15

trauma
  archetypal imagery manifest in, 62–63, 67, 69
  complexes and, 61–62, 66–67, 126
  defined, 58, 126
  difficult psychedelic experiences and, 53–55
  dissociation and, 58–61, 61–62, 128–29 (*see also* dissociation)
  flashbacks and, 56, 61, 70
  Grof on abreaction for, 57, 125, 126–28, 129, 130
  Jung on integration for, 125, 126, 128–30, 175
  manifest in
    daimonic images, 58, 59, 61, 62–63, 64, 65, 67
    dreams, 58, 59, 61, 62
    psychedelic experience and, 53–58, 62–65, 107, 132–33, 169–71
  psychedelic psychotherapy for, 11, 53, 57–58, 167–68
  psychotic reactions to, 54, 55, 67
  See also under Kalsched, Donald

unconscious, the (unconscious mind)
  collective and personal, 18, 31, 32 (*see also* archetypes)
  compensating function of, 32–33, 121, 123, 138, 153, 155–56, 163
  defined, 30, 31, 179–80 n. 38
  "Indivisibility of the Personal and Collective Unconscious, The," (Williams), 32
  interpreting symbolic content of, 98–99, 117, 122, 139, 140, 142, 154, 201 n. 11
  manifestations of as meaningful, 38, 40, 59, 98, 102, 103, 121–22, 139
  manifest in psychedelic experience, 24, 25, 39, 62–63, 163–65, 169–71
  overwhelming manifestations of, 36, 40, 141–42
  integration of, 141–42, 168–69
  lowered threshold of consciousness and, 30, 44, 101, 104–5, 173
  in psychedelic experience, 30, 47, 80–81, 101, 102, 141, 157, 173
  in psychosis, 36, 97, 102, 103, 104, 105, 157
  resistance to integrating, 12, 27, 44, 57, 76, 158–59, 161–62
  wisdom of, 31, 32, 33, 38, 127, 139, 168
  See also consciousness: unconscious, the, and

von Franz, Marie-Louise, 75, 124

Washburn, Michael, 85, 191 n. 16
White, Victor, Jung's letter to, 14–15, 49
Wilber, Ken, 191 n. 16
Williams, Donald Lee
  Border Crossings, 180 n. 44
Williams, Mary, 32
  "Indivisibility of the Personal and Collective Unconscious, The," 32
Winnicott, Donald, 59
Wulff, David, 5, 114

Yahweh, 73, 74, 76, 124. *See also* God

Made in the USA
Las Vegas, NV
11 April 2024